# SPECIAL NEEDS

## IN THE

# EARLY YEARS

# SPECIAL NEEDS
## IN THE
# EARLY YEARS
## PARTNERSHIP AND PARTICIPATION

EDITED BY

# REBECCA CRUTCHLEY

SAGE

Los Angeles | London | New Delhi
Singapore | Washington DC | Melbourne

Los Angeles | London | New Delhi
Singapore | Washington DC | Melbourne

SAGE Publications Ltd
1 Oliver's Yard
55 City Road
London EC1Y 1SP

SAGE Publications Inc.
2455 Teller Road
Thousand Oaks, California 91320

SAGE Publications India Pvt Ltd
B 1/I 1 Mohan Cooperative Industrial Area
Mathura Road
New Delhi 110 044

SAGE Publications Asia-Pacific Pte Ltd
3 Church Street
#10-04 Samsung Hub
Singapore 049483

Associate editor: George Knowles
Production editor: Tom Bedford
Copyeditor: Solveig Gardner Servian
Proofreader: Andy Baxter
Indexer: Cathy Heath
Marketing manager: Dilhara Attygalle
Cover design: Wendy Scott
Typeset by: C&M Digitals (P) Ltd, Chennai, India
Printed in the UK

First published 2018

**Library of Congress Control Number: 2017949801**

**British Library Cataloguing in Publication data**

A catalogue record for this book is available from
the British Library

ISBN 978-1-4739-4883-9
ISBN 978-1-4739-4884-6 (pbk)

At SAGE we take sustainability seriously. Most of our products are printed in the UK using FSC papers and boards.
When we print overseas we ensure sustainable papers are used as measured by the PREPS grading system.
We undertake an annual audit to monitor our sustainability.

# CONTENTS

# LIST OF FIGURES AND TABLES

## Figures

## Tables

# ABOUT THE EDITOR AND CONTRIBUTORS

## Editor

**Rebecca Crutchley** has worked as an early years teacher, a local authority early years consultant and an early years SENCO. She currently leads the Early Childhood and SEN programme at University of East London. Her research interests include support and empowerment for children with SEND, and social justice issues for children from other potentially marginalised communities.

## Contributors

**Louise Arnold** has worked in a specialist school for children with SEND, as a personal assistant to families under the direct payments scheme in a pathfinder location, and as a play and support worker with disabled children with the Children's Society. She has also spent time abroad, in early years and primary settings in India, and contributing to research in Ethiopia regarding the status of child and disability friendly policy across Africa. Louise now lectures on the early childhood programmes at the University of East London, with a focus on children with additional needs. Her research interests include child and parent involvement in the creation of education, health and care plans, children's voices in research, emancipatory and participatory methods, and parental perspectives of support and provision.

**Beate Hellawell** has worked as primary teacher and early reading specialist. She has also trained teaching assistants, worked as a local authority SEN officer and more recently as senior lecturer at two universities. Her research interests include SEND policy enactment, professional ethics and partnership working. She has recently completed a professional doctorate in these areas.

**Ruth Hunt** has been a primary school teacher in inner London specialising in the early years and Key Stage 1, and is also a qualified forest school teacher. Ruth currently works at the University of East London, leading an undergraduate Early Childhood programme, and lecturing on behaviour and early years education. Her research interests centre on children, family and practitioner experiences and understandings of current educational practices and policies within UK schools.

**Estelle Martin** has worked in the early childhood and education field for many years including in programme leader roles, and associate/senior lecturer roles at Anglia Ruskin University, Canterbury Christchurch University, and most recently at the University of East London. Estelle gained her PhD in 2014, from the University of Kent, where her focus was on the social and emotional wellbeing of very young children. Estelle is also an Associate at University College London, Institute of Education and a visiting research fellow at University of East London. Estelle, who is also a BACP registered psychotherapist, now works as a freelance early childhood consultant and counsellor.

**Anna Newbold** has been a primary school teacher for 12 years and has a particular interest in EYFS and Key Stage 1 teaching. She currently works in a large inner-London primary school which has a Resource Base for Autism; she works with children who have a wide range of SEND, and also has a leadership role line-managing support staff.

**Athina Tempriou** has worked as a primary and secondary school teacher in Cyprus. She has also worked as a research fellow and subject leader in different schools in the UK. She is currently a senior lecturer at the University of East London. Her research interests include raising awareness for children with SEND, inclusion and diversity, as well as in service training on autism for teachers and support staff.

# ACKNOWLEDGEMENTS

My thanks go to the children, parents and professionals whose experiences have contributed to this publication. I would also like to thank the co-authors of the book for their professionalism and commitment to the publication, and for their patience and understanding. Thanks also to the team at SAGE who have been hugely supportive in guiding us through the writing and publication process. Finally, to our families and friends for their understanding and support.

This book is dedicated to my mum, whose dedication to working with children with SEND throughout her career, inspired my initial interest in this field.

Rebecca Crutchley

# GLOSSARY OF KEY TERMS AND PHRASES

The following table provides an 'at a glance' summary of some of the key terms and phrases which are discussed further in the following chapters.

| Term | Description |
| --- | --- |
| Affirmative Model | Disability rights advocates assert that both the social and medical models (see below) fail to appreciate the interplay between a child or young person's medical needs and the impact that these needs have within their social environment. As such, these models homogenise and pathologise special needs and disabilities. The affirmative model reflects a competence-based approach which seeks the perspectives of children and young people in sharing their experiences, and promotes their empowerment and agency (Swain and French, 2000). |
| Common Assessment Framework (CAF) | The Common Assessment Framework is a tool for professionals to share information about children's needs and support plans that have been prepared for them. Introduced in pilot local authorities in 2004 and centralised across all local authorities by 2008, the CAF has been revised as the eCAF, or the Family CAF, in many local authorities in recognition of the holistic nature of children's and families' needs. After 2012 the national CAF/eCAF was terminated with the recognition that local authorities could develop their own integrated information sharing systems, although many still use the original format. |
| Code of Practice | The Code of Practice was initially introduced in 1994, and has been updated at regular occasions thereafter, with the current version produced in January 2015. It sets out the legal requirements and recommended practice for professionals working with children with SEND from the ages of 0 to 25. |
| Disability | The Code of Practice defines disability thus: 'A child of compulsory school age or a young person has a learning difficulty or disability if he or she: has a significantly greater difficulty in learning than the majority of others of the same age, or has a disability which prevents or hinders him or her from making use of facilities of a kind generally provided for others of the same age in mainstream schools or mainstream post-16 institutions.' (DfE, 2015c: 16) |

| Term | Description |
|---|---|
| Early Intervention | The umbrella term for interventions and support packages introduced at an early age aimed at ensuring maximum impact on the development and learning of children with SEND. |
| Early Learning Goals | The 17 attainment goals which children are assessed against at the end of the Reception year. Children are judged to be at an emerging, expected or exceeding level of attainment. |
| Early Support Programme | The Early Support Programme was piloted in nine local authorities and expanded to 45 community partners across England and Wales thereafter as a response to the Together from the Start framework (DfES, 2003). It aims at providing support and advocacy for children with complex or multiple needs through the allocation of a key worker who would work in partnership with the family to co-ordinate services and monitor the impact of intervention programmes. |
| Early Years Development Journal(s) | The EYDJ is a developmental assessment tool originating from the Early Support Programme which aims to support parents and carers to collate information about their child's developmental progress allowing them to be key contributors in a parent/professional partnership, and to avoid the anxiety of repeating their child's story to many professionals over and again (see Chapter 7 for more detail). |
| Early Years Foundation Stage | The statutory framework for all early years providers of education and care for children aged 0–5, unless exempted by the DfE. |
| Early Years Foundation Stage Profile | Statutory requirements for the assessment of children's progress and attainment at the end of the Reception year. |
| Early Years Outcomes | Non-statutory guidance for assessing children's progress and development across the three prime and four specific areas of development in the early years. |
| Education Health and Care Plan (EHC) | One of the significant changes to SEND provision of the Children and Families Act 2014 was the replacement of the Statement of SEN with the EHC. The plan covers children aged 0–25, therefore also replacing learning disability agreements for children and young people in post-16 institutions (discussed in more depth in Chapters 1 and 3). |
| Evidence-based Interventions | Interventions which can be clearly demonstrated to have had a positive impact on children and young people with SEND and improved outcomes (social, educational) for them. These approaches to interventions for children with SEND have been used in health and social care for many years, and have been influenced by the a series of reports and evaluations of SEND provision (see Chapter 1). |
| Every Child Matters | Every Child Matters was a framework focusing on five holistic outcomes for all children aged 0–19. Although the framework was replaced in 2010, many service providers continue to work towards ensuring that its key principles are maintained. |

*(Continued)*

*(Continued)*

| Term | Description |
| --- | --- |
| Graduated Response | This is the name for the process of implementing and reviewing interventions aimed at meeting the learning and developmental needs of children with SEND. The approach has four phases:<br><br>• Assess.<br>• Plan.<br>• Do.<br>• Review. |
| Individual Education Plan (IEP) | Although there is an increasing move away from IEPs to whole-school provision mapping (see below), many practitioners and teachers have maintained individual education plans to allow them to provide appropriate interventions for children with SEND using SMART (see below) targets. |
| Inclusion Development Programme (IDP) | The IDP was a raft of support packages and training programmes for professionals working with children with SEND from early years through to secondary school which was introduced by the Labour government from 2007 following the publication of Removing Barriers to Participation (DfES, 2004a). The IDP is discussed in more depth in Chapters 1 and 7. |
| Integrative Model | The integrative model seeks to combine the medical and social models of disability by recognising the social barriers faced by people with disabilities as a result of their specific impairment. |
| Medical Model | The medical model was for many years the traditional model of inclusion, whereby the barriers to full participation in society were attributed predominantly to the medical needs of the child or young person. Also referred to as the deficit model, this perspective has been criticised for failing to acknowledge social barriers, and for its focus on 'fixing' a child or young person's disability. |
| Multi-agency Working | Professionals from different disciplines (e.g. health, social care and education) working collaboratively through effective information-sharing processes to meet the holistic needs of the child and his/her family. The requirement for professionals to work through multi-agency partnerships was stipulated in the Children Act 2004, following the Laming report into the death of Victoria Climbié and is reiterated in the 2015 Code of Practice (DfE, 2015c). |
| National Service Frameworks | The National Service Frameworks are a series of strategy documents from the National Health Service outlining how key health issues and concerns (including children's medical and health needs/disabilities) will be addressed. |
| Person-centred Reviews | Traditionally used in health and social care to enable people with disabilities to contribute to their individualised support provision, person-centred reviews have more recently been used in schools and settings to capture the child's voice and empower children, young people and their parents/carers to be fully participatory in decisions which affect them. Person-centred reviews are discussed at length in Chapter 3. |

| Term | Description |
|------|-------------|
| Provision Mapping | Provision mapping allows schools and settings to provide an overview of the SEND support provided to all of the children on their SEND register. An example of a provision map is provided in Chapter 7. |
| Parent Forums | Parent forums are parent-led advocacy groups which support families of children with SEND to ensure that their children's needs are met. From 2013, there has been a National Network of Parent Carer Forums (NNPCF) whose aims are: <br><br> • to ensure that good practice, knowledge and shared expertise about parent participation continues to grow and strengthen; <br> • to develop a cohesive and coherent structure to sustain and develop the effectiveness of parent carer forums across England; <br> • to strengthen the pan disability, parent led model of local forums and boost our collective voice. <br><br> (www.nnpcf.org.uk) |
| Special Educational Needs | According to the 2015 Code of Practice, a child has SEN if 'they have a learning difficulty or disability which calls for special educational provision to be made for him or her' (DfE, 2015c: 15). <br><br> 'For children aged two or more, special educational provision is educational or training provision that is additional to or different from that made generally for other children or young people of the same age by mainstream schools, maintained nursery schools, mainstream post-16 institutions or by relevant early years providers. <br><br> For a child under two years of age, special educational provision means educational provision of any kind.' <br><br> (DfE, 2015c: 16) |
| SEN Areas of Need | The 2015 Code of Practice which accompanies the Children and Family Act 2014, defines four broad categories of need for children with SEND: <br><br> • Communication and interaction. <br> • Cognition and learning. <br> • Social, emotional and mental health. <br> • Sensory and/or physical. |
| SEN Support | The Children and Families Act 2014 replaced Early Years (School) Action and Early Years (School) Action Plus with one broad category of support for children whose SEND did not qualify for an Educational Health and Care Plan (see above). These two categories of SEND are grouped under the broad description of SEN support. |
| SMART Targets | Used to identify intervention support programmes for children with SEND, SMART stands for Specific, Measurable, Achievable, Realistic and Time-bound. Many schools and settings now use the acronym SMARTER, with the 'E' standing for Evaluate and the 'R' meaning Revisit. |

*(Continued)*

*(Continued)*

| Term | Description |
| --- | --- |
| Social Model | The social model emerged in the 1970s from the Union of the Physically Impaired Against Segregation (UPAIS) and was further developed in 1983 by Michael Oliver. The social model stresses that many of the barriers to participation experienced by children and young people with disabilities and SEN were caused by social barriers such as inappropriate teaching approaches, inaccessible buildings and discriminatory attitudes (Oliver, 1983). |
| Statement of SEN | Statements of SEN were first introduced in the Education Act 1981 (following recommendations made in the Warnock report of 1978). They stipulated the educational, medical and social care support provided by the local authority to enable children with significant SEND to have their needs met. They have since been placed with Education Health and Care plans (see above, and discussed further in Chapters 2 and 3). |
| Team Around the Child (TAC) | A TAC is a team of multi-professional staff who work in partnership with parents to plan provision for children with SEND and/or other additional needs, e.g. child protection issues. |
| Team Around the Family (TAF) | As above but with support from a multi-professional team to address the needs of the whole family. |
| UNCRC | United Nations Convention on the Rights of the Child. A list of rights-based articles aimed at promoting children's rights across the world, in the areas of protection, provision and participation. The UNCRC was adopted by the UN in 1989 and ratified by the UK in 1991. |
| UNCRPD | A similar convention to the UNCRC but with a specific focus on promoting the rights of persons with disabilities. The UNCRPD was adopted in 2006 and ratified by the UK in 2009. |
| WIKI (Multi-media Advocacy) | WIKIs are interactive multi-media advocacy tools which provide information for multi-agency professionals about children and young people with SEND. Designed and developed by children and young people and their parents and carers, they enable professionals to recognise the whole child, and not simply their SEN or disability. |

# ACRONYMS FOR ORGANISATIONS

The following list of government and charitable organisations is designed to support readers of the book with relevant and useful further information introduced in the book's chapters.

ACE Advisory Centre for Education (www.ace-ed.org.uk)

ADHD Foundation (www.adhdfoundation.org.uk)

CDC Council for Disabled Children (www.councilfordisabledchildren.org.uk)

CSIE Centre for Studies in Inclusive Education (www.csie.org.uk)

DfE Department for Education (www.gov.uk/government/organisations/department-for-education)

DoH Department of Health (www.gov.uk/government/organisations/department-of-health)

DRC Disability Rights Commission (www.drc.org.uk)

DSA Down's Syndrome Association (www.downs-syndrome.org.uk/downs-syndrome-association)

IPSEA Independent Parental Special Education Advice (www.ipsea.org.uk)

NAS National Autistic Society (www.autism.org.uk)

NASEN National Association of Special Educational Needs (www.nasen.org.uk)

NCB National Children's Bureau (www.ncb.org.uk)

Ofsted Office for Standards in Education (www.gov.uk/government/organisations/ofsted)

PSLA Pre-School Learning Alliance (www.pre-school.org.uk)

TfC Together for Children (www.together-for-children.org)

# OTHER USEFUL ORGANISATIONS AND WEBSITES

Action on Hearing Loss (www.actiononhearingloss.org.uk)

Cerebral Palsy (CP) (www.cerebralpalsy.org.uk)

Communication Trust: Combination of over 50 organisations supporting those who work with children with communication difficulties (www.thecommunicationtrust.org.uk)

Foundation Years: Website for early years service providers and professionals (www.foundationyears.org.uk)

I CAN: Charity to support children with speech, language and communication needs (www.ican.org.uk)

National Portage Association: A home visiting educational service for preschool children (www.portage.org.uk)

SCOPE: Advocates for full participation of people with disabilities into mainstream society (www.scope.org.uk)

Royal National Institute for the Blind (www.rnib.org.uk)

SENSE: For children, young people and adults with deafblindness (www.sense.org.uk)

Special Needs and Parents (SNAP) (www.snapcharity.org)

For further information about careers in the early years or SEND field, visit the National Careers Service website (https://nationalcareersservice.direct.gov.uk).

# INTRODUCTION

## REBECCA CRUTCHLEY

The purpose of this book is to provide teachers, students and practitioners working in the field of early years and special education an insight into provision and services for children with Special Educational Needs and Disabilities (SEND). As can be seen from the biographies of the contributors, the chapters reflect the expertise and experience of professionals from a range of perspectives and as such we hope that the information provided will be useful for a wide audience.

As might be expected from the subtitle of the book, there is a strong focus on partnership and participation, reflecting the authors' commitment to the importance of working with children, parents and as multi-agency professionals to meet the needs of the children and families with whom they work. This commitment is reflected in the most recent legislation in the field, the Children and Families Act 2014, and the 2015 Code of Practice, and represents what might be called a shifting paradigm in approaches to working with children and families. While partnership with parents and multi-agency approaches are not new phenomena, the repeated statements stressing the legal requirements for schools and settings contained within the 2015 Code of Practice signify the renewed importance attached to these areas of professional practice. Therefore, there will be some exploration in each of the chapters of the extent to which this principle has been successful at empowering children and parents to participate fully and authentically in the development of SEND support and provision.

Each of the chapters provides a summary of key points to be addressed, and combines consideration of theoretical concepts with practical real-life examples through case studies of children, parents or professionals. In addition, each chapter offers the reader some reflective pauses, which offer the opportunity to consider some of the key issues in more depth, in the light of the reader's own experiences and understandings.

Finally, at the end of each chapter, there will be an annotated bibliography which will signpost readers to relevant additional material and suggest further resources to support understanding of the key themes and concepts explored.

The underpinning philosophy of this book is that children and young people with SEND must be regarded as competent and valuable members of society. An affirmative model of disability which acknowledges the shortcomings of the traditional medical model and the more recent social model of disability is the preferred model of inclusion throughout the discussions. This is not to say that the authors dismiss an integrative model of disability which recognises the interplay between medical needs and social barriers that can serve to curtail full participation in society for children and young people with SEND; rather it advocates that overcoming such challenges must involve wherever possible the active participation of children and young people with SEND, and not simply those who speak on their behalf. Initially proposed by Swain and French in 2000, the affirmative model of disability draws upon the idea of disability pride and recognises that even if all barriers to social inclusion were removed, perceptions of disability within mainstream society would continue to be patronising or disempowering, and as such they advocate an approach which recognises the strengths and competencies of children and young people as superior to their needs and challenges. Key principles of the Children and Family Act 2014 reflect a small step shift towards this paradigm, for example the reiteration of the importance of the child's voice during the assessment process. However, the extent to which systems and processes within schools facilitate this principle in an authentic and genuine manner remains to be seen.

## Chapter 1. Legislation and Policy: Towards a Participatory Partnership

In order to set the scene for the existing landscape in the field of SEND and early years provision, Chapter 1 provides an outline of the history of legislation and policy underpinning services and provision for children with SEND. The evolving trend towards a recognition of the rights of children with SEND to have access to an education which enables them to reach their full potential is summarised, alongside a consideration of the initial steps towards the involvement of parents and children in the assessment process. The chapter reinforces the viewpoint suggested above of a rights-based approach to SEND provision rather than a needs-based model.

## Chapter 2. Working with Parents: Principles of Engagement

The principles of working in partnership with parents are further explored by Louise Arnold in Chapter 2. This chapter will discuss the complexities of working with parents and respecting their perspectives and involvement while maintaining professional roles. The chapter also recognises the benefits and challenges of working collaboratively with parents with a wide range of experiences and perspectives of special educational needs and disability. Power balances between professionals and parents will also be considered and the challenge of maintaining effective relationships without compromising professional identity. In addition, the benefits of collaboration and participation between parents and professionals will be considered in the context of ensuring that participation is accessed equally across and amongst the parent community, and the role of parent forums in facilitating equality of opportunity when developing collaborative partnerships will also be discussed. Requirements for local authorities to share the 'local offer' with parents and carers (DfE, 2015c: 4.1) will therefore be included in this discussion.

## Chapter 3. Pupil and Parent Voice: Contributions to Assessment and Planning

Throughout the SEND Code of Practice 2015, there are references to the child being at the heart of the assessment process. Chapter 3 will consider the principles of children's rights which underpin this commitment in recent legislation. The chapter considers the practical realities of eliciting and responding to children's voice in an authentic and meaningful way, for example through the use of person-centred reviews and multi-media advocacy approaches such as WIKIs.

Although person-centred reviews have long been used effectively in health and social care for several years and more recently in schools and early years settings to capture children's perspectives and empower them to participate in decisions which affect them, particularly in periods of transition, the benefits and challenges of these approaches have often been overlooked. This chapter will explore the person-centred review process, particularly the use of multi-media advocacy for children with SEN and/or disabilities. With a specific focus on the contribution of pupil voice to assessment and planning in the early years, the chapter will consider how practitioners and parents can ensure that very young children's perspectives can be captured and used to inform practice and provision. The tools for eliciting children's perspectives outlined in the Mosaic Approach (Clarke and Moss, 2001) are discussed in the context of a children's rights perspective. Reflections on how the Mosaic Approach facilitates a shift from a medical model to an affirmative model of disability is also discussed.

## Chapter 4. Models of SEN Provision: The Inclusion Debate

This chapter will explore issues around the range and diversity of provision available to meet the needs of children with identified additional educational, social and health needs. Setting current practice in the context of inclusion agendas, this chapter will explore recent thinking around the ideals of inclusion, and the reality for children, parents and practitioners. Differing provision will be considered in light of children's rights, current curriculum drives and models of inclusion. The benefits and challenges of mainstream, special and specialist unit education models will be explored with reference to parent and practitioner case studies. The drive to inclusion following the publication of the Warnock Report in 1978 and subsequent concerns about the validity and appropriateness of this focus will also be discussed. Does the placement in a mainstream classroom necessarily facilitate inclusion for children with SEND, or should a broader definition of inclusion be considered which refers to a child's access to equality of opportunity based on their individual needs?

## Chapter 5. Leadership and Inclusion: Creating an Ethos, Culture and Provision

Effective inclusive practice within mainstream and specialist provision relies on the ethos, vision and commitment of the leadership team. This chapter will consider the role of the leader in advocating for inclusive practice and ensuring that the whole staff team promote an inclusive culture both in policy and practice. It will examine issues relating to staff training and development and partnership with parents, external agencies and the local community. Comparisons across international contexts are included to demonstrate a variety of inclusive models. There will also be some consideration of recent changes in school leadership across the UK, for example the introduction of free schools, and the academisation programme, and the benefits and challenges of these changes to educational provision. Finally, the chapter will consider leadership within the non-statutory early years sector and the role of these settings in identifying SEND in children from an early age, including the implications for relationship building and partnership working with parents and carers.

## Chapter 6. Professional Ethics: Partnership and Collaboration in the Early Years

This chapter considers how an appreciation of professional ethics contributes to safe and child-centred practice as well as to more effective partnership working with colleagues, parents and other agencies and the professionalisation of early years practitioners. A brief introduction offering a definition of professional ethics and its dimensions of justice, care and critique will be followed by exploring the role and limitations of ethical codes, codes of conduct and codes of practice. Case studies arising from the new SEND Code of Practice 2015 explore moral dilemmas, conflicts of interest between partners, power in relationships and attitudes of mind, all with a particular focus on SEND. Research ethics, issues of confidentiality and whistleblowing will conclude the chapter. Themes from other chapters in the book will be explored from a position of social justice and professional ethics.

## Chapter 7. Early Intervention and Transition

The phrase 'early intervention' has been used extensively to accompany policy initiatives aimed at supporting families with children with SEN and/or disabilities at the earliest possibility. Indeed there are both moral and pragmatic justifications for advocating early intervention. This chapter will explore the benefits and complexities of early intervention strategies, including the impact of diagnosis and intervention upon children, families, schools and external agencies. The chapter will also explore transition from early years provision to Key Stage 1, with a focus on how parents, professionals and children can work in partnership to ensure that the process is smooth and effective. Recent changes to assessment in the early years, through baseline assessment and the modifications of external assessments at Key Stage 1, will be considered and the influence and impact of top-down pressure upon practice and provision for children with SEND in the early years will be discussed.

## Chapter 8. CPD Opportunities for Staff Working with Children with SEND in the Early Years

There is debate around the current staffing arrangements for children with SEND, centring on qualifications, status and pay. This chapter highlights perceived status and training inequalities across and within settings between differently qualified staff, and the role that CPD might play in up-skilling the workforce. Initial training and practitioner standards are explored in the light of children's complex needs and the changing demands of inclusive educational practice. The introduction of the master's level SENCO qualification in 2009 is discussed with reference to possible empowering of a workforce as well as the potential to widen the gap between practitioner and manager training opportunities. This chapter argues for the need for the most qualified to work with the children with the most complex needs whilst acknowledging the challenges of the new funding structure for children with SEND within maintained schools and settings. Critical examination of opportunities for leadership and SEN training within the non-maintained sector will conclude the chapter.

## Chapter 9. Multi-agency Working: Partnership and Collaboration

This chapter explores the impact of working with children and their families in a multi-agency project, when education, social services and health collaborate together to provide a framework for person-centred ways of working. The family-based intervention with a solution-focused approach underpins the inclusion of children with SEND and their parents. The concept of a triangle of trust can be constructed to enable collaborative effective partnership working with colleagues, parents and other agencies. This framework promotes advocating children's voice, providing a listening culture for parents and practitioners across children's services.

# 1

# LEGISLATION AND POLICY: TOWARDS A PARTICIPATORY PARTNERSHIP

## REBECCA CRUTCHLEY

## CHAPTER OBJECTIVES

- How does the Children and Families Act build upon and extend previous legislation and policy?
- How does the Children and Families Act position parents and children as active participants in decision making?
- Why are the voices of children and families important?
- What are the challenges?

The Children and Families Act 2014 is the largest reform of services for children with special educational needs and disabilities for a generation. Significantly, the articles in the Act relevant to the development of provision for children with Special Educational Needs and Disabilities (SEND) aim to place children and families at the centre of the decision-making process. The 2015 SEND Code of Practice, which replaces the Code of Practice published in 2001, states that local authorities (LAs) 'must have regard to the views, wishes and feelings of the child or young person and their parents' (DfE, 2015c: para. 1:1).

In this chapter we will consider how the Act builds upon and develops existing legislation, examine the context within which the Act was developed and explore the benefits and challenges of activating child and parent participation. The Act incorporates the existing regulations stipulated in the Equality Act (DfE, 2010b) designed to protect children and young people with SEND against discrimination or prejudice.

Over time, special needs and disabilities have been viewed according to a range of different theoretical models and perspectives. As you read through the history of SEN legislation, summarised below, consider how the following models and perspectives are reflected. Further discussion of the impact of these models on provision for children with SEND is included in Chapter 4.

## MODELS OF INCLUSION

### The Medical Model

The medical model of disability positions a person's disability based on their individual impairment with a focus on how the impairment can be managed and, if possible, overcome. Critics of this approach claim that it fails to recognise the way that society impairs individuals with disabilities. The medical reference refers to the perceived expertise of the medical profession in developing solutions and interventions to support the needs of children and young people with disabilities.

### The Social Model

The social model of disability asserts that disability is caused by barriers existent within society which serve to prevent children and young people with disabilities and SEN from participating fully and having equal access to health, education and social care services.

The social model was initially conceptualised by the disability rights activist Paul Hunt in 1966, in his book *Stigma: The Experience of Disability*. However, the clear distinction between a medical model and a social model of disability was made through the work of Michael Oliver when, in 1990, he rewrote the questions to the UK Office for Population, Census and Surveys to consider the impact of disability from a societal perspective. Reframing questions such as 'Do your health problems prevent you from going out as often or as far as you would like?' to 'Are there any transport or financial problems which prevent you going out as far or as often as you would like?' repositioned the barriers faced by children and young people as externally rather than internally imposed upon them (Giddens and Sutton, 2013: 467).

### The Affirmation Model

Initially conceptualised by Swain and French (2000), the affirmation model rests on the premise that provision for children with SEND and consideration of their strengths and needs must evolve from their own perspectives and definitions of their disabilities. Rejecting the 'tragic' model of disability, the affirmation model recognises that disability is an integral aspect of a person's identity.

*(Continued)*

*(Continued)*

## The Bio-psycho-social Model

Also known as the integrative model, this model was developed by Engel in 1977, and recognises the interplay between environmental, biological and psychological influences which affect the way in which a child or young person's disability may be experienced. Crucial to this model is the recognition that children with the same condition will have diverse experiences of their disability due to the impact of these experiences. Recognising the individual child's strengths and needs and not solely their condition is therefore key to effective provision.

## A brief history of SEN legislation and policy

The following section will explore how legislation from the Education Act 1944 to the most recent, the Children and Families Act 2014, has addressed the needs of children with SEN or disabilities, with a particular focus on the extent to which successive policies have recognised the role of parents and children in decision making.

### The Education Act 1944

The Education Act 1944 was the first act of legislation to suggest that children with disabilities may benefit from schooling and that local authorities (LAs) had a responsibility to provide this. Before considering the impact of this Act to the evolution of the SEND field, it is vital to consider the context within which the reforms were developed, as this provides an insight into the influences underpinning such legislative change. The Education Act 1944 (also known as the Butler Act, after the then education minister) was part of a raft of social welfare reforms which recognised the ways in which society was changing as a result of the Second World War and in the immediate post-war period. Although the main focus of the act was to seek to redress social inequality imbalances in the education system (through the introduction of the 11+ and the Grammar schools system), there were, nevertheless, some references to children with SEND when the newly appointed education minister stipulated that LAs should have regard to the education of children who 'suffer from any disability of body or mind' (Ministry of Education, 1944: 5). As such 11 categories were identified to assist LAs in assessing appropriate educational provision. LAs were thus authorised to compel parents to have their children examined by medical professionals in order for this categorisation process to take place. The perspectives of parents on their child's skills and abilities did not appear to be of relevance. The 11 categories of handicap identified in the Education Act 1944 ranged from those children considered to be 'delicate', children who were diabetic, deaf and blind children, and children with a physical handicap. Although the categories recognised, to some extent, the requirement for specialist provision to be offered to children with additional needs, following these medical assessments many children were deemed 'inedu-cable' and placed in non-educational settings where the emphasis was more on their medical care than on their education. These apparently 'ineducable' chil-dren were categorised as 'educationally sub-normal' (ESN). This reliance on what we would now regard as the 'medical model' approach to children with SEND disempowered parents from taking an active role in decisions made about their child's education and instead gave authority to medical professionals who pathol-ogised the child's additional needs. Indeed, the role of children and their families was in some ways perceived to be problematic, as it was anticipated that some parents might reject the decision of medical practitioners if their child was deemed unsuitable for mainstream provision. As such, parents were compelled to sign a form, the Handicapped Pupils Form, effectively agreeing with the deci-sion made by the medical profession for their child to be 'educated' in alternative provision. Therefore although the Education Act 1944 asserted local education authorities' responsibilities to ensure provision for children regardless of their abilities, the nature of this provision was decided without consultation or consid-eration of child and parent perspectives and did not reflect equal access to educational opportunities on the same terms as their non-disabled peers. It is clear, then, that the legislation above reflects the authority invested in the medi-cal profession within society at the time, with little acknowledgement of the personal experiences of families raising children with disabilities. Furthermore, access to information regarding effective approaches to supporting children with disabilities was only just emerging, again from the medical profession who were therefore 'gatekeepers' of this expertise. Thus, according to Tomlinson (1982), children and parents' perspectives were not merely invisible, they were also seen as problematic. This failure to provide equal access to educational opportunities for the 'educationally subnormal' was further compounded by children being placed in residential settings far from their family and community, thus height-ening their vulnerability and isolation.

It was not until the 1970 Education Act (DES, 1970) (also called the Handicapped Child Act) that access to education started to be considered as a right for all children, regardless of ability, and as such special schools were further developed. One of the consequences of the 1970 Education Act was the transfer-ring of responsibility for provision for children categorised as educationally sub-normal (ESN) from health authorities to education authorities. The ESN category was sub-divided into educationally sub-normal severe (ESNS) and edu-cationally sub-normal moderate (ESNM). However, despite the responsibility shifting from health to education, the vast majority of children in both the ESNS and the ESNM categories continued to be educated in special schools where there was an emphasis on 'functional skills' rather than educational attainment. Nevertheless, the Handicapped Child Act did hint at the emergence of a develop-ing awareness that children previously deemed 'ineducable' could, with appropriate educational support and expertise, attain skills and knowledge perceived to be necessary for integration into society. Such perceptions were influenced by earlier comments made in the Plowden Report (1967), originally commissioned to address concerns about inappropriate pedagogy in primary schools as a result of pressure to meet the demands of the 11+ system, and which led to changes in teaching and learning practices in pre-school and early primary provision, which stated that 'Modern society accepts responsibility for the welfare of its handicapped members to a greater extent than did earlier generations and much has been done during the last 50 years to enable children suffering from all kinds of handicap to take their place in society as they grow up' (1967: 296).

Although there would appear to be the roots of a more social model of disability emerging here (see above), it is not clear from either the Plowden Report or from the Handicapped Child Act, if the environmental barriers referred to are poor parenting practices or barriers existent within wider society in general.

## The Court Report

So far much of the legislation discussed has focused on the development of provision for children with SEND within (or indeed separate from) primary and secondary school provision. The Court Report (1976) (titled *Fit for the Future*) by contrast could be described as the precursor to the early intervention approach (discussed in depth in Chapter 7) in that it advocated a developmental approach to assessment and provision for children with SEND and recognised the benefits of early health screening. Although the medical model still dominates in much of the report, for example, 'the arrangements may provide for the education of the pupils in special schools appropriate to the category to which the pupils belong or in schools not maintained by a local education authority' (1976: 33, 2b), there is nevertheless an emerging acknowledgement of the need to consider the social determinants of health and disease, and to act to mitigate such determinants, advocating a community-based approach rather than an institutionalised one.

## The Warnock Report and the Education Act 1981

Published in 1978, the Warnock Report was commissioned to explore provision for handicapped children and young people. The report findings were to influence SEND provision for many years to come. Warnock referred to the changes within society, which recognised more fully the rights of children and young people with disabilities. The report also outlined new approaches to assessing the needs of children, which signalled a move away from the previous reliance on intelligence quotient tests and to more holistic, multi-disciplinary assessments. The 11 categories of handicap (Butler, 1944; DfES, 1981) and the distinctions between degrees of educational subnormality (DfES,1970) were replaced within the broad continuum of the term 'special educational need', and crucially there was acknowledgement of the need to consider children's individual needs, rather than provide services based on the label or category previously ascribed. Significantly, partnerships between professionals and parents were advocated, while responsibility for ensuring appropriate provision for children with SEND was with local education authorities. Perhaps the most significant recommendation from the Warnock Report was that children with SEND should, wherever possible, be integrated into mainstream provision. This, more than any other act of legislation, heralded the drive to inclusion that has characterised SEND educational provision thereafter. While there is a clear shift in the Warnock Report away from a medicalised perspective towards children and young people with SEND and a recognition of the importance of parent's perspectives, the report (and the subsequent Education Act of 1981, which enshrined the committee's recommendations in law) has been criticised for, amongst other things, not raising the expectations for children with disabilities sufficiently. For example, as Tomlinson notes (1982), Warnock appears to convey the message that the workplace cannot accommodate handicapped workers, suggesting that educational goals and targets would be set accordingly with a continued emphasis on functional life skills rather than academic attainment. Similarly, the statement below suggests that appropriate provision for children with SEND remained constrained by financial priorities.

> In present economic circumstances there is no possibility of funding the massive educational resources ... which would be required to enable every ordinary school to provide an adequate education for children with serious educational differences.

(Department for Education and Skills, 1981 quoted in Tomlinson, 1982: 54)

Warnock herself, in 2005, questioned the appropriateness of the drive to inclusion for all children with disabilities, stating that special schools were still the most appropriate educational setting for children with profound or multiple disabilities, and appearing to question the ability of mainstream schools to accommodate the needs of all children with SEND. Nevertheless, despite the criticisms levelled at the Warnock Report and the 1981 Education Act, several key principles were conveyed by the committee which continue to be relevant today, for example the importance of suitable educational provision appropriate to the needs of the individual child, the significance of holistic, multi-disciplinary assessment methods, and the role of parents as partners in decisions made about their child's educational future.

## The Salamanca Statement

In 1994, the United Nations Educational Scientific and Cultural Organization (UNESCO), working in collaboration with 92 government representatives and 23 international organisations, developed the Salamanca Statement, aimed at stating a clear commitment to 'Education for All'. UNESCO recognised that provision for children with SEND cannot occur in isolation but needs to be developed alongside reform of 'ordinary schools' and through changes in attitudes and perspectives towards inclusion for children with diverse needs and aptitudes. For example, section 2 of the Salamanca Statement clearly outlines the committee's commitment towards inclusion, stating that all children have a 'fundamental right' to education and must be given the opportunity to reach their potential. Furthermore the statement recognises that all children have unique characteristics, interests, abilities and learning needs and that education systems should be sufficiently flexible to respond to this diversity. The statement advocates that children with SEN should be assured access to 'regular' schools where the pedagogy is appropriate to support their learning and development, and through which discriminatory attitudes within schools and wider communities can be challenged (UNESCO, 1994).

However, while the intentions of the Salamanca Statement were laudable and widely welcomed in the field of special education, there have been concerns raised, not least by UNESCO itself, five years after the statement was produced, that insufficient progress has been made in assuring education for all (UNESCO, 1999). The significance of a rights-based approach rather than a needs-based approach is further reflected in subsequent legislation, and has been influential amongst parent advocate groups and disability rights activists in campaigns for these rights to be realised.

Furthermore, in the UK, successive legislation and policy guidance has shown an ongoing commitment to addressing inequalities in education opportunities for children with SEND, as outlined in the examples below.

## Evaluation Reports and Guidance Documents

As legislation aimed at enhancing provision for children with SEND was introduced, evaluation reports of current provision and guidance materials which reflected changes to legal requirements for schools and settings in regard to inclusion began to emerge, aimed at capturing the key challenges faced by children with SEND and their families and assisting educational providers to meet the revised requirements. Table 1.1 provides a brief summary of the key reports.

**Table 1.1**  Guidance and publications

| | |
|---|---|
| *Special Educational Needs: A Mainstream Issue* (Audit Commission, 2002) | This report evaluated the progress made by local authorities in addressing the needs of children with SEND and made ten recommendations aimed at ensuring that all children regardless of gender, ethnicity or family background received appropriate support. |
| *Supporting Families Who Have Children with Special Needs and Disabilities* (Sure Start, 2002: 5) | As this guidance was produced by Sure Start, its aim was to ensure that Sure Start programmes were delivering on their commitment to support children with SEND and their families |
| *National Service Framework for Children* (DoH, 2003) | This framework set out 11 standards to be met in addressing children's health needs, eight of which were specifically directed at children with disabilities or complex health needs. |
| *Removing Barriers to Achievement: The Government's Strategy for SEN* (DfES, 2004a) | The Labour government's programme for a 'sustained strategy' of support for children with SEND and their families, focusing on 'partnership working between local authorities, early years settings, schools, the health service and the voluntary sector and incorporates our strategy for improving childcare for children with special educational needs and disabilities' (p. 4). |

| | |
|---|---|
| *Improving the Life Chances of Disabled People* (DfES, 2005) | Joint report by the Department for Work and Pensions (DWP), the Department for Education and Skills (DfES) and the Department of Health (DoH) charged with addressing the barriers to effective life chances for people with disabilities. |
| *Inquiry into Special Educational Needs* (IPSEA, 2005) | Critical report by Independent Panel for Special Education Advice which evaluated the impact and effectiveness of Government SEN strategy. |
| *Aiming High for Disabled Children* (HM Treasury, 2007) | Additional (Labour) government strategy with a focus on:<br><br>• access and empowerment;<br>• responsive services and timely support; and<br>• improving quality and capacity. |
| *Inclusion Development Programme* (DCSF, 2009c) | A series of guidance documents focusing on different areas of SEND aimed at supporting practitioners working in the early years sector through to secondary stage. |
| *The Bercow Report* (Bercow, 2008) | A report into the causes and consequences of Speech Language and Communication Needs (SLCN) in the early years. |
| *Raising Standards, Improving Outcomes* (DCSF, 2008b) | Published as guidance to accompany the Children Act 2006, and aimed at reducing inequalities between children aged 0–5 years. |
| *Healthy Lives, Brighter Futures* (DCSF, 2009a) | A health-led initiative which recognised that steps needed to be taken to address inequalities arising from the social determinants of health, including for children with SEND. |

## PAUSE FOR REFLECTION

• How is the medical model still evident in some examples of provision for children with SEND in schools and settings?

• How effective do you think the social model of disability has been in changing society's perception of children and young people with SEND?

• How might the social model empower parents and children to be active participants in the development and provision of services for children with SEND?

## The Equality Act 2010

Although this Act focuses beyond provision for children with SEND, it is worth noting that it recognises disability as one of its protected characteristics, and as such this Act (which supersedes all previous disability discrimination legislation) places requirements on schools (section 6) and all other public institutions to make reasonable adjustments relating to three key requirements (DfE, 2010b):

- To develop amendments to any provision, criterion or practice.
- To make changes to physical features.
- To offer auxiliary aids and services.

## The Code(s) of Practice (1994, 2001, 2015)

As noted earlier, one of the key legacies of the Warnock Report was the shift away from IQ-based assessments of children's capacity for learning towards a holistic approach which recognised the parent's and to a lesser extent the child's voice in decision making. Guidance for schools on effective assessment of children with SEND was initially published in the Code of Practice in 1994. This was the first in a series of guidance documents which accompanied relevant legislation and advised schools and settings on their responsibilities to ensure provision was made to meet the needs of all children. The first Code of Practice (DfES, 1994) advocated a five-stage process for assessment, known as the Graduated Approach. It also introduced the statementing process for the first time for children whose needs required significant additional support, and initiated the role of the Special Educational Needs Coordinator (SENCO). Subsequent Codes of Practice have developed the guidance in line with legislative change. The most recent Code of Practice published in January 2015 (DfE, 2015c, amended May 2015) outlines how schools and settings must meet the legislative changes introduced in the Children and Families Act 2014, the details of which are discussed later in the chapter.

## The Changing Role of the SENCO

The DfE 1994 Code of Practice and its 2001 revision formally introduced the role of the SENCO, outlining this role as:

- overseeing the day-to-day operation of the school's SEN policy
- coordinating provision for children with special educational needs
- liaising with and advising fellow teachers
- managing learning support assistants
- overseeing the records of all children with special educational needs
- liaising with parents of children with special educational needs
- contributing to the in-service training of staff
- liaising with external agencies including the LEA's support and educational psychology services, health and social services, and voluntary bodies.

(DfES, 2001: 56)

The SENCO role has continued to evolve as an increasing number of children with SEND begin to attend mainstream schools and in response to the multi-agency framework (discussed more in Chapter 9) which required professionals from education, health and social care to work in partnership to support children's development and learning. In 2009, the workload and responsibilities of SENCOs (in statutory school provision at least) were recognised further with the introduction of the National SENCO award, a Master's level qualification which became a compulsory requirement for professionals working in this role in maintained schools. This award has been praised for its recognition of the complex and challenging role of the school SENCO, in particular the acknowledgement that in order for the roles and responsibilities of the SENCO to be conducted effectively they must be members of the school leadership team (SLT), and must be supported through policy and practice by the values and ethos of the headteacher (Griffiths and Dubsky, 2012). However, for non-maintained early years settings, there have been concerns that since the National SENCO award can only be completed by qualified teachers, the valuable work of inclusion workers in private, voluntary and independent early years settings (PVI) remains unrecognised and the role of staff in these settings in the initial assessments and intervention support provided for children with SEND and their families is under appreciated. For example Marrs-Grant (2015) advocates a broad range of training opportunities for SENCOs in PVI settings, from level 4 qualifications through to Master's level, while simultaneously stressing the need to safeguard the role of the Area SENCO (qualified teachers who support PVI settings with their SEND provision). Despite these differences between the maintained and the non-maintained sector, all provision needs to comply with the legal requirements of the 2015 Code of Practice. Further discussion on access to training is provided in Chapter 8.

As the role of the SENCO has continued to develop and increase in status and responsibility, the role has become increasingly more managerial, thus the role of the class teacher (or key worker in early years settings) as the member of staff accountable for the progress and development of children with SEND has increased in importance. The many references to 'quality-first teaching' in the 2015 Code of Practice reflects this accountability. Emanating from Ofsted's report into SEN (2010) which suggested that provision within the classroom needed to be considered as a contributory factor in the under-achievement of children with SEND, the focus on quality-first teaching coincided with the re-categorising of children with additional needs, from School Action/School Action Plus (Early Years Action/Early Years Action Plus) to a more generic category of 'SEN support', alongside SEND funding changes (see below).

To conclude this section on the development of the Codes of Practice since the initial Code in 1994, consider this paragraph from the 2015 version:

> When a child is very young, or SEN is first identified, families need to know that the great majority of children and young people with SEN or disabilities, with the right support, can find work, be supported to live independently, and participate in their community. Health workers, social workers, early years providers and schools should encourage these ambitions right from the start. They should seek to understand the interests, strengths and motivations of children and young people and use this as a basis for planning support around them.
>
> (DfE, 2015c: 19)

---

**PAUSE FOR REFLECTION**

- Consider the shift in expectations for children with SEND compared to comments made in the Warnock Report which recommended counselling for parents whose children were identified as having SEND.

- How is the social model of disability reflected in this paragraph?

---

## Impact of Educational Policy upon SEND Provision

Provision for children with SEND is strongly influenced by changes in educational policy in general. For example, the introduction of the National Curriculum and age-related attainment targets have been criticised by disability rights campaigners for establishing a 'normative' developmental pathway which may not be appropriate for children with SEND and immediately creates a deficit model of their attainment. The publication of school league tables and parental choice in schooling places schools in competition with each other and may deter them from admitting children with SEND and/or entering them for examinations. Finally, the academisation of the state school system with the freedom for schools to set their own admission procedures has raised concerns that the availability of mainstream school placements for children with SEND could be jeopardised (Norwich, 2014)

## Development of Early Years Education and Care and SEND Provision

As noted earlier, much of the legislation discussed refers to SEND provision within the maintained primary and secondary education sector. However, it is important to recognise concurrent developments across the early years sector in England during the same time period, not least because the recognition of the importance of early intervention placed considerable responsibilities upon early years providers to provide inclusive education provision for children with an increasingly wide range of needs. In addition, many of the principles of effective partnership with parents initiate from practice within early years settings as it is often during this period of education and care that a child's SEN may be first identified (Wall, 2011). Therefore sensitive relationship building between parents and professionals needs to be developed. As will be shown, however, despite recognition from successive governments of the importance of early identification and intervention for children with SEND, allocation of funding to support practitioners to meet the needs of children and families has been adversely affected by the removal of 'ring-fencing' for SEN services since 2010, and the reduction in the number of Children Centres (see below) created to serve as multi-agency service hubs. As discussed above, the impact on the PVI sector, has been further exacerbated by their inability to access the full range of SENCO training opportunities offered to maintained sector early years providers (nursery schools and foundation stage units in primary schools) due to the requirement after 2009 for SENCOs to be qualified teachers, very few of whom work in the PVI sector. This is despite the fact that 80 per cent of children under three are cared for in the PVI sector (Lloyd and Penn, 2013).

## Sure Start and the Evolution of Children Centres

Following the election of a Labour Government in 1997, there was considerable investment in early childhood services, influenced largely by research from the High/Scope Perry project in the USA (Schweinhart et al., 1993), which revealed the economic benefits in later years of investment in high quality early education and care, notably reduced unemployment, reduced drug and alcohol dependency, reduced anti-social behaviour and criminality and reduced educational intervention services. Further evidence has been highlighted in the Effective Provision of Pre-School Education (EPPE) project (Sylva et al., 2010) which has demonstrated that high quality pre-school environments, particularly those led by graduate level staff, where practitioners engaged in ' Sustained Shared Thinking' produced long term positive benefits for children's cognitive development and personal, social and emotional development. In addition the introduction of the Sure Start Local Programmes (SSLPs) initiated the introduction of community based programmes and intervention projects in the 30 per cent most deprived areas of the country. Initial projections were for there to be 250 Children Centres each serving 600–800 children and families. The initial SSLPs had a strong emphasis on parental partnership and community decision making. As reported by Naomi Eisenstadt (2011), the original director of Sure Start, local parents were involved in the decision making and planning process from the start, through the introduction of partnership boards where service providers and parent carers would discuss the needs of local families and communities. However, due to perceived concerns about financial accountability within the SSLPs, and the complexities involved in evaluating the impact of the programmes, the provision of services was removed from local community management into local authority Children Centres (although some voluntary providers remained), culminating in the development of 3,500 centres by 2008 (Eisenstadt, 2011). It should be noted that since the recession in 2008, and the election of the Coalition Government (continued by the Conservative Government in 2015), Children Centres in many local authorities have been closed or had their services combined in a hub/spoke model following the removal of ring-fenced funding for Children Centres. As such Children Centres across the country have been merged, with services serving a larger population or in some cases closed altogether (Butler, 2013). Since this time, the Education Improvement Grant (EIG), which did not include the 2-year-old offer (funding for this is now part of the dedicated schools grant) steadily decreased from £3.3 billion in 2010/11 to £1.5 billion in 2015/16 (National Children's Bureau, 2015) and was recently subsumed into general LA funding allocations. Although the early evaluations of Children Centres were inconclusive about the direct impact the programme had on the most vulnerable families (Eisenstadt, 2012), including those with children with SEND, nevertheless it was recognised amongst the service providers that the expectation for professionals to work in collaboration with each other and more significantly in partnership with parents, offered the opportunity to enhance relationships with key stakeholders and facilitate greater communication and shared understandings of children's needs. The co-location of these services in the initial phases of the Children Centre programme greatly facilitated this collaboration.

Subsequent phases of the Children Centres were able to reduce the services provided under a revised core offer; however, there was a clear direction of travel towards inter-agency cooperation which reflects the widest remit facilitated by such mechanisms as the Common Assessment Framework and the Lead Professional role. Thus the multi-agency approach had a significant impact on service provision for vulnerable children, including those with SEND, and perhaps more significantly on perspectives and attitudes towards inclusion. The abandonment of the Every Child Matters (ECM) agenda, following the election of the Coalition Government in 2010, may have removed the five outcomes, but multi-agency approaches continue to be promoted at policy level and in professional practice (see below). Concerns raised by professionals from the fields of early education and special educational needs about the cuts to Children Centre funding (Butler, 2013) have been challenged by the DfE, who stress that their commitment to early education is reflected in their manifesto pledge to increase funding for 3-year-olds' places from 15 hours to 30 hours per week (due to be rolled out in September 2017) and to continue the expansion of the 2-year-olds' provision for vulnerable families (including families with children with SEND). However, in addition to the questions raised by the National Day Nurseries Association (2017) in their response to the DfE report on childcare and education in England (DfE, 2017), about the affordability and capacity for providers to offer the 30 hours (only 63 per cent of private nurseries and 44 per cent of school-based providers have so far pledged to offer the extra 15 hours), other professionals in the field are critical of the qualification levels and expertise amongst staff in the PVI sector and within school-based settings, where many of the children now access their early education and where early identification of additional needs is imperative in order for support to be most effective (Hillman and Williams, 2015).

## Early Education Curriculum Development

Alongside structural change to services for children under five, including those with SEND as outlined above, came curriculum change. In 2000, the Curriculum Guidance for the Foundation Stage was introduced for children aged 3–5 (DfES, 2000), followed by the Birth to Three Matters in 2003 (DfES, 2003), and finally in 2008, the combined Early Years Foundation Stage (EYFS) framework for all children aged 0–5 regardless of the early years setting they attended (DCSF, 2008c). Significantly, these successive curricula frameworks, despite their 'age/stage' expectations, were promoted as inclusive curricula suitable for the assessment and provision for all children, regardless of ability (see Chapter 4). The play-based approach stipulated in the EYFS enabled an individualised approach to learning where activities and interventions could be planned and amended according to children's particular needs and interests, while the introduction of the key worker approach, whereby each child (and their family) would have an allocated member of staff to assess and monitor their progress, aimed to enable a source of communication and partnership between home and nursery. Further support materials which aimed to improve teacher's expertise when working with children with SEND were developed through the Inclusion Development Programme (DCSF,

2009c) (with support materials on autistic spectrum disorders, Down syndrome and speech and communication delays amongst others) and the raft of National Strategies (Early Years) publications which offered a wide range of materials and training packages for practitioners working with children in mainstream and special school provision across the PVI and maintained early years sector, for example Learning, Playing and Interacting (DCSF, 2009b) Not only did these support materials aim to address the need to raise expertise and knowledge across the early years sector, through the introduction of formal qualifications such as the Early Years Professional Status (since evolved into the Early Year Teacher Status), it demonstrated a recognition of the importance of enhancing assessment and identification and support for children with SEND and their families. The Inclusion Development Programme is discussed in more depth in Chapter 7.

## Early Support Programme

Initially a pilot project and introduced in 2003, in response to the Together from the Start agenda (DfES, 2003), the Early Support programme (DfES, 2004a) was introduced for children with severe or complex needs, whereby the family are allocated a support worker (key worker) to navigate the SEND support services available to them. There was recognition therefore that access to services was patchy and complex and that partnerships with parents and carers were crucial to effective and appropriate provision for children with SEND. Although the nationalisation of the programme ended in 2015 due to reallocation of central government funding, organisations such as Council for Disabled Children and the National Children's Bureau continue to work with LAs using the principles of the Early Support programme. The Early Support programme is discussed in more depth in Chapter 7. The principles of the Early Support programme are embedded in the Children and Families Act 2014.

As can be seen from the above discussion, there has been consideration of child and parent voice in previous legislation and documentation. So, how does the most recent legislation build on this? As mentioned at the start of the chapter, the Children and Families Act marks a considerable change in service provision for children with SEND and their families, not simply in the context of education but in the health and social care services too. It would be useful therefore to consider the key influences upon the development of these SEND reforms.

## Background to the Children and Family Act 2014

As suggested earlier, it is important to acknowledge the social, political and economic contexts within which the SEND reforms were developed. The year 2008 marked the start of a global recession which had an impact on service provision across the UK, while the election of a Coalition Government in 2010, followed by the election of the Conservative Government in 2015, led to a shift away from previous frameworks, including the abandonment of the Every Child Matters Framework, which had outlined the five outcomes which all services working with children and young people should strive to achieve.

In the lead up to the parliamentary presentation of the Children and Family Act 2014, the newly established Coalition Government launched the green paper

'Support and Aspiration' (DfE, 2011a) which was a consultation document eliciting the views and experiences of professionals working in the SEND field, and of parents and children who have been recipients of SEND provision and services. The report made a range of proposals based on this consultation exercise, many of which form part of the Children and Families Act, for example greater autonomy for children with SEND and their parents/carers, improved communication between local authorities and parents about services available to them (the local offer), improved identification of SEND, and a combined education, health and care (EHC) plan to replace statements and learning disability agreements. The 'Support and Aspiration' paper reaffirmed many of the concerns parents had raised in the 2009 Lamb Enquiry (Lamb, 2009) which had been tasked specifically with assessing parents' and children's experiences of SEN services. Notably that many felt disempowered and excluded from the system of support for children with SEND which was seen as being dominated by the voices and perspectives of professionals.

In 2010, the Office for Standards in Education (Ofsted), the body responsible for monitoring performance in schools and educational provision, including childcare, across England and Wales, published a report into provision for children with SEND across the early years, primary, secondary, and health and social care services entitled *The Special Education and Disability Needs Review: A Statement Is Not Enough* (Ofsted, 2010). While recognising some examples of excellent practice, it was nonetheless critical of much of the provision provided, and concluded with the controversial comment that too many children are being labelled as having SEN when they just need better teaching. Although there was opposition to this comment from the teaching unions, the comment did in fact echo parents' own comments, that once their child had received an identification of SEN, this label served to determine the level and nature of support, rather than the individual needs of the child.

Similarly influential during the same period is the Salt Review (DCSF, 2010), which examined the education experiences of children with profound and multiple difficulties (PMLD) and expressed concerns about the level of expertise of professionals working with children with the most complex needs. The report recommended raising the status and specialism of staff working with children with PMLD, and acknowledged the need for this expertise to be shared across the special school and mainstream sector. Interestingly, despite the acknowledgement of the importance of parent and child voice in subsequent legislation, none of the 23 recommendations in the Salt Review explicitly recognise the importance of professionals being skilled and trained to work in effective partnership with parents and carers.

Nevertheless the recommendations from the reports such as those cited above coupled with the cost of intervention services for children with SEND during a period of economic recession sets the backdrop for the SEND reforms.

## Key Changes to SEND Provision in the Children and Families Act

The Children and Families Act consisted of ten parts, of which only part 3 is directly relevant to the theme of this book. In addition, there are both explicit

**Table 1.2**  Summary of key changes in the Code of Practice (2015)

- The Code of Practice (2015) covers the 0–25 age range and includes guidance relating to disabled children and young people as well as those with SEN.
- There is a clearer focus on the participation of children and young people and parents in decision making at individual and strategic levels.
- There is a stronger focus on high aspirations and on improving outcomes for children and young people.
- It includes guidance on the joint planning and commissioning of services to ensure close co-operation between education, health and social care.
- It includes guidance on publishing a Local Offer of support for children and young people with SEN or disabilities.
- There is new guidance for education and training settings on taking a graduated approach to identifying and supporting pupils and students with SEN (to replace School Action and School Action Plus).
- For children and young people with more complex needs, a co-ordinated assessment process and the new 0–25 Education, Health and Care plan (EHC plan) replace statements and Learning Difficulty Assessments (LDAs).
- There is a greater focus on support that enables those with SEN to succeed in their education and make a successful transition to adulthood.
- Information is provided on relevant duties under the Equality Act 2010.
- Information is provided on relevant provisions of the Mental Capacity Act 2005.
- There is new guidance on supporting children and young people with SEN who are in youth custody.

(DfE, 2015c: 14)

(clearly stated) changes to provision and implicit (underlying principles) shifts in focus which are worth discussing, in terms of the impact upon professionals, parents and indeed children and young people with SEND. Table 1.2 offers a summary of some of the key changes to SEND provision in the Children and Families Act 2014 and the related 2015 Code of Practice.

---

### PAUSE FOR REFLECTION

- What are some of the key principles underpinning the changes to SEND provision in the Children and Families Act 2014 and the 2015 Code of Practice?

- What challenges may be presented to practitioners working in the SEND field by the changes outlined above?

---

## The SEN Code of Practice 2015

The Code of Practice (DfE, 2015c) was revised in January 2015 (and April 2016) to reflect changes initiated by the Children and Families Act. The new code stipulated the requirements in relation to the local offer, the EHC plans and to supporting children through 'quality-first' teaching and evidence-based interventions.

The graduated approach of 'assess, plan, do, review' was maintained, and further emphasis was placed on classroom teachers being accountable for the performance of all children in their class. In order for a child to be considered for an EHC plan, schools are now required to demonstrate that they have implemented appropriate evidence-based interventions to support a child's needs and there has been little or no impact on the child's developmental progress.

---

### PAUSE FOR REFLECTION

- What are some of the possible challenges of teachers being required to demonstrate that they have implemented all possible evidence-based interventions?
- What impact might the repetition of the 'assess, plan, do, review' cycle have on children with SEN?

---

### CASE STUDY

Katy is an assistant head teacher and early years manager in a primary school and Children Centre in North London, who has significant experience of implementing the new reforms. While she is positive about some of the changes to the SEN Code of Practice, particularly the commitment to working with children and their families, there are concerns that the focus on evidence-based interventions and the commitment to demonstrate that all reasonable steps have been taken to support a child before additional external support through the EHC plan can be achieved, risks delaying crucial support for children. Furthermore, providing evidence that a child has not made progress despite the interventions put in place can be quite challenging, particularly when sharing this lack of progress with parents. Katherine admits that in order to access additional funding, a deficit model of the child is required which runs contrary to the 'strengths-based' principles behind the assessment process (see Chapter 3). In addition, parents and professionals may have differing views about the child's needs and strengths, and partnerships are at risk of being jeopardised unless a high degree of sensitivity is present.

---

### PAUSE FOR REFLECTION

- What are the skills and qualities required by Katy to ensure that parents and carers feel empowered to be part of the assessment process?
- How might she demonstrate the additional needs of children with SEND in a positive and non-stigmatising way?

## Criticisms and Concerns

While there has been widespread support for many of the key developments introduced to support children with SEND, notably the increased emphasis on children's and parents' involvement, there have also been concerns raised about some of the key changes to the Code of Practice. For example, concerns have been raised about how the new funding arrangements for schools can ensure that appropriate support can be provided for those children whose SEN does not meet the threshold for an EHC plan, but which require considerable additional support (e.g. those previously on Early Years/School Action Plus who are now placed in the SEN Support category). Similarly, an EHC plan is only available for children and young people who have both a disability and a SEN, or who have just a SEN. For children who have a medical need or a disability but no SEN, best practice guidance for schools is stated in the Code of Practice, but this is not statutory. Disability rights groups have also commented that the Local Authority can only enforce the education requirements of the EHC plans and not the health or social care provision, which may lead to parents continuing to battle to have their child's needs met in these areas. The expansion of the Academies programme since 2014 has added additional considerations for parents of children with SEND. For example, Special Academies can admit pupils without the need for an EHC plan (funding arrangements in Academies are different to LA-run schools, and is not dependent on EHC plans being in place). While this may be interpreted as a positive move for parents awaiting their child's EHC plan, particularly those in the early years, it may also deny the parents the right to appeal against provision in the school if there is no paperwork stipulating the school's responsibilities (Apsland, 2014).

---

### CHAPTER SUMMARY

This chapter has explored some of the historical and current legislation and policy impacting on the provision for children with SEND and their families. The emergence of a partnership approach has been considered and the principles underpinning the reforms to SEND services have been outlined.

---

## Suggested Further Reading

The books listed below offer some further information and guidance on the key points raised in this chapter.

Nutbrown, C. and Clough, P. (2013) *Inclusion in the Early Years*. London: Sage.
As the title of the book suggests, this book considers inclusion for children with SEND in the early years in its broadest sense. With careful consideration of key issues and practical examples of best practice, the book is essential for practitioners currently in the field and those training to enter the profession.

Tutt, R. and Williams, P. (2015) *The SEND Code of Practice 0–25 Years, Policy, Practice and Provision*. London: Sage.
This is a really clear and concise summary of the key changes to SEND provision following the introduction of the Code of Practice 2015 and the implications for practitioners working in the field of SEND.

Wearmouth, J. (2016) *Special Educational Needs and Disability: The Basics*. London: Routledge.
Although this book does not focus specifically on SEND in the early years, it nevertheless provides a detailed and clear account of recent changes to SEND provision and what they mean for professionals in the field.

# 2

# WORKING WITH PARENTS: PRINCIPLES OF ENGAGEMENT

## LOUISE ARNOLD

### CHAPTER OBJECTIVES

- Explore what it means to work in collaboration with parents and carers of children with special needs and disabilities.

- Consider the importance of effective collaboration and partnership.

- Discuss some of the key challenges.

- Provide some practical and realistic strategies and examples of best practice of involving parents in their children's learning and development and in the evaluation and design of services.

## The Diverse Family

When we refer to parents, we are not necessarily just considering the child's birth mother and father – families are different and diverse, but all deserve to be treated fairly. The Equality Act 2010 protects people from discrimination, and must be abided by in workplaces, schools and in wider society – all parents must be treated fairly and respected in their role. The National Children's Bureau uses an inclusive definition of 'parent' in their document *Principles for Engaging with Families* (2010), which reminds practitioners and professionals that the person or people who have 'a responsibility for, and loving relationship with children in their care' (p. 8) are described as the parent, but that this covers carers and key adults too, as well as parents who do not live in the family home. The Children's Workforce Development Council states that the term 'parent' must also be extended to the guardians of looked after children (CWDC, 2008).

In particular, we are considering the parents of children with special educational needs or disabilities (SEND). Refer to the Glossary at the beginning of the book for definitions of key terms, including SEN, disability, and the SEN areas of need. For the purpose of the chapter, we will be referring to 'parents of children with SEND'; however, we recognise that this is not a homogenous group, and that children and their parents must be treated as individuals with unique needs and wishes. It is important for practitioners to be aware of how a child (and their parents) construct their identity, so as to avoid causing offence; some people identify as 'having autism', whereby their diagnosis is a small part of their overall identity, whilst others would prefer to be called 'autistic', where this is a significant element of their identity, leaving behind the negative connotations of their diagnosis, and the difficulty with 'person-first language' that individuals can feel (Shakespeare, 2014). Either way, as proponents of the more recent models of disability, the affirmative model, or the integrative model (again see the Glossary for definitions), there is room for us as practitioners to be flexible and adaptive with our language, according to the preferences of individual families.

We are also going to consider a multitude of groups who work with children and families, and consider practitioners from a variety of services and settings, including schools, nurseries, after school clubs, and more one-to-one practitioners, such as play workers, personal assistants, therapeutic specialists, and students who may want to pursue one of these careers after their studies. It is important to consider a wide range of roles, since professionals need to work in partnership with each other as well as children and parents, so an understanding of different roles and responsibilities helps aid professional cohesion. The SEND code of practice (DfE, 2015c) re-emphasises the crucial nature of multi-agency working; professionals working together to ensure that appropriate, joined-up support is provided for children with SEND and their families, to ensure the best possible outcomes (CWDC, 2008).

The majority of children with SEND live at home with parents; the 2001 census estimated that 99 per cent live at home with their family (ONS, 2001), however, there are also a subset of children with SEND who are looked after children and live with foster parents or at residential settings like children's homes or care institutions. Each of these situations has implications for parents, in terms of stress and day-to-day concerns. For parents who have their child living at home, there can be issues such as the higher cost of raising a child with SEND; Dobson and Middleton (1998) found it could cost three times as much as raising a child who is not disabled. Parents of children with SEND who are also carers because of additional health conditions or complex needs can experience further stress. The source of stress for many parents of children with SEND is said to be not simply the additional caring or treatment duties for their child, but more often the associated difficulties such as lack of access to information about their child's support, not being able to talk to a professional about their concerns, and dealing with feelings of isolation and powerlessness (NAPP, 2009b). The implications of this are serious for practitioners; it is imperative to be aware of these potential issues, and be part of the solution rather than the problem.

---

**PAUSE FOR REFLECTION**

- Think about your own practice. Have you had to adapt your practice to suit the needs of a family? Could you imagine a situation where you might need to?

- Think about your own experience. Do you feel you are given sufficient time to reflect upon your own practice?

---

## The Importance of Working Together

First, we have a legal obligation to work in partnership with parents and families. This is a concept that has developed over many years, with interest in the impact of parental involvement taking shape in the 1970s, from the perspective of breaking the cycle of poor parenting (Crowley and Wheeler, 2014) leading to (among other things) low educational achievement, and followed up with a review focused on raising parenting standards (Pugh, 1980). In the following years, the focus was firmly on supporting parents, and working with them towards the best outcomes for their children. Parents of children with SEN were specifically discussed in relation to the need for equal partnerships with schools in the Warnock Report, where a chapter entitled 'Parents as Partners' explored the importance of communicating with parents as individuals, valuing their contributions, and supporting them with 'information, advice, and practical help ... promptly and consistently' (Warnock, 1978: 152). Though the language may have changed between 1978 and now, many of the principles advocated in the Warnock Report are woven through more recent documents.

The Children Act 2004 updated existing legislation affecting children and families, and made further provision for considering parental involvement. This was supported by the findings of the EPPE study, which may be summed up by this quote: 'What parents do is more important than who parents are' (Sylva et al., 2004). This means that whatever the background of the parents, or the circumstances they themselves have experienced, or been deprived of, being involved in their child's education can cancel out these negative effects.

The importance of parental involvement in their child's education was built upon with *Every Parent Matters* (DfES, 2007a), which also announced the government's plan to be more proactive in supporting parents to get involved. It gave examples of how this was already happening in schools, and how this could be extended. In 2009, however, the Lamb Inquiry was commissioned by the government to investigate reports that information was not being shared with parents of children with SEND – information relating to services that they had a right to access. The findings showed a lack of trust in professionals and in the SEN system as a whole, with parents reporting that they were having to fight for what their child was supposed to be entitled to. Recommendations were made in terms of partnership, that there was a need for parents to be engaged as opposed to just being given information, and there was heavy emphasis on face-to-face communication. The complications of the system of securing support for children with SEND were raised again in 2011 in *Support and Aspiration* (DfE, 2011a). This document also announced the EHC plan as an option for replacing the 'statement of SEN', indicated that parents would have more choice and control in issues such as where their child is educated, and pledged to invest in the short breaks scheme. Choice and control was a theme in another 2011 publication, *Supporting Families in the Foundation Years* (DfE and DoH, 2011), but focused more on early intervention (with all children under five, not just those with SEND) and again pledged to give parents more control over how services are run and accessed. In 2014, the Children and Families Act provided the legal basis for many new initiatives and developments in the field of early years and SEND, followed closely by the *SEND Code of Practice: 0–25 Years* (DfE and DoH, 2015). This puts the young person and their family at the centre of the process of securing provision for support, and obliges professionals to consider parental views at every stage of creating the EHC plans, with the right to appeal decisions at every stage. This shows that throughout the developing legislation and guidance, children, young people and their parents have been placed firmly at the centre of professional practice, and practitioners are legally obliged to work together with parents for the benefit of the child or young person.

We also have a moral obligation to work in partnership with parents and families, as this is widely seen as good practice and impacts upon the outcomes for children.

Desforges and Abouchaar (2003), in their review of the evidence around the impact of parental involvement on pupils' outcomes, overwhelmingly found that when parents are involved and engaged in their child's education, both with the school and at home, this significantly impacts the achievement of the child in a positive way.

Among others, Wilson (2016) writes extensively about parents being viewed as crucial partners in their child's learning and development; this can be extended to contexts outside of formal education. As well as impacts upon outcomes in formal education, some of the other benefits of practitioners and parents working in partnership include benefits for the child, for practitioners and for parents.

## Benefits for the child

An inclusive environment and ethos can impact upon relationships with practitioners and other children, extending social networks and building confidence (NCB, 2006).

Building trust and strong relationships sets an example for the child about working together with others for mutual benefit, and positive role models.

There are positive outcomes for children in terms of accessing support and moving forward with goals and aspirations. Practitioners are unable to influence how a child behaves at home, or indeed how the parents react, but if the setting has a functional partnership with the parents, the shared ethos and expectations around behaviour, with consistent messages to the child, can ensure that the child is able to manage their behaviour themselves (Brunton and Thornton, 2010), contributing to quality of life outcomes.

## Benefits for Practitioners

Positive outcomes for practitioners can include gaining a partner in the parent, so they are able to use information given to them by the parent in planning activities and learning opportunities for the child (Wall, 2013). This also means that interventions or strategies being used by the practitioner can be shared with the parent to use at home, or strategies being used by the parent can be shared with practitioners, alongside in-depth knowledge about how the child has responded at home. There are also more voices and perspectives involved in planning strategies regarding, for example, behaviour, eating difficulties, speech and language interventions, and combined efforts to implement them, which can contribute to more success. The EPPE study (Sylva et al., 2004) found that settings that shared outcomes with parents in addition to shared methods had much higher chances of success.

## Benefits for Parents

There are also positive outcomes for parents in terms of raised self-confidence with increased knowledge and involvement with their child's learning and development (Wall, 2013), and seeing their child's achievements growing with their increased participation can strengthen and reinforce their commitment (see Figure 2.1). As above with practitioners, they gain a partner in celebrating their child's successes, and in rethinking a plan if it has not had the desired outcome.

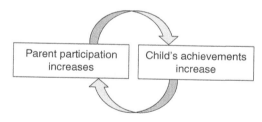

**Figure 2.1**   Parental participation increases as the child's achievements increase, and the child's achievements increase as parental participation increases (adapted from Ward, 2013)

## Wider Benefits

By working in partnership with parents, more targeted services can be devised that might be used more widely, which results in cost effectiveness (Contact a Family, 2012) and this can be related to service-level interactions too; if parents are collaborators in writing policies within a setting, or arranging meetings, the level of satisfaction with the service will be higher. SE7, a group of local authorities chosen to trial the vision of the SEND reforms as 'pathfinders' (Marrs-Grant, 2015) outlined three key ways that professionals work with parents and carers. Their definitions were:

*Consultation* – Professionals decide on questions they would like to know the answer to, and then ask parents for their response.

*Participation* – Parents and carers are invited to meetings and asked to share their experiences and opinions.

*Co-production* – Professionals work together with parents and carers to decide on outcomes, and then produce plans and recommendations together.

(SE7, 2011)

If parents are invited to participate under a co-production model, they can feel more included in the community of the setting and have some level of ownership over the policies and practices, potentially impacting upon how invested they feel in their child's education.

The reality of working in partnership can be more complex than the legislation and guidance suggests, and this is explored further through the chapter.

---

### PAUSE FOR REFLECTION

- Think about your own practice. Can you remember a time when you dismissed the view of a parent without considering it thoroughly? What could you have done to ensure that the partnership was more equal? See the SE7 definitions – which way do you most often work with families?

- Think about your own experience. Are practitioners in your setting given sufficient time and opportunity to form relationships with parents and families?

---

## Securing Support

The process of securing support for a child can be lengthy and complex, and it can be very alienating for families. There can be multiple services and levels of assessment involved, which can include assessment by an educational psychologist, clinical psychologist, speech and language therapist, or an occupational therapist, to name just a few.

## Diagnosis and Assessment

For parents who receive a diagnosis for their child that they were not expecting, or were hoping not to receive, it can be a very distressing time. Some have described this as similar to a bereavement, with families experiencing the stages of grief described by Kubler-Ross (1969): denial, anger, bargaining, depression and acceptance. This would clearly have an effect upon the relationship of parents with practitioners, depending upon which stage they feel they are in at a specific time. This has been challenged by others, who assert that it is similar to a more cyclical cycle of grief, as described by Olshansky (1962) whereby the feelings of sadness return at every 'missed milestone' (NAPP, 2009a), and is characterised by a feeling of 'chronic sorrow'.

Kearney and Griffin (2001) found that in addition to the periods of sorrow experienced by parents of children with SEND, there were also clear feelings of joy and optimism, despite much of the existing research focusing on the negative elements of raising a child with SEND. Again, the impact of this on the child and their parents needs to be considered, with practitioners remembering that it is wholly unhelpful to assume that a parent is feeling a particular way. It is important to strike a balance between acknowledging how a parent may be feeling and not perpetuating the 'tragedy' model of disability (Swain and French, 2000) which many have described as contributing to their feelings of hopelessness. Keen and Rodger (2012) advocate having a 'goal-setting meeting' with parents who have received a diagnosis for their child – their book focused on children who have been diagnosed with autistic spectrum disorder, but goal-setting can be a really helpful tool with all children. See the 'Encouraging Partnership with Parents' section below for more ideas.

## Statements to EHC Plans

Before 2014, children who were eligible for support were given a statement of special educational needs (informally known by the shortened term 'statement') which outlined what they were entitled to and how this would be delivered. This process was seen to be too complicated and lengthy, and focused upon deficits in the child's development rather than strengths, aims and outcomes (Ofsted, 2010).

Under the legislation from 2014, statements have been replaced by Education, Health and Care plans (EHC plans). According to the Children and Families Act 2014, the EHC plans are child and parent focused, and claim to put them at the heart of the process (DfE, 2014a). This means that although professionals and practitioners can request an EHC plan for a child, the parents can also request a plan, and in either case, the plan is supposed to be in place within 20 weeks of the referral being made (as opposed to 26 weeks for the statement). There are opportunities throughout the process for parents to see the plan and appeal if they feel it does not adequately represent their views. The SEN Code of Practice advocates the full involvement of children with SEND and their parents in 'decisions about their support and what they want to achieve' (DfE, 2015c: 11). When viewed with the SE7 definitions in mind, this most closely resembles 'co-production', where outcomes are decided together, and plans are created based on those shared and agreed outcomes. The SEN Code of Practice states that children with SEND and their parents can expect a system that is 'less confrontational and more efficient' (p. 11) and where provision is put in place as soon as possible. This hints at the difficulties parents have faced in the past in terms of accessing support and navigating the system.

As part of preparing for the EHC plan (either transferring from an existing statement to a plan, or creating a new plan), a meeting should be held where the child, with their parents and other significant adults in their life, has the opportunity to express their aspirations and aims, with the EHC plan outlining these aspirations and goals, who is responsible for helping the child to achieve them, and the timeframe that this should be completed in. This process is explained in more detail in Chapter 3, in a discussion about eliciting the views of the child. Each local authority (LA) has their own way of constructing the EHC plan, but as a minimum it must have these 11 specific sections:

A – Views, interests and aspirations

B – Special educational needs

C – The health needs

D – Social care needs

E – Outcomes

F – SEN provision

G – Health care provision

H – Social care provision

I – School placement

J – Personal budget (if a personal budget has been requested)

K – Related reports and assessments

These sections can be presented in whatever way the LA feels is most appropriate; for example, section A may look different depending upon the age of the child, with space for drawings for younger children and more formal writing spaces for older children.

The Local Offer is another important part of the provisions made in the Children and Families Act (DfE, 2014a). This outlines the support and services available in a particular area, and professionals are obliged to share this information with children with SEND and their families. It can contain information about specialist education, health and care services, transport facilities, and services to support young people develop independent living skills. Children with SEND and their parents can use the information in the local offer to support the decisions they make in the EHC plan, for instance, where they would like to go to school or college (section I). The local offer is also supposed to be transparent, making eligibility criteria for services clear, giving information about who and where to go for complaints and appeals, as well as how decisions are made and who has overall responsibility for them (Silas, 2014). IPSEA (2014) have provided some critique of the local offer, in that there is not often the required level of transparency, and there is confusion over what is the duty of the school and what is the duty of the LA, which has also been detected on online parent forums (Apsland, 2014) who are critical of how few professionals themselves are aware of the local offer, unless they are employed by a pathfinder location where it has been established for longer.

The personal budget was also introduced in the Children and Families Act (DfE, 2014a). A personal budget is available by request of the child or their parents, and is the amount of money that the LA allocate in order to meet a person's needs – in this case, the personal budget would be the money allocated in order to work towards the agreed aims and outcomes written in the EHC plan. This is outlined in section J, and can include information on outcomes, arrangements and duration. Personal budgets ideally provide a move away from the 'one size fits all' approach of social care to a more personalised system of individual outcome-focused support (Glasby and Littlechild, 2016).

This is another reason it is important to have an EHC plan that is representative of the aspirations of the child and their parents, since it dictates to some extent how and where the money can be spent. As part of the personal budgets scheme, young people or their parents can also receive direct payments in order to arrange their own support, rather than having the LA arrange it for them. Examples of this are being able to hire a flexible carer or personal assistant for certain hours each day, or accessing a respite or after-school facility. One of the difficulties with direct payments is that it can be difficult to find adequately qualified, trained or experienced candidates to take on the role (NAPP, 2009a), which can represent more work for parents. It is important for practitioners to support parents with these arrangements by sharing information about services available locally, for example local charities that will assist with criminal record (Disclosure and Barring Service – DBS) checks and interviews for personal assistants, and hold information on care agencies.

## CASE STUDY   THE JONES FAMILY

Jay Jones has a diagnosis of cerebral palsy, epilepsy and moderate learning disability. He attends a special school and lives at home with his mother (Ms Jones) and two younger siblings. He has an EHC plan, which outlines his needs (medical, educational and social) and his long-term and short-term outcomes. Jay's medical needs include requiring rescue medication administered by a trained professional, should he have an epileptic seizure.

Jay expressed as part of the process of creating the EHC plan that he would like to learn to swim, and be able to go swimming after school on a Friday after school. This has been written into the EHC plan, and Ms Jones has been allocated a personal budget to help her meet the outcomes on the EHC plan. Under the personal budget, Ms Jones can request to receive direct payments, so that Jay's specific needs can be met, rather than him having to access a service that might not necessarily suit him. This means that Jay can have swimming lessons, and Jay and Ms Jones can together choose and pay a carer who can accompany Jay to the swimming pool. They could choose a carer who had specific skills, experience and training so that Jay's needs would be met, for example, somebody trained in administering rescue medication. They could also choose a carer that Jay likes and wants to spend his leisure time with. Jay and Ms Jones could receive support in recruiting and employing a carer, performing required DBS checks and managing the direct payments from the LA. There are also charities that support families in acting as employers, which can be accessed via the LA. Jay's choice and control is exercised, with support from those who know him best, in order to meet specific outcomes that he identified as part of his EHC plan.

The reality of obtaining support for children with SEND is that it can take longer than expected, and families can face additional challenges, long waits and disappointments. In addition, creating plans that reflect the wishes and aspirations of those individuals and their parents can be a difficult balancing act, and practitioners need to acknowledge this, and the limitations that are present from the LA in terms of funding and wait time, as managing parent expectations.

---

**PAUSE FOR REFLECTION**

- What kind of issues could arise if a child or parent is not aware of their local offer, and the kind of services they can access?

- Can you envision a situation where a child or parent would be disappointed with their EHC plan? What could lead to this? How could this be resolved? Think realistically, considering financial implications too.

---

## Power and Voices

Balancing child voices with parent and professional voices is important, not only because the child has a legal right to an opinion on decisions that affect them (United Nations, 1989) and practitioners have a legal obligation to work in a person-centred way (DoH, 2009a), but also because an inclusive and child-focused ethos is woven through all guidance documents and practitioner policies. It is assumed that as practitioners working with children with SEND and their parents, you will want to consider their views and opinions in all aspects of the support you provide. Daly et al. (2009) frame this as treating children and their families with kindness and respect, and emphasise the need to nurture these partnerships.

Historically, professionals would advise parents on a matter, and they would act upon this information (e.g. in terms of behaviour strategies) or relay this to their child. This would be an example of professionals or practitioners taking the role of 'expert' and parents taking their guidance. Callan and Morrall (2009) have discussed this 'expert' role in the context of early years settings, whereby the professional sees the child's home life through a deficit lens – what the parents are not doing, what the child is not receiving – and the professional makes the decisions without the input or involvement of the parents or the child.

**Figure 2.2**   Single-channel communication

Information is given to parents by the professionals, and this is acted upon by the parents or passed to children, hence the single direction arrows in Figure 2.2. Information from the parents or child is not sought.

The model that many are working towards now is described as 'triadic' because all three groups are considered equal in their participation. As you can see from Figure 2.3, there are arrows representing a relationship between the child and their parents, a relationship between the parents and professionals, and a relationship between the child and the professionals.

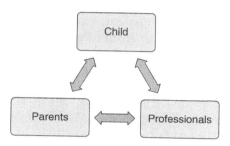

**Figure 2.3**   The triadic model of communication

The importance of functional relationships between each of the parties is key, with any breakdown in communication meaning that the relationships can become unequal, which distorts the dynamic. The parents and practitioner need to have a functional relationship to avoid giving the child mixed messages, and to ensure that they are working in equal partnership and respecting each other. Supporting the parent–child relationship might also be important for practitioners, to ensure that the parents are valuing the child's feelings, as well as ensuring that the parents have support in any difficult discussions with the child (Hughes and Read, 2012). This is also explored as the child–parent–practitioner triangle by Ward (2013), who expands this to include social context; the relationships will be different for every practitioner and parent, and much of this can be due to the variety in experiences and backgrounds, which is why varied strategies and methods are useful in constructing effective partnerships.

An alternative model is the Pen Green Loop.

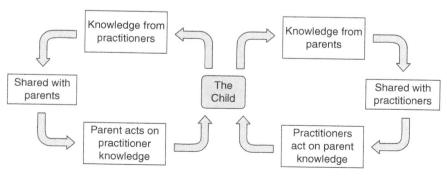

**Figure 2.4**   The Pen Green Loop (adapted from Whalley and the Pen Green Team, 2007)

Figure 2.4 assumes that parents and practitioners each have valuable knowledge that can be acted upon by the other, in order to support the child; the practitioners being experts in their field (early childhood, SEN, social work, play therapy or whatever their specialism might be) and parents being experts in their child (with in-depth lived knowledge about their child's likes and dislikes, routines, food preferences, verbal and non-verbal communication habits, behaviour triggers and soothers, and family structure). When using this model, the child is at the centre of all processes, with parents and practitioners acting upon information received from each other to ensure that the best outcomes for the child are reached.

There are links here to the Team Around the Child (TAC) process, used by many early years and education settings. The process was outlined in the 'Team Around the Child and Lead Professional' guide (CWDC, 2009) and supported in a policy context by the Children and Young People's Workforce Strategy (DfES, 2007b). This process is used in the creation and review of EHC plans, as well as at annual progress reviews. Some local authorities call it the Team Around the Family (TAF) process, but either choice signifies the centrality of the child and their family, with those around them working together for the best outcomes.

---

### PAUSE FOR REFLECTION

- Look at these models of participation again. Which one most closely represents the style of practice carried out in your setting? Could the children in your setting benefit from the principles of an alternative model?

- Consider some of the difficulties associated with this model of working. Are children's views always valued? Who has more power of these three groups? Why?

---

## Difficulties That Can Arise from Collaborative Working

Sometimes, working collaboratively can be difficult, for the parents as well as the professionals. This can be for a multitude of reasons, some of which we will focus on in depth here. Wall (2013) states that as professionals, we must not assume that parents are not interested, but focus on removing barriers to their participation. This is key to working together; to assume that most parents would want some level of participation, and make sure that their contributions are invited, welcomed, valued and taken seriously. Creating environments where the ethos is inclusive and there is a sense of shared responsibility will help to avoid an 'us and them' culture (Callan and Morrall, 2009). Rather than assuming that parents do not want to be involved, instead explore why they may not be involved, and focus on providing support to encourage involvement (Ward, 2013).

Differences in culture or belief can be a tricky subject. If a parent has a belief about the origin of the child's needs or disability that conflicts with the beliefs of the professionals, the process of intervention or support might not be smooth. Special educational needs and disability are constructed differently in different cultures, and without a shared definition there can be differences in opinion about how best to intervene, or whether that is appropriate.

There can also simply be differences in opinion on what is best for the child. Sometimes parents just disagree with what practitioners propose, or vice versa. Again, mediation is important here, as is a strong foundation for the partnership, and respect between all parties.

### Reluctance of Parents to Be Involved

Parents may be disengaged from the process and not want to be involved, but again this can be for a variety of reasons. For example,

> a parent could have anxiety over what is best for their child, and would rather that the professionals involved in the case made decisions relating to their child's support arrangements. In this case, it would be important to ensure that the parents have sufficient and appropriate information so that they are able to make informed decisions, rather than taking the easy route of making the decision you think is best.

In addition, a parent may have previous negative experiences of partnership with professionals (Callan and Morrall, 2009) and be sceptical about the usefulness of working together or sharing information. For example, the *Review of Best Practice in Parental Engagement* (DfE, 2010a) found that schools do not always value the engagement that parents already have in supporting their child's learning. In this case, the first priority would be making time to build a relationship with the parent and rebuilding their trust in the school or setting.

Parents may be experiencing difficulties with work or family commitments, and be unable to attend meetings or appointments; this should not be taken as a reluctance to be involved, but they should be accommodated as far as possible, whilst recognising that sometimes issues might be time sensitive, so alternative plans may have to be made or alternative methods of communication used. Parents might also have their own health concerns, or have a carer role for their child, which, as discussed earlier in the chapter, can contribute to stress levels and impact upon availability. It is also important to consider parents who are disabled themselves, and whether there are accessibility issues for that parent in terms of physical accessibility (e.g. to meeting rooms) or documents or reports issued (always ask if a parent would like a report or document in an alternative format).

There are certain additional difficulties that families from traveller communities can face too, including issues of fixed address (and how that affects correspondence with various education, health and social support services as well as parent support networks) or periods of time that the child may spend out of education in terms of picking up the curriculum or forming or maintaining social networks. Practitioners must be sensitive to the unique needs of individual families, and be proactive in making arrangements to ensure that partnerships can continue. Practitioners must also consider families in transition – facing homelessness, divorce, the birth of a new child, suffering a bereavement – so that they are able to be proactive in offering support and flexible in providing opportunities to meet.

### Reluctance of Professionals to Involve Parents

Sometimes, professionals do not want to involve parents in decisions or processes related to their child. Again, this can be for a multitude of reasons, but some of the more common are explored here:

> *Professional superiority complex* – professionals may think that they know better than the parent about what would be best for the child. This supports the model in Figure 2.2, where the practitioner constructs themselves as an expert, and is in direct contrast to the model in Figure 2.4, where both parties respect that the other has knowledge and information that is beneficial.

> *Lack of confidence in professional role* – sometimes the reverse is true; The *Review of Best Practice in Parental Engagement* (DfE, 2010a) found that sometimes teachers lack the confidence required to work with parents, which can impact upon relationships and communication.

Occasionally, the best efforts of those involved are not enough, and one party can feel as though they cannot participate, or would rather not participate, and relationships can become strained and break down. When this is the case, it can mean that the focus is directed from the best interests or the most positive outcome for the child to resolving arguments or disagreements. Unhelpful approaches from practitioners include the tendency of some to presume they know and understand everything about SEN, the processes and policies, and especially the child. This can be alienating to parents, who can feel that their knowledge and skills are not appreciated or welcome. This also overlooks the fact that the parents spend the most time with their child, and know them best – which gives them a unique insight into much of the child's behaviour. It is also important to consider that practitioners working regularly with the child may observe different behaviours to those reported at home, so working together and sharing information is crucial in order to build up a full, contextual picture of the child's abilities, development, preferences and how best to support the child at home and elsewhere.

---

### PAUSE FOR REFLECTION

- Think about your own practice. Have you tried to work with a family who seemed like they were not interested in being involved? Or a professional who was not cooperative? What did you do? Could you have handled this situation more carefully?

## Encouraging Partnership with Parents

Remember that different professionals have different working practices; as a teacher, social worker, personal assistant or playworker for example, you will have different roles and different relationships with families of children in your care. If you work in a school or nursery for example, there are usually internal policies governing partnership (which may or may not have been written in collaboration with parents themselves) and these sometimes dictate the level and type of contact between practitioners and parents.

If you work on a one-to-one basis with children and families, the local authority will often provide guidance, but if you work in a more informal way with children, as a personal assistant or carer, then there may not be policies so much as personal or parental preferences in working practice. This is something to discuss with the family or agency you are employed by, to ensure that everybody has an understanding of expectations and roles.

According to the statutory framework for the EYFS, every child needs to be allocated a key person who is responsible for helping the child to settle in, and who will ensure that the learning experience is meeting the child's needs (DfE, 2014b). This applies to state schools (both maintained and non-maintained), independent schools, all settings on the early years register, and those who are registered with an early years childminder register. The key person must also 'seek to engage and support parents and/or carers in guiding their child's development at home' (DfE, 2014b: s.1, p.10). For children with SEND, the key person liaises with the SENCO in order to implement and monitor programmes of support (DfE and DoH, 2015). This means that there need to be functional relationships between practitioners and parents in order to continue to meet the child's needs.

In a wider context, the SEN Code of Practice (2015c) states that feedback must be gathered from children and young people as well as from parents and families in order to review provision and services in the LA, so partnership should be encouraged at all levels. Of course, because of the different roles and ways of working, effective parental partnership will look different to each professional. We will explore methods to encourage effective partnerships in different spheres but on similar timelines, remembering that there is no one-method-suits-all approach (Ward, 2013) that will work for everybody in every context.

### When You First Meet a Child or Family

As a general rule, avoid starting a conversation by asking about a child's diagnosis or about what they are unable to do, but instead ask about them as a person: What do they like doing? What is their preferred communication method? What is your family story? This means that communication starts in a positive and ability-focused way, rather than from a deficit approach. Where appropriate a home visit might give the practitioners a chance to get to know the child and parents in the home environment, allowing all parties to form relationships and build confidence. In terms of starting at a school or setting, transition is a crucial period and it is important to manage transitions well (Hughes and Read, 2012) as it can impact upon the child's confidence, attainment and ability to settle. See Chapter 7 for further information on transitions.

### At Annual or Progress Reviews or in Annual Reports

Schools are obliged to provide a progress report each year, as well as meet with parents at least three times per year if their child is receiving SEN support (DfE, 2015c), and EHC plans need to be reviewed yearly too so this can be a crucial opportunity to develop the partnership face to face with the parents, and the child too if they are present. Ensure that the annual or progress review is held at a time when the parents will be able to attend if they would like to, and that plenty of notice is given to all parties so that as many people will be able to attend as possible. It is good practice to ask parents about their preferences before arranging a meeting, and to consider the child's needs in terms of time and length of the meeting, and the location it is to be held at.

Goal setting is an important practical activity (Keen and Rodger, 2012) that focuses on abilities as well as goals that the child would like to achieve, or which the parents would like to help the child work towards. This fosters effective partnerships too, as all parties have shared goals to work towards.

Sometimes a parent might feel they need some guidance in their parenting outside of the usual support provided by the parent–practitioner partnership, or the practitioner may feel that the parent could benefit from further support. In this case, they can be offered parenting courses or classes (Hughes and Read, 2012), though the best chance of success in this would be approaching the situation with a 'supportive, non-judgmental attitude' (DfE, 2010a: 7). Consider that some parents may require more support than others, whether it is a matter of preference, or difficulties in their own lives, as explored earlier in the chapter, so tact and understanding is required.

### When a Child Is Leaving a Setting or Provision Has Finished

Again this is a period of transition, which can be difficult for the child and their parents once relationships have been created. Transitions are explored in further depth in Chapter 7. Be careful to manage the relationship carefully to avoid the parent or child becoming over-dependent on the support.

### More Specifically for Education Settings

Daly et al. (2009) advocate ensuring that all setting up for activities is done before parents drop their children off, so that staff are free to talk to parents, as well as having staff positioned near the door, in order to create an environment where parents are welcomed and able to speak to a practitioner if they want to. It can also be helpful to invite parents to work or volunteer in the setting (Daly et al., 2009) so that they are familiar with the ethos and working practices of the setting, and can grow in confidence in terms of participating in more formal ways. Parent forums or parent councils are becoming increasingly common at schools and early years settings (Carnie, 2011). These are spaces where parents are able to be involved in the running of the school or setting and influence policy and practice, and can be encouraged to be proactive in their child's education at school level. Forums or councils also foster more equality in partnerships between parents and school staff.

### For Families Who Are 'Hard to Reach' or Are Finding It Difficult to Be Involved

Planning practical activities that may involve children too rather than discussions can encourage more participation in parents (Ward, 2013); this might be due to the more informal set up, as opposed to the very formal context of a meeting, review or appointment. Organising family workshops with rules and a specific focus (Brunton and Thornton, 2010) or fun days with other families invited can create a less formal environment where parents and children may be able to relax more and focus on the activities, lessening the anxiety they could feel in formal spaces. Simple acts such as inviting a parent to an event face to face rather than via a letter or email can ensure that they feel welcome, as it is a more personalised gesture.

---

### PAUSE FOR REFLECTION

- Are parents involved in planning transition activities at your setting? Has their advice been sought about what they found helpful or unhelpful?

---

### Communication

It is important that communication channels remain open, and flexible to the needs of the child and family. Practitioners can use email, telephone calls, letters, home-to-school diaries, face-to-face meetings or text messages, but first check if your workplace or employer has a policy on communicating with parents. It can also be helpful to follow the family's lead on communication; if they prefer to telephone you rather than communicate via email, then you should follow suit.

---

It is important that the most appropriate method of communication is used for individual families. Consider which method of communication you would suggest for the families in the following cases:

- A family who have English as an additional language.
- A family who reside across several different households.
- A family with no fixed address.
- Parents who have limited literacy skills.
- Parents who have an intellectual disability.

Murray (2015) writes about the importance of school staff communicating good news to parents, and keeping relations positive. This means that if an issue with the child's behaviour arises, a relationship has already been established with the parents and they are more likely to take the issue seriously. Daly et al. (2009) recommend being prompt with communication (in terms of replying to parent queries, or reporting an accident or injury) to ensure that the partnership feels reciprocal.

This also means that, as discussed above, the environment around the child remains positive and supportive, with all parties working together to support the child in the most effective way possible.

---

### PAUSE FOR REFLECTION

- Are you always as inclusive as you can be in your communication with the parents and families that you work with? What could you do differently to improve the communication channels?

- Have you worked with parents who speak English as an additional language? How did you ensure they were included? Or how could you ensure that you are being inclusive in future?

---

## Maintaining a Professional Role

Whilst most practitioners will want to go above and beyond to support families, there are boundaries and limitations to the role that practitioners play in a family's life. It is important to stay reflective, and refer families on to other kinds of support if this feels more appropriate. This may not always mean referral to other formal services like parenting courses or therapeutic interventions, but instead to more informal sources of support such as online parenting support forums or local support groups. Many parents can find it very comforting to be in the presence (online or in person) of others who have experienced similar situations to them, and as a practitioner you may not be the person who can (or should) provide this kind of support.

---

### ALWAYS REMEMBER

- Parents want what is best for their child, and their words or actions could be affected by anxiety, anger, having had bad experiences with practitioners in the past, or other, unrelated difficulties – always speak to them respectfully and give them the benefit of the doubt.

- Parents are busy too – make sure they can be around when important decisions are going to be made. Be flexible and understanding when planning meetings or appointments.

- Parents are also people, and may prefer to be referred to by name in formal situations, rather than as 'mum' or 'dad' – ask them.

- A child might be one of a large caseload or class group to you, but they are still an individual and their welfare is their parents' main priority. Avoid phrases that might depersonalise them, like 'this happens all the time' or 'your child is not the only person we have to consider'.

- It is important to have empathy, and to imagine yourself in a similar situation to those you are working with, but avoid telling somebody you know how they feel because the chances are that you don't, and this can sound inauthentic and patronising.

- Sometimes a case or a situation might feel stressful, but it is important to contain this – keep things calm and confidential. Breathe deeply and maintain accurate, unbiased records – do not rant to other colleagues or send emails or other communications when you are stressed out.

- Be honest – if you do not know the answer to a question, then say that, but make it a priority to find out, and get back to the person who asked you. If it is not your area of expertise, refer them to an appropriate person.

## PAUSE FOR REFLECTION

- Have you asked parents what they like about the practice in your setting, and what could be improved? Why/why not? Has this been helpful, or do you think this could be a helpful process?

- The definition of 'parent' was explored in the beginning of the chapter. Why is it important to expand on the traditional definition?

- How many different ways of communicating with parents and families can you think of? Which ones are appropriate for professionals to use?

- Think about current policy. Has anything changed? What impact does it have upon practitioners and parents working in partnership?

## CHAPTER SUMMARY

In this chapter, we have explored different ways of working with, communicating with and partnering with parents. We have considered the differing structures and needs of families, and ways in which we as practitioners and professionals can accommodate these into our work, for positive and fulfilling outcomes for the children and families we work with. We have also reflected upon problematic aspects of working together, and ways that difficulties can be overcome, as well as the benefits that partnership can bring.

## Suggested Further Reading

Murray, D. (2015) 'Working in partnership with families, parents and carers', in Martin-Denham, S. (ed.), *Teaching Children and Young People with Special Educational Needs and Disabilities*. London: Sage.
This chapter focuses more specifically on working with parents in a school setting and includes lots of helpful advice for practitioners who want to build relationships with parents of the children in their setting.

Keen, D. and Rodger, S. (2012) *Working with Parents of a Newly Diagnosed Child with an Autism Spectrum Disorder: A Guide for Professionals*. London: Jessica Kingsley.
This book goes into more detail about the difficulties that parents face after their child has been diagnosed with ASD. It provides useful information and guidance for professionals.

Wilson, T. (2016) *Working with Parents, Carers and Families in the Early Years: The Essential Guide*. London: Routledge.
This book focuses specifically on practitioners working in education settings, and has a chapter on parent forums and parent councils that is very detailed

# 3

# PUPIL AND PARENT VOICE: CONTRIBUTIONS TO ASSESSMENT AND PLANNING

## REBECCA CRUTCHLEY

## CHAPTER OBJECTIVES

- What are the principles of effective assessment for children with SEND in the early years?

- How can the graduated response approach be used effectively to provide appropriate interventions for children with SEND?

- How can schools and settings ensure children and parents are fully involved in the assessment process?

- How can person-centred plans be used to encourage greater levels of participation from children, parents and carers?

As discussed in previous chapters, there is a clear requirement in the Children and Families Act 2014 and the 2015 Code of Practice for children to be at the heart of the assessment process, and for parents and carers to be fully involved when decisions are made about their child's SEN support and provision.

This chapter will consider why this is so important and provide examples of how schools and settings have successfully incorporated child and parent voice into assessment procedures in their settings.

## The Early Years Curriculum

Since the introduction of the Curriculum Guidance for the Foundation Stage in 2000 (DfES, 2000), followed by the Birth to 3 Matters Framework in 2003 (DfES, 2002), which were combined to produce the Early Years Foundation Stage in 2008, and its subsequent revised versions thereafter (DfE, 2012, 2014b), observational assessment has been considered key to assessing the needs of children in the early years. The Early Years Foundation Stage framework (DCSF, 2008c) recognised that children in the early years develop in different ways at different rates, and age-related expectations should be flexible enough to take these varying patterns of development into account. There was also a clear statement in the Early Years Foundation Stage Framework that it was intended as an inclusive curriculum which was appropriate for supporting provision for children with additional needs, and for observing and assessing their development. Key principles and commitments from the framework reflect this position, as can be seen from the principle of the unique child, one of its four key themes. Similarly guidance on the principles into practice cards included in the framework encourage practitioners to ensure that 'the diversity of individuals and communities is valued and respected. No child or family is discriminated against' (DCSF, 2008c). Schools and settings should also ensure that they are 'working in partnership with other settings, other professionals and with individuals and groups in the community to support children's development and progress'. Although the statutory framework has been reviewed twice (DfE, 2012, 2014b) since these principles were developed for the original EYFS framework in 2008, they remain core to the underpinning philosophy of the EYFS curriculum.

## Principles of Effective Assessment

The principles of effective assessment in the early years as outlined in the *Early Years Foundation Stage Profile Handbook* (STA, 2017: 7) are cited as follows:

- Assessment is based primarily on the practitioner's knowledge of the pupil.
- Knowledge is gained predominantly from observation and interaction in a range of daily activities and events.
- Responsible pedagogy must be in place so that the provision enables each pupil to demonstrate their learning and development fully.
- Embedded learning is identified by assessing what a pupil can do consistently and independently in a range of everyday situations.
- An effective assessment presents a holistic view of a pupil's learning and development.
- Accurate assessments take account of contributions from a range of perspectives including the pupil, their parents and other relevant adults

(DfE, 2016b: 7)

The guidance for effective assessment is intended for all pupils in the early years foundation stage, and not specifically for children with SEND. However, it is anticipated that these principles of assessment are equally relevant for the children with additional needs. Many would argue that the perspectives of parents are particularly crucial when assessing and planning provision for children with SEND. Indeed this principle is repeated throughout the 2015 Code of Practice (DfE, 2015c).

Thus continuous, ongoing formative assessment combined with summative assessments at timely intervals (e.g. once a term) continue to be the dominant approach for assessing the developmental progress of children in the early years. It is worth noting that from September 2016, schools have been able to choose their own process for summative assessment rather than the current nationally imposed early years foundation stage profile. However, it is expected that schools will continue to adhere to the principles of effective assessment as cited above.

## FORMATIVE ASSESSMENT

Ongoing, continuous assessment of children's learning which informs day-to-day practice and provision. Formative assessment can include observation, annotated drawings, photographs and videos, adult–child interactions, focused group activities.

## SUMMATIVE ASSESSMENT

Time-bound assessment of a child's attainment and progress based on the collation of evidence from formative observational assessment methods, measured against a set of developmental criteria, for example early years outcomes or early learning goals.

## Methods of Observational Assessment

As reflected in the principles of effective assessment cited above, holistic assessments of children's developmental progress are key to gathering a clear and accurate picture of the child's strengths and areas for development. This evidence can be gathered through a variety of observational assessment processes and through dialogue and discussion with all of the adults involved in supporting the child, particularly the child's parents. Many of the key principles of engagement with parents, and the rewards and challenges associated with parental partnerships, are discussed in Chapter 2 but the overarching philosophy underpinning this engagement is reflected in the 'parents as partners' commitment in the EYFS which states that 'parents are children's first and most enduring educators. When parents and practitioners work together in early years settings, the results have a positive impact on children's development and learning' (DfE, 2014b). The following section outlines some examples of observational assessment and considers how these can be used in partnership with parents to collate a full picture of the child's competencies and abilities.

## Observational Assessment

Observational assessments aim to capture a 'snapshot' of the child's abilities in a range of different domains, for example, their interactions, dispositions, competencies, and areas for development. During observational assessment it is crucial that the observer records exactly what is observed and avoids making assumptions about what they have seen. Analysis of what the observation reveals about the child's development and learning is ideally discussed through collaboration with other staff, and where possible with parents. Observations are collated over a period of time and shared with parents through the child's development records, which should be freely available for parents and carers to access. Inviting parents to read through their child's observations can be an effective way of sharing how the child demonstrates their skills and abilities in a group-based setting and what these show about his/her developmental progress. Having an open-access approach to children's development records at the start of a child's entry to an early years setting can ensure that information about the child's development is communicated on a regular basis, which can facilitate effective partnership working and ensure that discussions about a child's needs take place within well-established and trustful parent–practitioner relationships. Observations from the setting can be compared with the child's behaviours in the home environment, for example with their siblings, to build a fuller picture of the child's learning and development in a range of contexts. This can be particularly important for children with SEND, who may display different behaviours at home and school, due to differences in the learning environment, or where they feel most settled and comfortable.

Table 3.1 provides an example of some of the main type of observational assessment in an early years setting.

**Table 3.1**  Examples of observation methods

| | |
|---|---|
| Narrative | These are 'open ended' observations which aim to capture how the child responds to their learning environment, e.g. how they interact with their peers and in response to adult interactions. |
| Focused | Focused observations aim to observe a specific aspect of a child's development either for a fixed period of time or in response to a directed activity, e.g. the child's use of verbal language skills during a language intervention activity. |
| Time sampling | Time sampling aims to gather information about a child's interests and engagement over a fixed period of time and can be useful when assessing the extent to which the learning environment is able to provide engagement and stimulation for the child's stage of development. |
| Event sampling | These types of observations aim to monitor the number of times an event happens over a fixed period of time in the learning environment. They can be particularly useful to assess a child's use of verbal or non-verbal communication during a free play activity, or for monitoring a specific behaviour. |
| ABC sampling | ABC stands for Antecedent, Behaviour and Consequence. These types of observation can be useful to understand the potential triggers for inappropriate or challenging behaviour in the early years, in order for staff to minimise the occurrence through careful adaptations to the learning environment or routine. |
| Tracking | As the name suggests, these observations track the child's behaviour over the course of a specified time, e.g. a whole morning or an hour of the session. The intention is to monitor the child's engagement with different learning opportunities within the environment to assess their concentration, focus and engagement. |

This is not an exhaustive list of observational processes, and most early years settings and schools will use a variety of approaches in order to develop a holistic picture of the child. Information gained about the child from these observations will be used to inform the summative assessments (see below), and to plan for future provision in the free-play learning environment and through interventions (or 'next steps') to address areas for development in the child's learning.

In addition to observational assessment, early years settings and schools use a variety of approaches to develop a full picture of the child's knowledge, ability and skills. For example, photographs or videos of the child in a range of contexts (indoor/outdoor, free-play/focused activity) can be an effective way of capturing the child's engagement and interest in a particular activity. Discussions with the child about the photographs/videos and their recounting of the activity is crucial to developing an understanding of the significance of this 'snapshot' and what it suggests about the child's competencies in a range of developmental areas. Such annotations can also be used to illuminate the child's thinking processes during drawing activities. The case study below provides an example of this.

## CASE STUDY

Tommy is four years old, and attends a pre-school in London. He shows his key worker a drawing he has completed which consists of a series of straight lines, parallel, perpendicular and intersecting. To the untrained eye, they appear to show a collection of random straight lines. The key worker asks Tommy to tell her about his picture. He explains that they show the underground lines, the overground lines and the train line to Paris! When the key worker asks for more information about the train line to Paris, he replies, 'You can take this train to Paris and get fresh croissants'. The discussion with Tommy revealed considerably more about his knowledge of his local environment (and further afield!) than could be gleaned by simply looking at a drawing of straight lines.

## PAUSE FOR REFLECTION

- How could practitioners working with Tommy use this information from the discussion with his key worker to provide further activities to continue developing his thinking?

- How could they involve parents in the planning of future provision?

## Listening to Children: The Mosaic Approach

Developed by Clarke and Moss in 2001, the mosaic approach was originally intended as a tool for the engagement and participation of young children in educational research. However, key principles of the approach are highly relevant for observation and assessment of children in early years settings and classrooms. A key underlying principle of the approach is the conceptualisation of children as competent 'social actors' who have the capacity to make informed decisions about issues which affect their lives, thereby offering clear comparisons with the affirmative model of disability cited earlier in Chapter 1. For very young children, this may require adapting processes for them to be able to express their perspectives and opinions in age-appropriate ways. Thus Clarke and Moss recommend a range of child-centred approaches to eliciting children's views:

- Drawings (and annotated conversations)
- Annotated photographs
- Storying (children creating their own stories)
- Role play
- Focus groups (group-based discussions with children which reduce adult–child power hierarchies).

Further information about the mosaic approach and its application as a tool for observational assessment can be found in the recommended reading section at the end of this chapter.

## Development Matters and Early Years Outcomes

The Development Matters statements were initially developed by Early Education (www.early-education.org.uk) to accompany the first EYFS framework in 2008. Although non-statutory, they have been extensively used by early years settings, schools and childminders as a tool for observing and assessing children's development and learning and for planning future provision to support children's progress across the areas of learning of the EYFS. Revised alongside the revisions of the framework in 2011–12 (Tickell, 2011) and 2014, the Development Matters statements reflect the three prime and four specific areas of learning of the EYFS. Table 3.2 cites the prime and specific areas of the revised Early Years Foundation Stage (DfE, 2012).

**Table 3.2**   Prime and specific areas of the EYFS

| Prime | Specific |
|---|---|
| Personal, Social and Emotional Development | Literacy |
| Communication and Language | Mathematics |
| Physical Development | Expressive Arts and Design |
| | Understanding the World |

One of the key benefits of the Development Matters statements for practitioners and parents is that they take into consideration the observation, assessment and planning cycle, thus rather than simply listing a series of expected levels of development at particular ages and stages they offer guidance and support on the practitioner's role in supporting children's learning, for example through enhancements to the learning environment and one-to-one interventions. Following the reduction in the number of early learning goals during the revision of the EYFS in 2012 (maintained in 2014), which is discussed further below, a streamlined guidance document for practitioners was published aimed at supporting staff in assessing children's learning according to these new early years outcomes (DfE, 2012). However, as this revised guidance simply lists the expected level of attainment at different ages and stages of development, it has limited usefulness for practitioners wishing to know how to support children with SEND who may be operating at a level below the expected level of attainment.

Perhaps a more welcome revision in the 2012 Early Years Foundation Stage was the explicit inclusion, for the first time, of the importance of children's *characteristics of learning*. These are summarised as: active learning, creating and thinking critically, and play and exploration. These later additions to the framework were widely welcomed by professionals working in the early years field as they reiterated that long-held view that how children learned was as important (if not more important) than what children learned. These characteristics of learning remain a dominant philosophy underpinning the curriculum, although professionals in the field have warned that they risk being compromised by the imposition of outcomes which are unrealistic and unobtainable. Concerns have been raised, for example, about the revised 'expected' level of attainment in the revised early years outcome descriptors (Norbury and Gooch, 2015; Ang, 2013). However, the characteristics of learning can be particularly helpful when assessing the developmental progress of children with SEND, whose pattern of development may not follow a conventional trajectory as they can alert practitioners to a child's lack of motivation or difficulty accessing play-based learning which may indicate that the child requires support to engage fully with the learning environment (Dubiel, 2012).

## Early Learning Goals

As noted above, during the information gathering which accompanied the initial review of the EYFS by Dame Claire Tickell in 2011, concerns were raised about the excessive paperwork involved in assessing children's developmental progress in the EYFS, with many complaints focused on the extent to which the paperwork prevented practitioners from working alongside children to support their learning. As such the early learning goals in the original early years foundation stage profile (completed at the end of the foundation stage in Reception class) were reduced from 69 to 17. For each of these 17 outcomes, staff are required to make a 'best fit' judgement as to whether the child is at an emerging, expected or exceeding level of attainment. The *Early Years Foundation Stage Profile Handbook* (STA, 2017) provides exemplification materials to assist staff with this process of assessment, and reiterates the expectation that observational assessments, alongside contributions from children, parents and other relevant adults, are included in order to provide a full picture of the child's development across a range of meaningful contexts. Judgements should therefore be made using the following information:

- knowledge of the pupil
- materials which illustrate the pupil's learning journey, such as photographs
- observations of day-to-day interactions
- video, tape or electronic recordings
- the pupil's view of his or her own learning
- information from parents or other relevant adults.

(STA, 2017: 12)

## Early Years Outcomes

Communication and language

> *Listening and attention*
>
> *Understanding*
>
> *Speaking*

Physical development

> *Moving and handling*
>
> *Health and self-care*

Personal, social and emotional development

> *Self-confidence and self-awareness*
>
> *Managing feelings and behaviour*
>
> *Making relationships*

Literacy

> *Reading*
>
> *Writing*

Mathematics

> *Numbers*
>
> *Shape, space and measures*

Understanding the world

> *People and communities*
>
> *The world*
>
> *Technology*

Expressive arts and design

> *Exploring and using media and materials*
>
> *Being imaginative*

(DfE, 2013a: 2)

The importance of the characteristics of learning (see above) is reiterated in the EYFSP handbook, in the requirement for practitioners to write a 'commentary' which states how the child engages in the learning environment. Guidance for practitioners includes statements such as:

'Using what they know in their play' describes how pupils use play to bring together their current understandings, combining, refining and exploring their ideas in imaginative ways. Representing experiences through imaginative play supports the development of narrative thought, the ability to see from other perspectives, and symbolic thinking'.

(STA, 2017: 12)

The commentary section of the EYFSP is deemed to be particularly useful as children transition from Reception to year 1, and also for children with SEND, some of whom may be assessed as emerging for many of the 17 early learning goals, which may offer only a partial picture of their development; for example, it may not reflect their perseverance, motivation or interests.

The 2016 handbook also reiterates that for children with SEND in the early years (0–5), assessment of their developmental progress should be conducted using the EYFS early learning goals, and that alternative assessment tools should not be used (see below). However, there is some guidance, albeit quite limited, about specific adaptations which can be used to support this process. For example the guidance refers to mobility aids, communication aids, magnification and computer software and ICT support. There is a recognition in the guidance that children with SEND may have reports on their developmental progress from many other professionals, and it recommends that these reports are used to support practitioners in reception class to make the 'best fit' judgement.

## Assessment using the P scales

As mentioned earlier, the EYFS framework is designed to be an inclusive framework for providing learning activities for all children aged 0–5 and for assessing their learning and development accordingly. However, at the end of the EYFS, as children transition from early years to the primary curriculum, for children with profound or multiple learning difficulties the expectations of the primary curriculum can be unrealistic and inappropriate to their stage and rate of development. P scales (QCDA, 2009) can be used to assess children according to more relevant steps in their development, and enable practitioners to plan more meaningful and relevant learning opportunities for these children. P scales consist of an eight-stage developmental scale for English, Maths and Science, which precede the National Curriculum expected attainment levels at Key Stages 1 and 2.

Recent revisions of the EYFS in 2012 and 2014, while maintaining the themes, principles and commitments, have also introduced a move towards a 'school readiness' agenda (DfE, 2012, 2014c), which has concerned many in the early years sector not simply because it suggests a shift away from the perspective that the period between the ages of 0 and 5 is important in its own right and not simply as a preparation for a later stage in the child's life, a long-held tradition in the early years community, but also because it prescribes a set of skills and competencies which may be inappropriate for some children with SEND. This concern has led some in the field to suggest that school readiness should focus on whether the school is ready to meet the needs of the child, as well as whether the child herself is ready to start school (UNICEF, 2012). The introduction of a standardised baseline assessment, due to be introduced in September 2017, which is welcomed in terms of its stated intention of improving the early identification of additional needs, has nevertheless caused concern due to its prescription of the expected attainment for children at the start of the foundation stage, many of whom will be in the process of transition from home to school. For children with SEND these periods of transition can be particularly challenging, especially for those children who do not respond positively to changes in their routine.

The assessment processes discussed above relate to the procedures and principles for assessing the development of all children in the EYFS regardless of their additional needs. However, this combination of formative and summative assessment is similarly reflected in the 2015 Code of Practice when it refers to the graduated response as the key approach to supporting the learning needs of children within the classroom. This cycle is to be used for children in both mainstream and special school settings. Previous Codes of Practice (DfES, 2001b) used the same continuous pattern of assess, plan, do, review. The same cycle has been the model for assessment in the early years foundation stage curriculum since 2008 (DCSF, 2008c). Therefore many professionals working in the field of SEND and/or early years provision will already be familiar with this approach.

There are, however, some key differences in how the graduated response should be used under the 2015 Code of Practice:

- There are much more rigorous timescales for teachers and support staff to comply with when implementing the graduated response.
- There is a clear requirement to focus on measurable outcomes as a result of the planned support intervention.
- There is an expectation that interventions will be evidence based, i.e. that they have been demonstrated to have been successful at meeting student's needs when previously implemented.
- There is far greater accountability when evaluating the impact of the intervention, as schools and settings have to demonstrate that they have explored every possible intervention in order to meet the learning needs of children with SEND.

(DfE, 2015c: 86)

---

## PAUSE FOR REFLECTION

- What strategies can practitioners use to demonstrate that an intervention has been successful?
- What are the benefits and challenges of a reduced timescale for the implementation of the graduated response?

Figure 3.1 provides further thought for reflection on how teachers and early year practitioners can assess the effectiveness of their processes in light of the graduated response.

---

*Assess*

- Do we have appropriate systems and tools to assess and track pupils in different subject areas?
- Are staff suitably trained in these systems and tools?
- What data can we use to form a baseline?
- What criteria will we use to decide that a child should receive SEN support?
- How can we assess the teaching, curriculum and teaching environment?
- Are pupils and parents involved at this stage?
- Do we include strengths as part of the assessment process?

*Plan*

- Are pupils and parents fully involved in the planning stage?
- Does planning take account of strengths as well as difficulties?
- What are key outcomes for the pupils?
- Are outcomes specific?
- Do plans include a timeframe for review?
- Are suggested interventions evidence based, and can they help meet key outcomes?
- How will the plan be recorded so all staff can access and use it?
- Are all appropriate staff trained in delivering the intervention?

*Do*

- How can staff (teachers and TAs) be supported to deliver the intervention?
- How can we monitor and track any progress made during the intervention?
- How can pupils and parents be encouraged to take some responsibility for working towards aspects of the outcome?
- Are there any training needs raised by the above?

*Review*

- What evidence will be used to check if outcomes have been met?
- How can pupils and parents be involved in the review process?
- How can we identify next steps?
- What is the overall outcome of the intervention?

---

**Figure 3.1**    Evaluating the graduated response

(adapted from Packer, 2013)

## From Statements to Education Health and Care Plans

As we have seen, one of the major changes in the Children and Family Act 2014 was the replacement of statements with EHC plans for children aged 0–25. The next part of this chapter will consider the rationale for this change, and some of the implications for children and families.

It is clear from the 2015 Code of Practice that there was a commitment from the Department for Education that children already in receipt of a statement would continue to be supported during the transition to the new system, and that their statement would be replaced with the new plan. Similarly young people in post-16 provision who were supported through the learning difficulty assessment (LDA) would transfer to the EHC plan, due to the age range for the latter being extended to 25. The timescale for this transition states that LAs should have converted all statements to EHC plans by April 2018, and all LDAs by September 2016. This extension was widely praised across the statutory and post-16 sector and from parents for the recognition that there have traditionally been inconsistencies in support during the transition from compulsory to non-compulsory provision (Bullen, 2015).

Where there have been criticisms is in the perception that the threshold to be eligible for an initial EHC assessment is perceived to be considerably higher than was required for a statement (Harris, 2015). This is further exacerbated by the increased level of evidence that schools need to demonstrate to evidence the interventions they have implemented to support a child's needs through the graduated response cycle. There are real concerns that although rigorous timescales are in place, the evidence required to justify application for an EHC may sabotage the ability of schools and settings to comply with the timescales, thus potentially jeopardising the EHC application. Guidance aimed at supporting parents and practitioners to understand the new requirements stressed that the timescale required to complete the plan should not compromise efforts to hear and respond to the views of parents and children (DfE, 2015c).

## Developing an EHC Plan

The EHC plan process to a large extent follows the same procedure as the previous application for a statement. Where the procedures differ is in the way that the assessment is administered. For example, the use of child-friendly language and the avoidance of professional jargon which may prevent the process from being accessible to parents is evident throughout the documentation. LAs can design their EHC plans according to their own requirements. There is no nationally approved plan which is standardised across the country. However, the templates used must comply with the underlying principles outlined below.

---

### THE FOUR UNDERLYING PRINCIPLES OF AN EHC PLAN

The EHC template must include:

(a) the views, wishes and feelings of the child and his or her parent, or the young person;

(b) the importance of the child and his or her parent, or the young person, participating as fully as possible in decisions relating to the exercise of the function concerned;

(c) the importance of the child and his or her parent, or the young person, being provided with the information and support necessary to enable participation in those decisions;

(d) the need to support the child and his or her parent, or the young person, in order to facilitate the development of the child or young person and to help him or her achieve the best possible educational and other outcomes.

(DfE, 2014a: s. 19)

---

## CASE STUDY  SAMPLE EHC PLAN

This example of the different sections included in an EHC plan from one of the 'pathfinders' involved in piloting the new approach offers an insight into how parents and children can be involved in the process:

- Personal information
- List of people present and their role/relationship to child
- Summary of views, interests and aspirations of child and parents
- Summary of child's strengths and needs
- Summary of health needs which relate to his/her SEN
- Summary of social care needs which relate to his/her SEN
- Outcomes sought to meet these needs, including steps towards meeting the outcomes, and how they will be reviewed
- The special provision required to meet the outcomes (education, health and social care needs)
- Placement
- Personal budget allocated in the child's plan
- Summary of evidence provided in the EHC plan.

(adapted from Nottinghamshire County Council, n.d.)

## Hearing the Child's Voice

The clear message in the 2015 Code of Practice that the child's voice must be considered during the assessment/review process reflects a children's-rights perspective which has become more influential in policy and legislation since the

**Table 3.3**   Children's voice (Norwich, 2014)

| UNCRC | UNCRPD |
|---|---|
| **Article 13** | **Articles N and O** |
| The child shall have the right to freedom of expression; this right shall include freedom to seek, receive and impart information and ideas of all kinds, regardless of frontiers, either orally, in writing or in print, in the form of art, or through any other media of the child's choice. | Recognizing the importance for persons with disabilities of their individual autonomy and independence, including the freedom to make their own choices.<br><br>Considering that persons with disabilities should have the opportunity to be actively involved in decision-making processes about policies and programmes, including those directly concerning them. |

*Sources*: United Nations, 1989; UNESCO, 2006

UK signed the United Nations Convention on Children's Rights (UNCRC) in 1991 (UNESCO, 1992). In addition, the statements encourage practitioners to acknowledge the competencies of children with SEND, and to consider approaches to ensuring their voices are heard, for example through the use of alternative communication methods (see below). These principles of self-determination are reflected in the United Nations Convention on the Rights of People with Disabilities (UNCRPD) (UNESCO, 2006) (ratified by the UK in 2009) and suggest a shift from the traditional medical/social model of disability to a more affirmative model. Table 3.3 summarises the key articles from the UNCRC and the UNCRPD and how these reflect a more affirmative perspective of children with SEND.

### The Child's Voice

As discussed above, the statements regarding the voice of the child in SEND assessments and review, and more significantly the emphasis on strength-based approaches incorporated into the person-centred review process, to some extent reflect a shift towards an affirmative model of inclusion, initially advocated by Swain and French (2000). This model recognises that although the social model of disability was important in highlighting the social and environmental barriers to inclusion, that it nevertheless retains a 'personal tragedy' perspective whereby the disability or SEN is perceived as something to be 'resolved' or overcome in order for a child or young person to be fully included in the system. However, as welcome as this may appear, the affirmative model can only truly be realised when curriculum models and assessment processes in mainstream and special schools reflect broader sets of outcomes, rather than the narrow descriptors currently in place which can serve to reinforce a deficit model of SEND (Norwich, 2014).

### Strategies for Hearing the Child's Voice

Augmentative and alternative communication methods (AAC) can be used to elicit the perspectives of children with SEND who are not able to communicate verbally. AACs can be categorised as 'aided', for example communication boards, communication books, voice output communication aids (VOCAs) and eye-pointing software, and 'unaided', for example signing or Makaton. There are many websites and organisations which provide additional information about suitable software for supporting the preferred communication methods of children and young people with SEND, but what is important is that the child/young person and their parent/carer are supported to use the resources and that within the school or setting teachers and SEN staff are similarly trained and supported to deploy the required communication aids effectively. Further consideration of the importance of appropriate training for SEN staff is discussed in Chapter 8.

Unlike the statementing process, parents can request an EHC plan independently of the school or setting their child attends. While this is to be admired, there are concerns from parent advocacy groups that this places parents with more detailed knowledge of the SEN system at an advantage over other parents and perpetuates a situation where those who press hardest have their children's needs met over those who are unable to navigate the complexity of the SEN system effectively, for example those for whom English is not their first language. These issues are discussed in more depth in Chapter 2.

## Person-centred Reviews

Person-centred plans have been used in adult social care and health contexts for many years, following the publication of the White Paper *Valuing People* (DoH, 2001) and its subsequent revision (DoH, 2009a). It is only in more recent years that local authorities have started applying the principles of person-centred approaches to an educational context. Initially used mainly for periods of transition from primary school to secondary school, the approach has become more main-stream and key features of the person-centred planning approach can now be seen in the four principles cited in the development of the EHC plan as mentioned in the 2015 Code of Practice (see above).

What is important to remember about the person-centred planning approach is that it is not just about changing the wording on relevant paperwork to improve its accessibility for parents. For many practitioners, the approach requires a radical shift in mindset from one which focuses on a professional-led assessment process to a collaborative approach, where parents and children's views are considered equally.

The key aspects of the person-centred review process are shown below and illustrate the expectation that children and parents are fully involved in the process from the outset.

---

### PERSON-CENTRED REVIEW MEETINGS

- Who's here sheet
- Like and admire sheet
- Important to and important for sheet (now)
- Important to and important for sheet (in the future)
- My objectives sheet – you need to list these prior to the meeting
- My support sheet – you need to list these prior to the meeting
- Changes to my EHC plan

(adapted from London Borough of Waltham Forest, n.d.)

---

Having stressed this point, it is clear that the paperwork facilitates this shift in mindset, but a truly person-centred approach can only be successful if the review meeting is conducted in a collaborative and non-hierarchical manner. For example, each of the categories above will be headlined on a large sheet of paper, posted to the wall (or on a touch-screen interactive whiteboard if necessary), each participant at the meeting will be provided with a coloured marker pen (including the child/ young person) and at any time during the meeting they can contribute a suggestion or concern. The steering of the meeting by a professional, which can reduce active participation from children and/or their carers, can thus be reduced, offering the potential for a more equal partnership between parents and professionals.

---

**PAUSE FOR REFLECTION**

- What might be some of the challenges of conducting a person-centred review with a child with profound or multiple difficulties?

- What strategies could practitioners use to listen to the voices of very young children?

---

## Incorporating Person-centred Principles in an EHC Plan

For some LAs, the principles of person-centred planning have been fully incorporated into the design of the EHC plan. In addition, the use of WIKIs as an approach to eliciting the views and experiences of children and young people with SEND and their families has facilitated authentic participation and minimised power imbalances between parents and professionals.

### What are WIKIs?

The University of East London Rix Centre has been at the forefront of the development of multimedia advocacy in the form of WIKIs, interactive web-based information-sharing tools which incorporate audio-video information with written reports. Staff from the centre now work in partnership with schools, settings, children, young people and parents/carers across many LAs to embed these interactive advocacy web pages into person-centred review procedures. The principle feature of a WIKI is that it is designed, developed and thus 'owned' by children and young people with SEND and their parents/carers. Deciding on the information to include in a WIKI is the responsibility of the child or his parent/carer, so in addition to significant information about the child's social, emotional, educational and medical/health needs, WIKIs contain information about the child's lifestyle, preferences, hobbies and so on, thus building an holistic profile which supports professionals working with the child and their family to develop an in-depth perspective of the child as a whole person, and not just their additional needs. Thus the multimedia advocacy approach facilitates enhanced independence for children and young people with SEND and maximises the potential for them to fulfil their personal ambitions.

Below is an example of the front page text of a WIKI outlining the categories chosen for information sharing.

---

### WIKI CATEGORIES

- Who is important to me?

- How do I communicate?

- What am I good at?

- How best to support me?

- My goals

- My person-centred plan (EHC plan)

---

### CHAPTER SUMMARY

This chapter has considered observation and assessment processes for children in the early years, particularly those with SEND. Changes in assessment requirements as a result of the Children and Family Act 2014 and the 2015 Code of Practice have been considered and innovative approaches to working in partnership with children with SEND and their parents and carers have been outlined.

---

## Suggested Further Reading

Clarke, A. and Moss, P. (2001) *Listening to Young Children: The Mosaic Approach*. London: National Children's Bureau.

The original introduction to the mosaic approach, which details the approaches taken to capture the voices of children during the research process. The strategies used can be equally effective as a means of capturing the child's voice during the assessment process.

4Children (n.d.) 'SEN and disability in the early years: A toolkit'. London: Council for Disabled Children. Available at https://councilfordisabledchildren.org.uk/sites/default/files/uploads/documents/import/early-years-toolkit-merged.pdf (accessed 16.6.16).

A thorough and detailed discussion of the changes to SEN provision following the Children and Families Act 2014 and the 2015 Code of Practice. With practical guidance and checklists of effective practice, this is a useful resource for students and practitioners alike.

Early Education (2012) 'Development matters'. London: Early Education. Available at www.early-education.org.uk (accessed 21.7.16).

Although these descriptors were developed in 2012, they remain a vital tool for assisting experienced practitioners, students on placement and parents/carers when assessing the learning needs of all children in the 0–5 phase. With suggestions and strategies for planning further provision, and highly useful guidance on the characteristics of effective learning, this resource is definitely worth a look.

Macintyre, C. (2014) *Identifying Additional Learning Needs in the Early Years*. London: Routledge.
This is a highly practical book which supports practitioners working with children in the early years to identify and intervene to support the learning needs of children with SEND. There is clear recognition throughout the book of the need to find creative and appropriate ways to capture the child's voice, reflecting key principles of the 2015 Code of Practice.

Moylett, H. (2014) *Characteristics of Effective Early Learning: Helping Young Children Become Learners for Life*. Maidenhead: OUP.
Although the main premise of this book is the characteristics of learning, outlined in the revised Early Years Foundation Stage, the contributory chapters explore beyond this remit and consider useful and effective strategies to support all children's learning by tuning into their individual needs and building on their interests.

# 4

# MODELS OF SEN PROVISION: THE INCLUSION DEBATE

## RUTH HUNT

### CHAPTER OBJECTIVES

- What are models of disability and models of inclusion and how might these interact with or impact on people and systems?

- What is the current provision for children in the UK with additional needs (educational and medical/health needs) in light of inclusion priorities and with reference to models of inclusion?

- What are the issues raised by the practicalities of implementing the inclusion agenda?

- How do children, parents and staff currently experience inclusion?

Since the 1978 Warnock Report, inclusion has been the avowed educational goal for children within the UK with special educational needs, and/or medical or health needs, supported by the Salamanca Statement (UNESCO, 1994) which called for truly inclusive educational establishments. This chapter seeks to outline some key perspectives on inclusion within UK schools, and by doing so aims to problematise any concept of what inclusion might mean or imply. This chapter recognises that the practicalities of inclusion are emotive and often debated, and aims to highlight the multiple perspectives of what inclusion should or might be that may exist within an educational setting or community. By doing so, the chapter also discusses how far the practical out-workings of the inclusion agenda reflect the original intention, and ponders whether inclusion in its social justice sense is possible within an education system designed around universal academic attainment.

Discussion of inclusion causes us to question assumptions and norms within schooling and can be uncomfortable. It causes us to ask questions about what any type of education is for. How we answer that question depends on our particular history, worldview and era. For some, education is emancipatory, and the curriculum is designed to provide learning that empowers and brings opportunity and choice; for others, education is to create future workers, education to these people ought to be shaped by the needs of the workplace; for still others, education is a means of occupying children outside of the home, allowing the family adults responsible for them to work outside of the home and be economically productive; for others, education serves to create community and build society, whether as a social leveller by comprehensive education or by stratification via public, private and state schools.

Any individual's view on education is likely to be a complex mix of ideas and influences, unique to their own situation and influences. Just as there is no consensus as to what education is for, there will be many different answers as to what inclusion is and what it might be for. This chapter seeks to outline some of the historical and current views of what inclusion is (or might be), the ideologies behind inclusion and views on the purpose and practicalities of inclusion.

Drawing on Bronfenbrenner's ecological systems theory (1976), whereby a person's self is shaped by their immediate social systems and wider communities and values over time, people's experience of inclusion and ideologies around (dis)ability may influence their own feelings about inclusion. Staff working in a well-resourced Children's Centre, who have had long experience of working with children with particular needs and who have good links with professionals from physiotherapy, occupational therapy, health and speech fields, are likely to have a different view of inclusion than staff from within a four-form entry primary school which shares TAs between year groups and has few links with local services (see Figure 4.1).

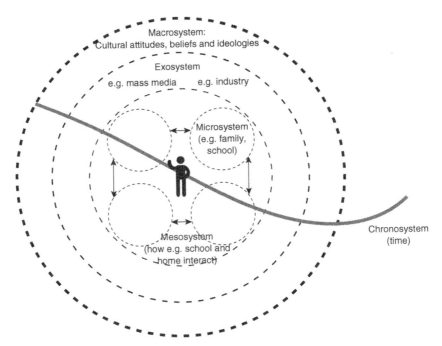

**Figure 4.1**    Ecological systems theory diagram (Bronfenbrenner, 1976)

**PAUSE FOR REFLECTION**

- What systems, concepts, organisations and people would you add to the ecological system diagram above to represent factors that might influence our understanding of inclusion?

- Think back to your own school days. What was your experience of inclusion?

- How might that influence how you feel about inclusion as an adult?

A parent who has been happy with the experience of their child in a special school and who feels part of a thriving school community may have a different view of inclusion to that of a parent who feels that their child has missed out on mainstream school life by being in a special school and who has not met any other parents due to the bus pick-up system of their child's school.

In addition, inclusion is ideological, and therefore staff, parents and children's views and understanding of inclusion are necessarily influenced by the ideologies of their society and their own personal beliefs. Inclusion is ideological in as much as it contains strands of universal equality, social justice and a sense of social responsibility for all in society. By demanding equal inclusion of all children in education, inclusion automatically advocates for more consideration of difference; for funding and resourcing to be made available on an unequal basis by automatically providing additional resources needed to ensure equal access to the curriculum. For those who see the state as having a duty to provide for all in society, inclusion as a fully-funded model ideologically demands that the full cost of additional support be met by the state. In contrast, those who see market-forces as being the proper societal narrative (i.e. profit and demand being key drivers), then a system of businesses bidding to provide resources at low cost and consumer (parent/child in this case) choice based on their own personal circumstances is more fitting. This simplistic binary vignette serves to illustrate the potential spectrum of beliefs of what inclusion might practically mean in terms of provision within educational settings. Whether we advocate for a particular understanding or model of inclusion within an educational sphere will necessarily depend on our ultimate views on what inclusion should be, how it should be brought about, and its purpose.

**PAUSE FOR REFLECTION**

- What is your initial reaction to how inclusive services should or might be provided?

Different or additional needs seem to be more readily and easily accommodated by the children-centred early years and primary schools (Rix et al., 2013). Different challenges to inclusion emerge as curriculum changes and demands on teachers evolve through Key Stages. The largest EHC plan cohort by age in 2016 were 15 year olds (DfE, 2016b), those who were about to take national tests (GCSEs), and when curricula become fixed according to outcomes. This could perhaps be interpreted as children's additional needs being recognised due to the inflexibility of the system rather than any change in the child themselves, although this is speculation.

In early years, despite reporting of levels and judgements based on children's 'attainment' (STA, 2015), there is a greater emphasis on child-led activities, and personalised learning as a constant thread (DfE, 2014b). Depending on the setting's values there may be little to no whole-group compulsory activities, which allow children to experience and explore in their own way without 'failing' a mainstream task. This flexibility of curriculum and expected range of ways of interacting with resources narrows as children progress through the school system. Elsewhere there are debates about the UK's curriculum (Early Childhood Action, n.d.), and particularly the English emphasis on formal learning before the age of six, in contrast to other countries (Germany, Denmark, Sweden) where learning is play-based and may not be compulsory until age six or later (NFER, 2013). The UK model impacts on inclusion by its early narrowing of the curriculum to focus on literacy and numeracy in formal ways (Fuchs and Fuchs, 1994). The increasing focus on technical skills and reporting children's achievements as a way of judging schools creates several issues when considering models of inclusion. Through measuring absolute achievement (DfE, 2014b) (i.e. the reaching of a pre-ordained, and seemingly ever-increasing, standard) rather than progress, children who start very low on the attainment scale, whether due to SEN, a health need or environmental factors, must make more progress than their peers in order to reach the expected levels. Whilst having high expectations for all children is shown to be a pre-requisite, for children to fulfil their potential (Proctor, 1984) it might be argued that starting points should also be taken into account. Therefore, children who may be socially happy in the foundation stage, and who may be successfully enabled to access provision within a Nursery or Reception setting, are required, by virtue of their age, to access more formal, less play-based activities. This more formal curriculum often includes a demand to cover certain content, which creates a time-pressure to ensure that children experience the full curriculum. This sets a pace for learning within the class, which may be faster or slower than individual children would wish. In addition, school classrooms for Key Stages 1 and 2 may be smaller, have no outside area, no drama or roleplay area, and be dominated by tables. Both curriculum and classroom create a framework into which children are expected to fit. This is a potential source of conflict or anxiety for all children, but it is brought into clear focus when considering children with additional needs. A child who enjoyed being outside and being very vocal can thrive within a foundation stage setting where there tends to be more room and different areas for children to be, and where there are statutory higher adult–child ratios (DfE, 2014b): children who want a quiet space to concentrate can move away for their louder friends and there can be designated quieter areas, and there are multiple staff members for children to interact with. The same child within a year 2 classroom on the second floor with tables close together may not find their sensory and physical needs met, in an environment where being seated and being quiet may be valued, and there may be a single adult (the class teacher) who has to spread their time between 30 children and may not feel confident to support all children's behaviour (Nye et al., 2016). Here it is not the child's needs that have changed, but the curriculum and organisation of learning. As learning becomes more formal and timetables less flexible as the child moves through the school system, the mismatch between needs and provision can become more pronounced. This may make inclusion seem to be difficult, but also underlines the role that structures play in our perceptions of inclusion: for those in the early years, inclusion might be seen as a normal (if under-resourced) expectation, by those working in older Key Stages, inclusion might be seen to be more problematic. The change of views here is not due to the children changing, but due to educational structures and settings changing.

## Models of Disability

Models of disability are relevant to inclusion debates, as they are pervasive beliefs which indicate how individuals and societies view those who have different physical, intellectual or emotional needs. This extends to how governments and schools see pupils with additional needs, and how committed or opposed to inclusion people might be. Values and priorities are influenced by how we think about disability.

### Medical Model of Disability

The medical model of disability can be seen as one which sees disability as arising from personal misfortune: malady, genetic defect or tragedy. The model takes the stance that people with disability are deficient in some aspect of their being, and that medicine and technology should be applied so that the individual can take a place in society (WHO, 2001). For those for whom medication makes a difference, for whom assistive technology overcomes their physical needs, this model seems pragmatic. However, careful notice must be taken of the constructions that underlie this model. The individual is treated as damaged, and separated from society by their (dis)ability. The person is less than a non-disabled person. They are somehow behind and separate – they need to catch up to societal norms, to use medical means to fit in. By each of these measures the perceived problem, deficit or difference lies with the (dis)abled individual. In this model there is no prompt to reflect upon the society that surrounds individuals. The medical model does not draw on Bronfenbrenner's (1976) ideas of people being impacted by all the organisations, constructions and relationships around them, providing a holistic view of a child with a disability. Instead, the medical model focuses on the perceived deficit that the individual carries.

The medical model, whilst advocating for good medical and technical support for people with a disability, places the burden of change with the individual affected by that particular need. It offers little help or support to a person who uses a wheelchair for mobility when faced with public buildings, such as schools, which are accessed only via steps. The medical model of disability is closely linked to the segregational, non-inclusive style of school which enforced special schools attendance for children with almost every kind of disability in the UK at one point. The blanket use of special schools as a default, whether the child had an intellectual or physical disability, presupposed that children with a disability were somehow different, with the implication of deficit attached to this difference. Specific curricula and expectations were applied, a distinctly medical 'treatment' model. Individuals with disabilities might be expected to fit around the mainstream, and the provision of accessible resources would be a matter of funding and personal equipment.

## Social Model of Disability

The social model of disability places a more direct emphasis on the barriers that society has (wittingly or unwittingly) erected towards people with different abilities. At its inception, it was hailed as revolutionary and paradigm-shifting (Gallagher, et al., 2014) as it transformed the way that people with disabilities were viewed. The disability was seen to be situated in the environment rather than within the individual (Gallagher et al., 2014: 1124). Placing the problem with the environment, that is society, meant that responsibility for altering or alleviating the problem belonged to society as a whole, rather than the individual. It also moved away from people being seen as deficient, and towards access and support being deficient, which was revolutionary. Working from a social model of disability, an inclusive school would consider what systemic barriers there were to children with disabilities, and how the school as a whole could overcome these, which chimes with some scholars' conditions for inclusion in schools (Ainscow et al., 2006). This model is not without its critics, and Ferri (2015) acknowledges the arguments between those who foreground the medical issues of disability and those who instead focus upon the social construction of ideas of disability. Anastasiou and Kauffman (2011) are vocal critics of the social model of disability, and argue, amongst other points, that medical concerns are always a factor, even if the impact of environment is conceded, which they are reluctant to. Their argument extends to schooling, and they express doubt that inclusion in what they term general (i.e. mainstream) education can be effective for students without radical change, citing past and present failures. These robust critical views are refuted as belonging to a medical model (Ferri, 2015), and yet seek to link medical and social models together, albeit with the medical aspect to the fore.

## Bio-psycho-social Model

The bio-psycho-social model is a conscious attempt by the WHO (2001) to integrate the medical model and the social model; it recognises that both models consider aspects of the person which the other minimises. This model was developed with health in mind, and so whilst it does consider holistic life experiences of individuals, this is done through the lens aiming to improve health needs. The model considers medical, personal and environmental factors as playing a part in people's overall health and wellbeing. In attempting to harmonise two models which are often opposed, it might be argued that this model downplays the societal urgency for action; however, its focus on multiple factors impacting an individual is a useful framework when considering education (de Camargo, 2011).

## Barriers to Inclusion: Educational Ideology

It is difficult to discuss the nuances of inclusion without discussing views on education in a wider sense. There has been much written on the neo-liberal agenda with regard to education. This term refers to the political agenda of creating markets for services, with weaker central control and more market-driven trends (Angus, 2015). This necessarily includes finances within discussion about services, alongside a need to evaluate and rank services and systems to prove efficacy. Academies, with their independence from LAs, control of their own budgets, and ability to set pay scales are an example of neo-liberal education ideology. The reduction of educational establishments to profit and loss and league tables creates an uneasy debate: how do we value those children who are expensive to educate because they require individual support or resources within the current system, how do we value those children who will not meet expected standards, and whose results are therefore seen as detrimental to the school league table?

Within this argument comes Tomlinson's (2012) provocative view that governments are hostile to those who are lower achievers, marking them as failures and penalising them if their educational career does not bear fruit; that is, as adults they do not find paid work. Judging people based on their ability to work or find work is inextricably tied to an ideology that valorises those who financially sustain themselves. That ideology carries the implicit assumption that any who do not work (for whatever reason) are not valued members of society. Tomlinson (2012) contrasts this view with what she terms 'humanitarian' influences, who seek to value people regardless of their wealth-generating capacity. Tomlinson's argument may feel uncomfortably blunt, but she raises the vital point that our view of education and inclusion is formed by the society in which we live, and the values of those who order our society through rules and laws. Schools and settings have pragmatic responses to an attainment-based educational culture: they might support children to reach a standard by investing in resourcing; they might apply to formally exempt low-performing children from test; they may take draconian steps of finding reasons to lawfully permanently exclude children. There is also a radical response: to use inclusion as a driver to rethink the entire education system to remove the punitive performative culture.

## What Do We Mean by Inclusion: Who Is It For?

When we speak of inclusion, our ideas of who 'ought' to be included tell us about our understandings of current cultural norms and differences. The Salamanca Statement (UNESCO, 1994) includes children with physical and intellectual and emotional difficulties, and makes specific reference to women, in recognition that in most of the world women experience additional exclusion. Views on inclusion within schools are situation based, depending on the cohort of students in the local area: for some schools, discussions and practice regarding inclusion centres on children with autism spectrum disorder (ASD); in other areas, inclusion of members of the traveller community is a priority; for others, including children with EAL is the most pressing need. Inclusion, when viewed in these terms, becomes less of an 'us and them' situation. Inclusion in its broadest sense is about providing quality education for all children, regardless of ethnic heritage, language, ability, physicality, gender or sexuality. Whatever the current local focus, there also needs to be strategic awareness that inclusion is not fitting one sub-group into a homogenous normal group, rather it is an ethos and practice which aims to remove inequalities and barriers to learning for all children.

For some, inclusion brings to mind situations such as those found in Rioux and Pinto's (2010) excellent and challenging survey of experiences of inclusion: pupils who are being actively excluded (in some countries) because they have additional needs which are largely physical, such as vision, hearing, mobility. These needs could be met with environmental changes, which whilst having cost and time implications, are matters of building redesign, software purchasing and braille book production. These require specialist technicians to create the resources, but it is clear what the resources need to do, and may not involve teaching staff. Some changes are either one-time events, such as marking step-edges with bright strips, or purchasing computer software, or attitudinal, such as remembering to say a person's name before asking a question so that a person who is partially sighted knows you are directing your remarks at them. Whilst others, such as ensuring sufficient lead-time on ordering new textbooks to ensure that there is time to create braille editions before the start of the school term, require some organisational rigour and ongoing funding, they have the potential to fairly easily become part of the rhythm of school life. It is clear that with a willing leadership team and staff (Ainscow et al., 2006), changes can be made, and with a funding stream, appropriate resources could ensure that buildings and materials are appropriate and available for all students.

When inclusion is framed in these terms, there can be impatience with a lack of progress on inclusion. Figures for children who have an identified additional need, indicate however, that 25.9 per cent of pupils with an EHC plan have ASD as a primary type of need, while 5.8 per cent have a physical disability, 2.7 per cent have a hearing impairment and 1.5 per cent have a visual impairment (DfE, 2016a). These percentages indicate that the most common primary need (and reason for an EHC plan) in England is ASD, which might indicate a more complex route to inclusion. Indeed, Ravet (2011), in her discussion of ideologies of inclusion for children with ASD, indicates that there is no single 'recipe' (p. 680) for the inclusion of children with ASD. Someone on the autistic spectrum is commonly termed as having autistic spectrum disorder (ASD), which some people with an autistic spectrum diagnosis find offensive and derogatory due to the inclusion of the word 'disorder'. Unfortunately as this term is prevalent in research studies, it is unavoidable in this chapter. The autistic spectrum, as the name implies, can include a range of learning needs and behaviours which may affect the individual with differing degrees of impact and complexity. For children with an EHC plan, ASD may be their primary type of need, but the outward markers, such as speech and language needs, or social and emotional mental health (SEMH) issues, may also be present. Inclusive teaching that supports children with these needs who do not have ASD may not be appropriate for children who also have ASD (Ravet, 2011), as for those children the speech and language needs are the external manifestations of the communication and processing needs associated with ASD, rather than the need itself. The range of courses and resources aimed at staff and parents of children with ASD is extensive. Whilst it could be argued that this is partly due to the marketisation of SEN (Tomlinson, 2012), it could also be seen as a testament to the sheer range of challenges that a spectrum diagnosis might bring. Whilst responding to a spectrum of communication needs, and indeed including children with a range of intellectual disabilities, increases complexity of classroom support, the Salamanca Statement (UNESCO, 1994) is clear that the majority of students could and should be educated within a mainstream environment.

---

### PAUSE FOR REFLECTION

Consider your own experiences in education and care settings:

- Was there an emphasis on inclusion being about all students?
- Were particular groups' needs highlighted or specifically catered for?
- Which minority groups were already considered 'mainstream'? How might that affect the support they received?

---

## Specific Inclusion Perspectives

Taking into consideration the multiple understandings and experiences that influence an individual's understanding of inclusion and what this might be, we now move on to consider some specific ideologies that have emerged from debates around inclusion. Despite the ongoing commitments to inclusive education (Warnock, 1978; UNESCO, 1994), the roads towards inclusion are not always clear. In discussing what inclusion is and what form it should take, two dominant perspectives have emerged, often presented as binary alternatives: children's rights and children's needs. These ideologies, which are often presented as competing (Ravet, 2011) in a similar way to medical and social disability models, have also come to the fore when considering other aspects of education and life, mobilised particularly by the UNCRC (United Nations, 1989).

## Children's Rights Perspective

Children's rights to social and educational inclusion are the driving factors of this perspective. The emphasis is on schools to change in order to accommodate children's needs (Ravet, 2011), in line with the UNCRC (United Nations, 1989). The separation of children from mainstream education is firmly cast as a breach of rights, and full resourcing supplied by schools/the state are an expectation (CSIE, 2015). With echoes of the social model of disability (Gallagher et al., 2014), a lack of inclusion is seen as a societal problem, which disadvantages individual children with SEND, but the locus of the problem remains firmly with schools and wider society. Advocates of this model, including CSIE (2015) are calling for a radical restructuring of education to enshrine inclusion within the ethos and fabric of the UK education system.

## Children's Needs Perspective

This perspective foregrounds the different resources and provision required to ensure that children are able to access curricula. This model is focussed on sustaining a spread of provision aimed at different groups with specific needs, for example specific provision for the deaf, or for those with physiotherapy needs. This model reacts to inclusion warily, questioning whether there is evidence that mainstream education benefits children (Ravet, 2011), in a way which echoes Anastasiou and Koffman's (2011) views of the social model of disability and inclusion. Whilst, during times of funding cuts, the desire to preserve specialisms might seem appealing, the CSIE (2015) argues for better funding to allow comprehensive services in multiple locations.

## Models of Inclusion

### Integration

Integration describes an approach whereby there are recognised cohorts of 'mainstream' children and 'SEND' children, whose education is co-located for at least part of the school week. The different cohorts exist within the same teaching space, but may be seated in distinct groups, have distinct curricula or timetables. The SEND group may be taught by different staff members, who may have specialised training and use distinct pedagogies. Expectations for the two groups differ, usually with the mainstream targets being more rigorous and academic. The SEND group may attend a specialised unit for the remainder of their time. This model proves

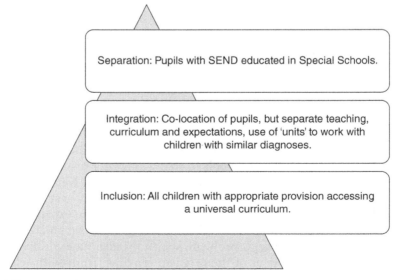

**Figure 4.2**   From 1978 to now?

controversial, and whilst it is emphatically not full inclusion, McCoy and Banks (2012) argue that such models may prove more effective in meeting pupils' socialisation and emotional needs and limit negative self-image of students with SEND surrounded by differently-abled peers. Whilst the Salamanca Statement (UNESCO, 1994) has a firm steer for full inclusion, nevertheless it too counsels that for a minority of pupils with distinct and profound learning needs, this model can create difficulties for staff and children: teachers report not knowing what is going on in dual units (Wilde and Avramidis, 2011), and this has the potential for units creating an 'us and them' thinking for mainstream teachers and children. (See Figure 4.2 for an overview of the models of inclusion from 1978 to the present.)

---

## PAUSE FOR REFLECTION

- What is your understanding and experience of how inclusion has changed over time?

- How do these descriptions match what you see, experience and read about in schools and settings today?

- What changes might be required to the current education systems to enable all children to be fully included? What challenges might there be?

---

## Inclusion

'Inclusion' in its broadest term is meeting the educational needs and rights of all children in mainstream settings (UNESCO, 1994). The Salamanca Statement (ibid.) makes it clear that this may involve re-thinking how education and curricula are organised and understood, and may include extra and different resourcing. Along with Ferguson (2008), Wilde and Avramidis (2011) caution that inclusion can have a variety of meanings. Wilde and Avramidis (2011) point to models of inclusion that required children with SEN's assimilation into a mainstream; that is, the support given aids children to reach into the mainstream world, rather than inclusion meaning a remaking of the mainstream world so that inclusion is a whole-class and whole-school action. Here again the wealth of terms can be seen; in this case 'assimilation' is used by the researchers (Wilde and Avramidis, 2011) to describe a lesser form of inclusion, which can also be seen as integration. This, some might argue, is not actually inclusion, and Ferguson describes a cohort supposedly included in mainstream who are integrated, that is, as he terms it '"in" but not "of"' (2008: 111) the class socially and educationally.

There is widespread acknowledgement (Wilde and Avramidis, 2011; Norwich, 2008; Ferguson, 2008; Fuchs and Fuchs, 1994) that even in settings committed to inclusion, this takes on different guises, ranging from those that are intentionally integrationist to those who achieve partial inclusion. Wilde and Avramidis (2011) capture the sense that the previous binary choice of mainstream or special education has transmuted not into a single inclusive avenue, but rather has fragmented into multifarious routes which are area and context specific.

Norwich's (2008) international research on inclusion underlined that the English national curriculum was perceived as a barrier to inclusion. This echoes the calls in the Salamanca Statement to alter not just material features of schools, but also to ensure that curricula are inclusive (UNESCO, 1994). To achieve inclusion within the UK curriculum in its current state, with the emphasis on age-specific knowledge, skills and ability, poses challenges. In a different context, Fuchs and Fuchs (1994) argued passionately that a focus on academic excellence, which in the UK we might equate to good league table scores, is not consistent with a drive towards equality. This returns the argument to the discussion of what education is for; if we extend Fuchs and Fuchs's argument, perhaps controversially, the decision needs to be made between summative achievements for league tables, and equality of opportunity regardless of intellectual disability. Indeed, Ferguson considers that there is a need to 'reinvent schools with new assumptions and more effective practice' (2008: 117) to secure inclusion, which within a state system such as the UK would require wholesale reimagining of educational structures and accountability. See Figures 4.3 and 4.4 for visual interpretation.

**Figure 4.3**   Integration as a stepping stone to inclusion

**Figure 4.4**   Integration as an end unto itself

---

## PAUSE FOR REFLECTION

- Which of these ideas about integration and inclusion do you currently hold? What challenges does this pose?

- Do you think integration can lead to inclusion (Figure 4.3)?

- How do you respond to the idea that inclusion requires a new way of thinking about education (Figure 4.4)?

---

### Integrative Approach

Ravet (2011) calls for a highly responsive and reflexive approach to supporting children with ASD, terming a combination of rights-based and needs-based approaches an 'integrative' approach (Ravet, 2011: 678). In this discussion, integration is used to describe an approach which uses specialist skills (in this case ASD specific training) within a mainstream environment. This argument can be a useful counterpoint to the seemingly binary needs and rights-based approaches, but also serves to demonstrate how even the language of inclusion is not clear: to some 'integration' is a half-hearted measure to contain SEN children within a mainstream environment, and is always second best. There are echoes here of the WHO's attempt at marrying medical and social models of disability into the bio-psycho-social model (2001). For Ravet (2011), an integrative approach means a highly personalised and responsive mainstream approach carried out by appropriately trained and resourced teachers. This might be seen to fit with Wilde and Avramidis's (2011) provocative views that current inclusion has created not the binary of 'mainstream' and 'special' education, but rather a raft of different educations delivered through different specialist teaching, which they do not see as full inclusion. Despite differently nuanced ideologies of inclusion, both Ravel (2011) and Wilde and Avramidis (2011) argue for mainstream teachers to be more specifically skilled as a cornerstone to achieving meaningful inclusive practice. This chimes with the Salamanca Statement's (UNESCO, 1994) drive to increase in-service training to facilitate inclusive schools. See Table 4.1 for a summary of these approaches.

**Table 4.1**   What do we see as 'inclusion'?

| | |
| --- | --- |
| SEN unit serving pupils from multiple mainstream schools – pupils spend some time in mainstream at different points in the week. Do not have relationships with peers in mainstream. | SEN unit attached to a mainstream school, pupils spend half a day in the unit, half a day in mainstream class. Children have some friendships with lower-achieving peers in mainstream class. |
| Children with SEND located in mainstream classes, work at a 'workstation' on different tasks to their peers, have an adult with them at all times | Children in class socialise with their peers, accessing the same curriculum and working with teachers, teaching assistants and their peers. SEND students achieve lower than other peers. |

### PAUSE FOR REFLECTION

- How far do these SEND support set-ups match your own experience in schools and settings?

- Would you call any of these examples 'inclusive'? Why/why not?

- How would you describe effective inclusion? As a visitor to a class what might inclusion look like?

- How far do any of these examples take into account a children's rights perspective?

- How far do any of these examples take into account a children's needs perspective?

## Experiences of Inclusion

When considering models of inclusion, and keeping Bronfenbrenner's ecological systems theory (1976) in mind, it is essential to consider how systems affect the individual. Inclusive education, after all, is a lived experience by a multitude of actors: children, parents and staff. Accordingly, there is no consensus around how inclusion is experienced, although research indicates some broad themes.

Children's views have been sought by researchers, with a host of responses, which are not easily categorised. McCoy and Banks's (2012) Irish study indicates that children with SEND in Ireland were found to enjoy school less than their peers without SEND, and point to socialisation and being exposed to prejudice within the school. They raise the important point that teachers and other staff may have inclusion in the forefront of their mind, but other pupils may not. It is clear that there is work to do on children's rights awareness within mainstream schools. It should, however, be noted that McCoy and Banks's (2012) cohort were not within early years age ranges, and children growing up in inclusive schools may construct ideas about disability and difference in a different way, although this does not lessen the potential distress for those experiencing negative peer reactions to inclusion with secondary schools. Social concerns were highlighted by children who were experiencing integration between special schools and mainstream schools (Frederickson et al., 2004), although this study was carried out prior to children's experience of mainstream schooling.

Parents of children with SEND are shown to be concerned about securing full support for their children (Tomlinson, 2012), especially in light of Attwood's (2013) claims that some forms of academisation allowed schools to seek independent status and thereby side-step their SEND obligations. Frederickson et al.'s (2004) investigation of a special school–mainstream school partnership as a transition to inclusion focussed on pupil, parent and staff hopes and concerns. Parents were optimistic about the positive social and educational benefits, although they carried concerns around specific support and home–school communications. In the same study, teachers did not show concern around home–school communication, but instead highlighted increased workload, a factor not considered a concern by parents. These differences in concern highlight the need for parent–school partnerships in order for realistic expectations to be expressed and set, and parallel or conflicting priorities discussed.

Within research on teacher views, perhaps the most striking is what Clough and Nutbrown (2013: 60) term the 'yes but' response to inclusion. They coined this term in response to interviews where staff agreed with inclusion in principle, but found the practical realities to be under-resourced or otherwise challenging. This is echoed in Kurniawati et al.'s (2014) research, which indicated that more experienced teachers expressed doubts about the practicalities of inclusion more than newly qualified colleagues. Kurniawati et al. (2014) theorised that this might be due to the more experienced teachers understanding the full impact on workload of inclusive or integrative practice. Not all newly qualified teachers had more positive views. MacBlain and Purdy (2011) found that only one-third of Post-graduate Certificate of Education (PGCE) students felt confident to meet the needs of children with SEND, with students echoing the emerging theme that they valued inclusion and personalised learning but failed to see how practically it might be done. The prevailing theme in teacher responses to inclusion highlights that at present resourcing does not match ideology.

Within any education system or process there will be tensions between expectations, demands and resources. Inclusion is no different, but as MacKenzie (2012) indicates, those working with children with SEND are seen to experience magnified stresses and happiness, as the profundity of some children's needs seems to magnify emotions.

## CASE STUDY 1   THE STUDENT

Sanjeet is a 7-year-old boy who attends Nelson School. Sanjeet is currently non-verbal and communicates using two or three word phrases using Picture Exchange Communication System (PECS). Sanjeet can order number cards from 1 to 3. Sanjeet enjoys bubbles, toys with flashing lights, and a brightly coloured xylophone. Sanjeet loves to climb, and does not have an understanding of risk or danger. Sanjeet becomes very distressed by noise, and currently bites other children if he is distressed or distracted by them. Sanjeet is in a dual placement with half a day in the specialist provision and half a day in mainstream class. In his mainstream classroom Sanjeet has a workstation that is positioned to give him an area where sensory distractions can be minimised. It also prevents him from hurting other children by isolating him from their tables. The specialist provision teacher says this arrangement will allow him to concentrate. Sanjeet has a teaching assistant assigned to him in the mainstream classroom to support his use of PECS, to ensure that he does not climb, run from the classroom or otherwise endanger himself, and to mediate Sanjeet's engagement with all learning tasks. Sanjeet does not appear to show any preference for members of his class, but becomes distressed if his one-to-one worker is absent and he must work with other staff members.

## PAUSE FOR REFLECTION

- What areas of education and school life is Sanjeet included in?

- What is Sanjeet currently excluded from?

- Working within current funding and curriculum demands, what would you recommend to Sanjeet's school?

## CASE STUDY 2   THE MAINSTREAM TEACHER

Class teacher Jeremy works in a two-form entry primary school in the suburbs. His school has an informal reputation amongst parents as being good with children with additional needs. Jeremy's year 2 class has 32 pupils, of whom one,

*(Continued)*

(*Continued*)

Jack, has an EHC plan and a diagnosis of ASD; another, Simon has SEN support and a diagnosis of ASD; two boys, Tyrell and Stefan, have SEN support and diagnoses of ADHD; one girl, Mariam, who has recently arrived in the UK and has limited English; and one child, Grace, with sickle cell anaemia who has extended periods of illness-leave. Jeremy's class has one teaching assistant, who works 12 hours a week with Jack. Jeremy believes in inclusion and works hard to provide appropriate materials and learning for all his students, and yet feels overwhelmed by the range of needs in his class. He feels guilty if he has not prepared separate work packs for Grace when she returns after having a sickle-cell crisis, and works late into the evening to ensure that he has resources to give her and her family. Jeremy implements clear routines which he hope helps Simon, Tyrell and Stefan, and gives them work that he has prepared for his lowest ability group, which they are sometimes able to complete unaided. Jack requires separate activities as he is not readily able to access written resources. Jeremy spends time each week using the computer in the staff room which has software that creates PECS for Jack, but relies on his teaching assistant to re-interpret much of the curriculum activities for Jack on a daily basis. Jeremy wants to be able to include all children fully, but feels the pressure of preparing children for SATs, and attempting to provide a range of resources for each lesson.

## PAUSE FOR REFLECTION

- Does the situation as described meet your expectation of inclusion? Why/why not?

- What would you change about this situation? Which of these ideas would be within Jeremy's or the school's control? What barriers might there be to changes?

## CHAPTER SUMMARY

This chapter has explored some key ideologies and views that underpin our understanding of models of inclusion with educational settings in the UK. The varied and shifting understandings of what inclusion is or might be have been highlighted. The lenses of social, medical and bio-psycho-social models of disability have been used to consider how integration and inclusion currently exist within school settings. This chapter does not argue for a particular model of inclusion, but highlights the complexity of the educational systems and the inclusion agenda. Ideas about inclusion are diverse, and any conceptualisation of inclusion in schools is dependent on multiple factors, including personal experience and ideologies of education and disability, rights and needs. Practices which within schools may be seen as inclusive, may in fact be integration or integrative. Inclusion in its most radical sense would require considerable change to the British education system.

## Suggested Further Reading

The list below offers some further information and guidance on the key points raised in this chapter.

Ko, B. (2015) 'Education, health and care plans: a new scheme for special educational needs and disability provisions in England from 2014', *Paediatrics and Child Health*, 25 (10): 443–9.
Useful short piece on what EHC plans are and what kind of support they mandate within mainstream classes.

Clough, P. and Nutbrown, C. (2004) 'Special educational needs and inclusion: multiple perspectives of preschool educators in the UK', *Journal of Early Childhood Research*, 2 (2): 191–211.
As the title of this article implies, this is a strong and helpful article which explores practitioners' perspectives on SEN and inclusion. This is helpful to read with the following more recent article by Fisher.

Fisher, H. (2012) 'Progressing towards a model of intrinsic inclusion in a mainstream primary school: a SENCO's experience', *International Journal of Inclusive Education*, 16 (12): 1273–93.
Helpful discussion of lived-experiences in schools.

Gallagher, D.J., Connor, D.J. and Ferri, B.A. (2014) 'Beyond the far too incessant schism: special education and the social model of disability', *International Journal of Inclusive Education*, 18 (11): 1120–42.
A challenging article which explores how models of disability inform/transform how children with SEN are taught.

# 5

# LEADERSHIP AND INCLUSION: CREATING AN ETHOS, CULTURE AND PROVISION

## ATHINA TEMPRIOU

## CHAPTER OBJECTIVES

- How can a school's leadership team encourage inclusive practice within the setting?
- Which characteristics of leadership styles found in research literature are perceived to support inclusive practice?
- What strategies help implement inclusive education in early years settings?
- What other factors can play an important role in promoting inclusive practice in a setting?
- Is working with external agencies considered an effective strategy for inclusion?

## Inclusion

As has been seen in previous chapters, it is very difficult to define inclusion. In previous years, different authors and researchers have made efforts, but it is very seldom that any two will ever agree entirely. The matter of inclusion is a versatile one and has been viewed as a rights issue (Norwich, 2008) and recent legislative developments have pushed educational inclusion as a social justice and human right for all children, especially children with SEN (Artiles et al., 2006).

Brodie and Savage (2015: 1) suggest there is not 'a unitary way of conceptualizing inclusion', albeit it can be perceived as the respect towards people's individuality and their full membership in the social, cultural and economic life of society. Additionally, they include the values, the difference and promotion of confidence for all people to make their choices, so that they can live in a healthy society, where their voices can be heard. Furthermore, Nangah and Mills (2015) declare that it is a fundamental part of supporting wellbeing in children, but the definition can differ based on settings, practitioners' values and approaches.

Thompson (2012) agrees with Ainscow et al. (2006) and suggests a framework that includes some main features of inclusion. These are:

- Reducing barriers to learning and participation of all students.
- Increasing the capacity of schools to respond to the diversity of students in ways that treat them all of equal value.
- The putting of inclusive values into action in education and society.

(Ainscow et al. 2006: 297)

Also:

- Training and enabling of professionals to develop communities of practice that support inclusion (Cornwall and Graham-Matheson, 2012: 49).

So, inclusion is a complex issue, but it is characterised by a tendency to reduce barriers to learning and to participation of all children in their setting and eventually in society. Also closely related to the idea of inclusion is the notion of inclusive education (IE) where it has been also identified as a multi-faceted issue (Lunt and Norwich, 1999), and it is very difficult to apply in policy and educational practice (Norwich, 2008). This difficulty was also shared and recognised in the House of Commons Education Select Committee report on special educational needs (House of Commons, 2006).

IE has been conceptualised by some researchers as identifying and removing barriers in order for all the children to participate in education (Ainscow et al., 2011; Mittler, 2012) regardless of their gender, social background, race, sexuality, disability or attainment in schools (Booth and Ainscow, 1998). Even more, it has been suggested that it refers to the development of policies and practices, as well as the culture in educational institutions, so that they are ready to respond to the diversity of students and treat them uniformly (Angelides et al., 2010). Moreover, Westwood (2003) and Salend (2005) suggest that IE relates to the organisation of the curricula in order to meet all the children's needs and to school improvement (Angelides et al., 2010).

The development of IE relies heavily on leaders, and their input has been acknowledged by a number of researchers as significant (Bailey and du Plessis, 1997; Guzman, 1997; Ingram, 1997; Praisner, 2003; Kugelmass and Ainscow, 2004; Ryan, 2006) because they foster new meanings about diversity and build relationships between schools and community (Riehl, 2000). The following part of the chapter will focus mainly on leadership and how the school leadership team (SLT) of a school can support IE in policy and practice.

## Leadership

Leadership is difficult to conceptualise and equally difficult to be defined. A substantial number of researchers view leadership from different angles. However,

Dickins defines leadership as 'an enabling process through which individuals can inspire, articulate, influence and implement a shared, collective vision of principles, policy and practice' (Dickins, 2014: 113). This is very useful to IE, since it emphasises the development of shared values and positive relationships between parents, children and staff members. Effective leadership needs to engage with all aspects of policy and practice in order to encourage and motivate others, having as main goal the best interest of the families and the children (Dickins, 2014). This argument is also shared by Booth and Aiscow (2002), who have suggested that a sense of acceptance, collaboration and safety exists when inclusive culture exists as well.

However, key to leadership development work is the necessity to develop leaders to change schools and educational systems. School development will take place when inclusive principles guide decisions and policies of everyday practices in schools in order to support the learning of all (Angelides et al., 2010) and inclusion is viewed as a whole-school phenomenon (Slee and Allan, 2001).

In early childhood education, however, there seems to be a confusion between leading and managing or whether the SLT does both. Here it is crucial to differentiate between leading and managing. Whalley (2011) clearly states that leadership involves sharing values with the team, developing a shared vision and taking responsibility for staff, families and children. On the other hand, management is characterised more as deploying staff effectively, planning for the centre and making decisions. In practice, the SLT to make changes needs to have both leadership and management skills (Whalley, 2011). However, other researchers have argued that leadership and management are closely intertwined due to the working environment framework, therefore it is difficult to distinguish each one separately.

## Styles of Leadership

There are many leadership styles stated in the literature, such as: transactional, transformational, distributed, democratic, pacesetting, visionary, coaching as well as others. For the purpose of this chapter, only some of them will be presented and analytically discussed. Therefore, transactional, transformational, distributed and democratic styles will be presented systematically.

One well-known leadership style is *transactional leadership*. This style of leadership is implemented in different educational settings. It refers mainly to the development of a relationship between leaders and subordinates, as an exchange process that is meant to provide rewards to the subordinates for their performance. Because of the basis of this process, this model has been criticised strongly because it promotes mediocrity, since the focus is on offering the minimum performance on the task given (Sousa, 2015).

Another well-known leadership style is *transformational*. This style is implemented in different organisations and its main characteristic is that there can be many leaders who contribute to goals and can be empowered to make decisions. This style has been recognised to motivate people emotionally to be part of the vision of the leader and to sacrifice their self-interest for the purpose of the organisation.

Leaders that follow this are encouraged to question their practice in order to enrich their professional capacity with new learning opportunities (Sousa, 2015).

Sousa (2015) postulates that for transformational leadership to happen, certain parameters need to be in place. For example, it is imperative that staff develop a collaborative and professional school culture that shares leadership; a culture that will share power and reduce teachers' isolation as well as use bureaucracy as a vehicle to support change. In addition, amongst the most important elements of this style is to encourage staff to internalise goals for professional growth and help teachers to work smarter by acknowledging that teachers also can contribute to solutions, not just the head teacher of a school (Sousa, 2015).

Undoubtedly though, following such a leadership style in the current educational system is not an easy task, since the system is characterised with heavy bureaucracy and a 'top to down' leadership ethic (Sousa, 2015). The top to down leadership style has been criticised by other researchers and was considered inappropriate in an age of diversity (Hargreaves and Ainscow, 2015).

On the other hand, Kugelmass and Ainscow (2004) describe the collaborative style of leadership and believe that it is a basic characteristic of inclusive schools, promoting collaboration at all levels (between students, teachers and the community). The aforementioned style links with the distributed leadership style and encourages participative decision making (Kugelmass and Ainscow, 2004; MacBeath, 2006) – to have leaders who promote inclusive cultures, then leaders need to distribute the power. This can happen by training leaders to respond to diversity and to change the structures in order to encourage equal participation for all children (Angelides et al., 2010). That said, Dickins (2011) asserts that a distributed model of leadership would be the best model for developing inclusive practice. Clearly, the role of the leader in this model is perceived as broad and it can be filled concurrently by more than a few people. Jones and Pound (2008) affirm that people in managerial roles should be seen as 'leaders of leaders' and believe that a broader concept of leadership can create a culture of 'inclusive leadership'. By adopting this, each individual can be given the confidence to be seen as a prospective leader in some aspect of practice. Woods (2004) agrees with this and suggests that links can be made between distributed and democratic leadership. The first is characterised by action at all levels on a basis of direction-setting strategies, while the latter implies consultation and participation.

---

### PAUSE FOR REFLECTION

- By reading about the characteristics of the aforementioned leadership styles which one do you perceive as the best to support inclusive practice in schools?

- Have you ever worked in a school where the leadership team was following characteristics of the above styles? Or following a particular style completely?

- If you were one of the members of the SLT, which style do you think you would have adopted, and why? Why not the others?

## Styles of Leadership in Early Years

In England, early educational settings are diverse and include nursery classes, primary schools, private and voluntary settings (Fabian and Dunlop, 2002).

In early years education the SLT usually consists of the head of the setting, who is responsible for the day-to-day management, the Deputy Head, the Assistant, the SENCO and early years foundation stage leaders (Siraj-Blatchford and Wah Sum, 2013). According to the Code of Practice, when a child is identified with special educational needs the individual practitioner, most of the time the child's key person, will be the lead professional to engage with parents as well as remain responsible for that child on a daily basis (DfE, 2015c).

It is increasingly acknowledged that the quality of services early years settings offer to young children and families is strongly related to effective leadership (Rodd, 1994, 1997; Jorde-Bloom, 1992; Clyde, 1995). However, it also widely stated that leading a children's setting is an intrinsically complicated and difficult task. This is because it includes facilitating the needs of families and children, and working collaboratively with external agencies and partners (LAs, governing bodies, advisory boards and parents) (Sharp et al., 2012). That said, and although there is a clear consensus on leadership, still an explanation is not given on how to achieve highly effective leadership in order to achieve the strategic aims of the stakeholders, including parents, colleagues, pupils, LAs and the local community (Durrant and Twyman, 2015).

In the recent revised SEND Code of Practice (DfE and DoH, 2015) there is a clear emphasis on the importance of leadership. Leadership that includes working with other professionals, including SENCOs, LAs, Governors, the National Health Service (NHS) and CCGs (Clinical Commissioning Groups) with a clear drive towards leadership for integrated working (DfE and DoH, 2015). Integrated working (IW) refers to 'everyone supporting children and young people to work together effectively to put the child at the centre, meet their needs and improve their lives (CWDC, 2008: 2).

Therefore the leadership and management of a setting is a very important factor for inclusion. The Every Child Matters agenda (ECM) challenges leaders and managers in order for them to build integrated teams that support the child and the family by placing them at the heart of the process. This process can be facilitated by leading colleagues from other professional backgrounds and finding a common ground to unite members who are bringing together different working practices and expectations (CWDC, 2008). Sylva et al. (2004) report that high pre-school provision which has integrated childcare and education can benefit children's cognitive and behavioural outcomes up to 11 years old. However, although IW is important to inclusion, what has been found is that parents and carers now have more choices available to them and this can result in more conflict between them and the professionals. The reason for this can be that although both parties want the best interest of the child, the way they view it and want to see it served can be very different (Brodie and Savage, 2015).

Siraj-Blatchford and Manni (2007) report the range and extent of the leadership role in early years and have recognised ten categories of effective leadership practice:

- Identifying and articulating a collective vision.
- Ensuring shared understanding, meanings and goals.
- Effective communication.
- Encouraging reflection.
- Monitoring and assessing practice.
- Commitment to ongoing, professional development.
- Distributed leadership.
- Building a learning community and team culture.
- Encouraging and facilitating parent and community partnerships.
- Leading and managing: striking the balance.

(Siraj-Blatchford and Manni, 2007)

On the other side, a more recent report published by the National College for School Leadership identified eight behaviours of highly effective leaders. These are presented in Figure 5.1.

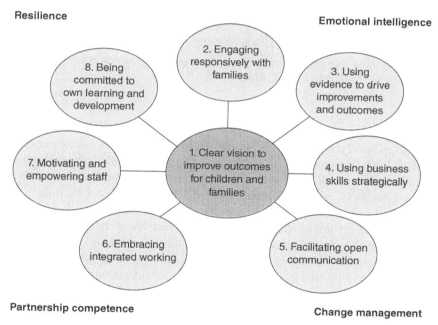

**Figure 5.1**  Eight behaviours of highly effective leaders (Sharp, 2012: 20)

What can be seen is that there are a lot of similarities between the two and that some characteristics have been identified by both. For example:

- vision and effective communication
- motivating staff
- promoting professional development, like a community of learning
- building partnerships between school and parents.

These four characteristics seem to be the common ones that both teams of researchers believe are indicators for effective leadership.

On the other hand, Goleman et al.'s book *The New Leaders* (2002) which focuses on leadership in the early years identified six leadership styles: visionary, coaching, affiliative, democratic, pacesetting and commanding. Each of these styles present positive characteristics as well as drawbacks if they are used poorly. But their argument is that in order for leaders to be effective they need to use a range of styles depending on the needs of the organisation and personal preferences. For a leader to be effective she needs to be able to implement comfortably at least four out of the six styles based on the circumstances (Cook, 2013).

---

### PAUSE FOR REFLECTION

- What characteristics do you find important for a leadership team to be effective in inclusion in the early years? What is your personal or professional experience of this?

- Were the leader(s) in your setting implementing a particular style of leadership? Or were they following characteristics of each style suggested above?

- Do you think that the leader(s) in your setting are supporting inclusive practice? If yes, how? If not, why is that?

---

## Strategies to Promote Inclusion by the Senior Leadership Team

It has been argued that the pursuit of inclusion should form a vital component of the school leader's preparation programme (Angelides, 2012; Jean Marie et al., 2009). Therefore, the SLT of a school needs to be prepared and ready to follow and implement inclusive practice. In order for this to be achieved there are certain strategies that can be implemented to support this. Initially, it has been suggested that the SLT of a setting needs to start by identifying the strengths of their setting instead of believing that they do not know anything about inclusion. Thus, they should build on the belief that there are practices already in place to support IE (Forlin and Loreman, 2014). Moreover, the SLT could encourage the belief that children with disabilities are not different and that diversity in classrooms can be an excellent opportunity for the teacher to learn new skills. The SLT will need to support the teachers in order to see this challenge as a learning opportunity (Forlin and Loreman, 2014). As Prizant (2015) has advised, teachers do not have to specialise in special education in order to understand children that have a diagnosis of SEN. It is regarded as very important that teachers do not view children with SEN based on a checklist of deficits rather than acknowledging their strengths and having a whole picture of who the child is (Prizant, 2015). There has been a recent move towards looking at children with SEN from neurodiversity perspectives. Specifically, children with SEN are characterised as having a different set of skills and abilities than their neurotypical peers. However, this fact should not necessarily imply that they are any less than others. On the contrary, with appropriate support children with SEN can be very successful and flourish (Prizant, 2015).

Another strategy that the SLT can adopt is the notion of a shared vision. This idea has been stressed by many authors, especially of SEN practices (Ekins, 2015). Hence, shared vision can motivate the team and provide energy to staff. However, it has to resonate with and be owned by the whole community, setting common goals and shared values. The vision needs to be informed by the pedagogy of the SLT, the knowledge of the setting as well as the needs of the community (Cook, 2013).

So, highly effective leaders in children's centres need to ensure that they have a clear vision of their setting which is interpreted in relation to their local needs, and this should be conveyed to staff and to external people coming to the centre in order to assist direction and progress. Even more, leaders who wish to be efficient need to include the child's and family's voice when decisions need to be made (Ekins, 2015). However, the process of developing inclusion and school vision needs to be seen as a working document. To be able to review and periodically turn back to it is important, so that external and internal changes to the school can be visible and useful changes can be made (Ekins, 2015). Nevertheless it is admittedly difficult to ensure that everybody has a clear understanding of the underpinning values and direction of the school in order to be able to support the vision's ongoing development and achievement (Ekins, 2015). Even more, to build a shared vision and cohesion among different groups of adults in early years is a challenge (Mistry and Sood, 2012).

SLT can build and reinforce team work. Team work refers 'to the process of all working together in a cooperative and purposeful manner' (Kaweski, 2014: 85). It is widely acknowledged that only when team members share their own expertise in an atmosphere of mutual respect where communication is direct, shared goals are heard and promoted and clear directions are given, that a setting can flourish (Picket et al., 2007). This is in agreement with Lipsky (1994), who suggested that IE is based on a fundamental principle of team work. However, it is worth noting here that there is not an expectation of teachers to be able to have all the expertise to meet the individual educational needs of the students in the classroom, rather that all professionals work together to achieve the best possible result for the child.

At this point it is important to clarify that 'team work' can refer to professionals working within a setting and external professionals from other settings or agencies. According to the newly introduced Children and Families Act 2014, different organisations must work together with the local council to get the right support for children with SEND. These organisations can be from the health and social care services (Children and Families Act – DfE, 2014a). The importance of team work cannot be more strongly emphasised rather than the newly introduced educational and health care plans. The UK government has recently introduced this in order to meet the needs of children with SEN in settings. EHC plans aim to place the families at the centre of the process as well as to ensure that there is an effective coordination amongst education, health and care services (Ko, 2015). However, this approach presents challenges, especially in coordinating so many professionals with different opinions and approaches to a child's future.

Additionally, children's centres can find it very difficult to operate under very difficult financial restraints where there are increased needs and high expectations of these services but lower levels of public funding (Brodie and Savage, 2015). Also, leading an early years centre where there is a high staff leaders' turnover (Brodie and Savage, 2015) is challenging. Therefore, if professionals change repeatedly, then this poses difficulties for building team work.

A research study conducted by Kugelmass and Ainscow (2004) that focused on leadership roles in schools drew evidence from three countries: the United States, the United Kingdom and Portugal. Intriguing findings showed that if the school staff embrace and accept the celebration of diversity and commit to offer educational opportunities to all students, then the students are enabled to participate in schools. Also when staff with different specializations were willing to work collaboratively, inclusive practice was able to be implemented more effectively. As a result, the leadership team of these schools was therefore redefined and empowered, since a sense of community and mutual trust was embedded. It is therefore suggested that strong school leadership which commits to inclusive values is of paramount importance to support and empower a collaborative culture (Kugelmass and Ainscow, 2004).

Another important strategy that contributes to the development of inclusive schools is writing a school inclusion policy – a policy that when written is linked to the school's vision and ethos. The SLT needs to involve all teachers in the process of identifying the objectives and the aims of this policy and indicate where to turn if help is required. This should be the guideline for the staff as well as parents and children who attend a setting. The policy needs not just to be written on paper, but also be an effective one that will be implemented in all areas of practice. Moreover, it should reflect governmental policies, the LA policies as well as the values and beliefs of the local community (Blandford and Knowles, 2013).

An idea that has been evident in many authors' work is that inclusion can be part of the school development plan (SDP) (Male, 2000; Burello et al., 2001; Powers et al., 2001; Kugelmass and Ainscow, 2004). Thompson (2012) asserts and reinforces the idea of an inclusion policy, arguing that the most consistent way of planning to achieve inclusion and school ethos can be via the SDP. However, for this to happen it needs to be embraced as a whole-school community theme and not of a particular class or a teacher, and it should be fully supported by the SLT of the school (Thompson, 2012 as cited in Cornwall and Graham-Matheson, 2012).

An all-inclusive SDP that has inclusion as a core value can be expressed over a period of time, and changes can happen. The SDP document should be practised via a distributed set of responsibilities and a communities of practice approach. If the SDP is seen as a vehicle towards change and improvement, then any move towards an inclusive culture needs to be strongly embedded in this and should reflect the values of the whole school community. If progress is to be made within it, then it should complement the school's standards agenda with a clear expression of the school inclusion policy. School leadership and management needs to be in tune with inclusive practice and staff that are committed to these values. Leadership that distributes responsibilities and parents and governors who are supportive would be of pivotal importance towards building a SDP. The head teacher, staff and the governors need to show enthusiasm for the idea of inclusion, even within the context of school inspection, league tables and legislation (Thompson, 2012 as cited in Cornwall and Graham-Matheson, 2012). This is strongly emphasised since it has been noticed in the last few years how early years settings are setting very high expectations on a standard's driven agenda rather than meeting individual student needs.

Another very significant strategy for promoting and reinforcing inclusion in schools and early years settings is building partnership with parents. Dickins (2014: 131) uses the term partnership 'in relation to how settings should work with parents'. The SLT needs to empower this relationship and to build up trust between the family and the professionals. This can be achieved via different routes, like planned meetings and structured conversations with parents to inform them about their child's inclusive placement. Also, it can be achieved when teaching staff at the school embrace this inclusive ethos within everyday practice.

The idea was equally recognised by the Department for Education and Skills in the SEND Code of Practice (DfES, 2001b), where the emphasis was on a 'culture of cooperation' in order to give the opportunity to children to reach their full potential. Even more, the Lamb Inquiry (2009) has strengthened the idea that a school needs to provide parents of pupils with SEND with ample information in order to enable them to engage in their child's schooling and recommends changes to the home–school dialogue in relation to the expectation and the planned outcome (Lendrum et al., 2015).

In 2009 the Achievement for All project was developed to provide better opportunities for children with SEND to achieve their full potential. This pilot initiative had three strands: assessing, tracking and intervention. The second strand involved structured conversations with parents (SCPs) and outlined a clear framework to help schools establish an open dialogue with parents about their child's learning. The results show that the developed framework appeared to be effective because it gave the parents a voice that was listened to, and it changed the dynamic of the relationship between school and home (Lendrum et al., 2015).

When the school is trying to build a partnership with parents it is essential to remember and remind staff about the parent's sensitivities as well. For instance, when parents have disabled children research has shown that parents experience their children's disability in individual ways (Wall, 2003). It is evident that some parents still struggle to overcome the effects of the negative interpretations of disability which are sometimes reinforced by the attitudes and the assumptions of the people around them (Wall, 2003). If professionals working with families are willing to comprehend, to listen and to build trust, then that can be perceived as a significant step forward for the families (Dickins, 2014). Even more, it is essential to remember that the language used with the parents needs to be one that they understand. In an Audit Commission study (2003) it was noted that parents of disabled children noticed that professionals talk in a language that they could not comprehend. Therefore, professionals need to consider that the level of language used with the parents needs to be the one that the parents can understand and communicate in more successfully.

## Leadership in International Perspectives

At this point, the idea of inclusion will be looked at from the perspective of a country in the European Union: Cyprus. The idea of inclusion in Cyprus is well embedded within the special education framework. Liasidou and Antoniou (2015) have conducted a research study in Cyprus about head teachers' views on inclusion. Results show that when head teachers embrace a culture that promotes learners' diversity, at the same time there is a lack of supportive networks for them in order to successfully implement transformative change. Additionally, they describe the situation as a lack of a coherent vision by the Ministry of Education and Culture of Cyprus (MoEC) (World Bank, 2014). The lack of vision for inclusion is also credited to the reality that no effectiveness indicators or accountability regimes exist in order to push for school development for inclusion (Sindelar et al., 2006). Also, the MoEC does not provide any directions or mechanisms to support vulnerable students, nor does it check whether teachers are effective in providing quality in their teaching (Sindelar et al., 2006). Therefore, the idea of IE in Cyprus does not seem to be promoted from the SLT of the schools, mainly originating from the fact that the MoEC does not offer the essential help.

## Continuous Professional Development

The SLT of a school has many responsibilities; among these is the continuous professional development (CPD) training of staff. This is a very important aspect of school life since it has been found that inadequate professional training may contribute to failure in successfully communicating with the children (Ellis and Beauchamp, 2012). Simultaneously, Busher (2000) highlights the significance of 'creating an inclusive school of developing staff abilities to improve the quality of learning opportunities student have' (as cited in Blandford and Knowles, 2013: 29). Hence it is the responsibility of the SLT to make sure that the most suitable professional is engaged with the children who need that expertise. It is somehow expected that the SLT will listen to other people in order to identify the challenges in practice as well as finding ways to adapt to these (Brodie and Savage, 2015: 191) and provide the best possible strategy. Therefore the SLT needs to identify who has the skills to work with children with SEN and to promote inclusion for them. If the staff need to be trained, then the SLT need to decide on their CPD training schemes. Admittedly though, it is acknowledged that primary schools (age range 3–5) are facing challenges in developing a coherent policy on CPD because there are so many different agencies and several functions to manage (Mistry and Sood, 2012).

Therefore, the CPD that the SLT will provide can emphasise detailed empirically-validated teaching strategies for particular curriculum areas, as well as social and emotional needs (Baker and Martin, 2008; Forlin and Hopewell, 2006; Leko and Brownell, 2009; Ross and Blanton, 2004). What is more, the SLT can ensure that professional development days provide teachers with opportunities to discuss pedagogy, curriculum, students' progress and instructional differentiation in addition to their own individual ongoing professional needs (Philpott et al., 2010). As research studies have shown, mainstream and specialist teachers prepare minimally when delivering individual support, particularly for students with specific needs (Golder et al., 2009; Leko and Brownell, 2009; Norwich and Lewis, 2001). As a result, if the school wants to adopt an inclusive culture, then essential links would need to be developed; for example, partnerships between mainstream and special education teachers so that they can start collaborating (Philpott et al., 2010). Issues related to CPD within the early years and primary sector are discussed in more depth in Chapter 8.

Moreover, a very important area that research has pointed out as needing attention is that leaders do not know enough about inclusive education, policies and legislation that can support the implementation of inclusive practices for children with disabilities (Pazey and Cole, 2013). So, SLTs that wish to support IE need to make sure that all school staff participate in professional development programmes about relevant legislation and policies that are linked to educating students with disabilities (Agbenyega and Sharma, 2014).

The significant aspect here is that CPD training can also apply to the leaders themselves. For example, there is now a dedicated training course called the National Professional Qualification in Integrated Centre Leadership that is available via the National College for School Leadership and is an opportunity that leaders can act upon (Siraj-Blatchford and Manni, 2007). So, CPD applies to leaders as well as staff (teachers and teaching assistants).

However, CPD is a large field of interest, but an exhaustive review of CPD is beyond the scope of this chapter. See Chapter 8 for further discussion.

## Local Community

It is very clear how important it is for a school to work closely with the local community and that this would reinforce the sense of belonging and wellbeing in the students. A study conducted by Barnes in (2008) focusing on schools that were embedded in local communities showed that there was a significant benefit from multi-agency working and improved outcomes for vulnerable children. To be precise, it highlighted the importance of improved accessibility of specialist trained professionals in supporting universal services, preferably working out of and within local schools and the community. In addition, the study presented a general agreement that a key worker or a collaborative team work approach that works within the community can be straightforwardly accessed by families and professionals. This has been suggested to be the best way forward to support vulnerable children (Barnes, 2008).

## External Agencies

An equally important matter for an effective inclusive leadership style is collaboration with external agencies. In the new Code of Practice (DfE and DoH, 2015), a need for all services and agencies to work together has been highlighted. A clear example of this are the EHC plans (Ekins, 2015). External agencies can help, support and promote inclusive practice in schools as long as the leadership team supports this.

These people are called the 'paraprofessional' team. These people can be health care and social services staff who provide interventions, support and therapeutic training for children in order to reduce barriers to learning. They adhere to the standards for SEN support and outreach services, and among those standards are the requirement to understand the school systems that promote inclusion for children with SEN and have good interpersonal skills in order to work as a team (Cheminais, 2006).

The school can also seek help from bodies like the Council for Disabled Children, the Special Needs Jungle, and the Professional Association for Childcare and Early Years (Brodie and Savage, 2015). These are some of the opportunities that the SLT needs to consider in order to develop the knowledge for an inclusive practice. There are many other agencies that the school can seek help from, like the Children and Adolescents Mental Health Service (CAMS), in order to give all children the opportunity to be included.

However, the issue of external agencies is beyond the scope of this chapter and an extensive review will not be provided.

## CASE STUDY

Michael is a 3-year-old-boy who has recently been diagnosed with autism spectrum disorder (ASD). Michael's family wants him to start nursery, so they were recommended a setting because of its excellence in inclusive practice. The family called the setting and arranged a visit. The parents and the child were stressed on the day because of the unfamiliar environment. However, the manager of the setting welcomed them with the SENCO and introduced them to the setting and explained that they would be given a tour there. The visit to the setting was very successful and Michael liked a particular class where there were a lot of sensory opportunities for him to explore play. The class teacher introduced the structure of the class to the parents while Michael was busy playing. The parents were reassured about both the educational and the social aspects of his learning at the setting. Additionally, the family was reassured that all professionals that need to be involved with Michael's learning are welcomed to the setting, and there was willingness from the school to work in an integrated approach for the child's own benefit. The family did not know, however, what professionals would need to get involved with Michael and how that would be accomplished. The manager suggested that Michael join the setting initially part time for two days a week for an easier transition. The manager also informed the parents that a meeting would be held with them and the class teacher in order to see how to support the child's needs in the most effective way.

## PAUSE FOR REFLECTION

- What else could the leadership team do to make the family feel more included to the setting?

- Who else could have been invited to the meeting?

- Since Michael is the first child of the family and has been recently diagnosed with autism, would there be anything else (information) that the setting could have provided the family with?

- Could the leadership team provide any information regarding inclusion strategies and approaches they implement for children with SEN?

- Should the leadership team of the school provide any further information to the family about how to best support Michael's needs for inclusion in the local community?

- Do you think that the leadership team is important in supporting an inclusive culture in your school setting? If yes, why? If no, why?

- What do you think are the main factors in providing a successful inclusive practice in school settings for staff, children and their families?

- How strong do you think that the voice of the parent or the child should be in school inclusion policy?

## CHAPTER SUMMARY

This chapter aimed at exploring and discussing the multi-faceted issue of inclusion and presenting a discourse of what the notion stands for. There is a strong consensus that the role of the SLT in implementing inclusion is vital not only in theory but also in practice. It is of fundamental importance that all staff, families and external professionals work together in an integrated approach for the child's own best interest. Advantages of adopting this approach were discussed as well as the risks within this framework. However, collaborative working with families and professionals needs to be the vehicle for supporting inclusion for children, and the best interest of the child needs to be at the centre of all actions. More importantly, and although a variety of leadership styles were presented, discussed and criticised, the leaders of a setting need to be able to assess the circumstances and decide the best one for their setting. Albeit distributed leadership was the one suggested as the best approach for inclusion, some early years settings will need to combine elements of different styles initially. The SLT needs to be experienced and knowledgeable enough to know the different leadership styles and decide which one would be the best for inclusive practice for their own setting. Finally, CPD, external agencies as well as the local community were discussed as factors that contribute towards inclusive practice in order to understand the effect that these have in reinforcing inclusion.

## Suggested Further Reading

The list below offers further information and guidance on the key points that were highlighted in this chapter.

Brodie, K. and Savage, K. (eds) (2015) *Inclusion and Early Years Practice*. Abingdon: Routledge.
This timely new text examines the key perceptions, perspectives and concepts around inclusion in the early years. It discusses how practitioners can be effective and acquire the

knowledge necessary to identify what makes each situation and circumstance unique and use this to develop strategies and approaches that are appropriate. Drawing on real-life experiences of practitioners, it considers the questions practitioners are likely to come across in their professional lives and how they might genuinely go about meeting the needs of all the children in their care. The book covers case studies drawn from current research and thinking points which encourage reflective practice. It will be essential reading for students on early childhood studies programmes and early years foundation degrees who wish to become reflective and critically aware practitioners.

Dickins, M. (2014) *A-Z of Inclusion in Early Childhood.* London: McGraw-Hill Education. This book is an excellent guide that presents principles and practice of inclusion in young children's care and education. By using an alphabetical approach, the book may be dipped into as required or read from cover to cover. The whole book is driven by the author's passion for inclusion since, as she states, 'we all have responsibility and a role to play in challenging discrimination and oppression'.

Cook, J. (2013) *Leadership and Management in the Early Years.* London: Practical Pre-School Books.
This book is part of the Early Childhood Essentials, which is a series designed to help those working in early education to develop the essential skills and level of professionalism in key aspects of practice. The book is a practical guide to building confident leadership skills via a presentation of real case studies of best practice in a range of settings.

# 6

# PROFESSIONAL ETHICS: PARTNERSHIP AND COLLABORATION IN THE EARLY YEARS

## BEATE HELLAWELL

---

### CHAPTER OBJECTIVES

- What is professionalism and what constitutes professional knowledge?
- What are the roles and limitations of professional ethics?
- How can professional ethics contribute to safe and child-centred professional practice?
- How can the 2015 SEND Code of Practice influence the professionalism of practitioners?

---

In this chapter we will explore how an appreciation of professional ethics can contribute to safe and child-centred professional practice; enable more effective partnership working with peers, parents and other agencies; and support the professional standing of early years practitioners and teachers. In the first part of the chapter, a brief exploration of ideas around professionalism and professional knowledge is followed by looking at professional ethics and the role and limitations of codes of ethics and codes of practice. The second part explores ethical knowledge. This includes the role of moral theories that can be used for justifying professional decisions, as well as the nature of ethical dilemmas and the recognition of moral stress. In the final part, an extended case study relating to the 2015 SEND Code of Practice explores implications for a professionalism that is defined and limited by professional codes, and considers moral dilemmas and conflicts of interest between partners.

## Professionalism and Professional Ethics

> ### PAUSE FOR REFLECTION
>
> - What does it mean to describe someone as an early years professional? How does it differ from being a practitioner or a worker?
>
> - Is this a helpful or harmful way of distinguishing between colleagues? Does it facilitate or hinder partnership working?
>
> - Do you think about yourself as a practitioner or a professional?

### Professionalism and Professional Knowledge

Conventional descriptions of professionalism focus on the requirement for professionals to demonstrate specialist knowledge and experience. The relevant profession itself is responsible for the training and for setting appropriate standards of competence. Following dedicated training – and alongside continuing professional development (CDP) – professionals in return enjoy a fair degree of autonomy in the daily pursuit of their professional practice. In this traditional understanding, the self-regulation of the profession goes hand in hand with ethical practice which individual professionals have internalised. The two components of professional ethical practice entail being guided by the knowledge base of the profession, and seeking the welfare and best interests of those who are served (Strike, 2007). However, this conventional understanding of professionalism has been challenged by more recent social policy reforms, which have significantly reduced professional autonomy and replaced the assumed internalised ethical practices of individual professionals with increasingly prescriptive codes of professional conduct and practice. The statutory SEND Code of Practice (DfE and DoH, 2015) is the latest example in this development.

SEND professionalism is caught up in the debate about what constitutes the specialist knowledge base for educators and whether teachers are in fact professionals, or rather semi-professionals or skills-based technicians instead (Burstow and Winch, 2014). Some commentators point to the increasing responsibility and complexity of meeting the needs of children with diverse SEND, and the specialist knowledge as well as valued dispositions those professionals therefore now need (Benedict et al., 2014). Others emphasise the importance of the practical knowledge SEND educators will develop after undergoing generalist teacher training (Florian and Black-Hawkins, 2011). These conflicting views are often informed by the models of disability individuals subscribe to (Mintz and Wyse, 2015). Medical and psychological positions of SEN (the medical model) assume discrete categories of need that require specialist theoretical knowledge to support diagnosis and interventions. Sociological perspectives (the social model) emphasise experiential knowledge which prioritises the need to know the individual child. The sociological approach draws on the concept of craft knowledge (Eraut, 2000) that distinguishes between theoretical knowledge and personal knowledge, including commonsense knowledge of people and memories of prior cases. Craft knowledge is not a derogative term that seeks to deny teachers' professional status, but particularly emphasises the knowledge that comes from focusing on dilemmas and the resulting dialectical character of knowledge (Florian and Black-Hawkins, 2011).

---

### PAUSE FOR REFLECTION

- What are the key points of difference between a medical and social model of disability?

- How does this inform understandings of the nature of professional knowledge?

- What do you think is the 2015 SEND Code of Practice's implied view about professional knowledge?

---

## Ethical Knowledge as the Defining Knowledge Base

Campbell (2003, 2008) proposes the concept of ethical knowledge (rather than knowledge relating to pedagogy or the individual child) as the defining knowledge base for educators and advocates a professionalism that is defined by both a collective and an individual sense of ethical responsibility instead. She argues that ethical knowledge should be viewed as practical wisdom, distinct from technical competence. Ethical knowledge offers 'tools for thinking about difficult matters' because 'the world is seldom simple or clear-cut. Struggle and uncertainty are part of ethics, as they are part of life' (2003: 9).

Urban (2008) and Urban et al. (2012) write in the context of the professionalisation agenda of early years practitioners and also argue for a relational professionalism that embraces openness and uncertainty, and that encourages the co-construction of professional knowledge and practices. Here the emphasis is less on the acquisition and transmission of theoretical knowledge or on following prescriptive guidance given in practice codes. A key feature of the proposed competent system is the support given to individuals to realise their capability for developing responsible and responsive practices that meet the needs of children and families in ever-changing contexts. Becoming 'competent' is seen as a continuous process that comprises the ability to build a body of professional knowledge and practices, and also to develop professional values. Although 'knowledge' and 'practice' are critically important, practitioners and teams also need reflective competences as they work in highly complex, unpredictable and diverse contexts. This may be particularly true when working with children with SEND.

---

## PAUSE FOR REFLECTION

- Both Campbell and Urban argue that uncertainty is something that professionals should welcome rather than avoid. Do you agree?

- How might this view influence partnership working with parents and colleagues from other agencies?

---

## PROFESSIONALISM

*Craft knowledge*: distinguishes between theoretical knowledge and personal knowledge which includes commonsense knowledge of people, insights gained from and memories of prior cases. Experiencing and reflecting on dilemmas develops craft knowledge.

*Ethical knowledge*: is distinct from theoretical knowledge or technical competence gained from studying and experience and is viewed as practical wisdom which accepts personal and collective ethical responsibility in complex and often uncertain professional circumstances.

*Competent system*: emphasises the co-construction of professional knowledge and practices and highlights the need for professional knowledge as well as the competence to reflect on professional practices and opportunities to develop professional values.

*Distinctive professions*: a profession with a special set of ethical principles and knowledge which is distinct from other professions. How various professionals engage in partnership working depends on whether they view their profession and ethical practice as distinct from each other or in common with other partners. Contemporary professionalism has undermined the ideas of distinctive professions.

---

## Professional Ethics and Codes of Practice

In the section above we explored links between different notions of professionalism and types of professional knowledge. In this section, we consider the relationship between professionalism and professional ethics. Carr (2000) argues that whether or not someone is a professional is to consider whether professional ethics is central to their role. Some writers see the 'elimination of a moral landscape' (Stronach et al., 2002: 130) as the biggest threat to contemporary professionalism, with values such as autonomy, trust and risk-taking removed from closely directed and inspected professional practice. These authors also make professional ethics pivotal to an understanding of what it means to be a professional.

Professional ethics are the 'norms and standards of behaviour of specific occupational groups, and the ethical issues and dilemmas that arise in their practice' (Banks, 2004: 3). The recent trend of inter-professional working in multi-disciplinary teams means that distinct roles and responsibilities are disappearing and this challenges the idea of distinctive professions with special sets of ethical principles. It is replaced by a new kind of accountability where organisational values might have to come before professional values and where the first loyalty will have to be with the employer rather than with a professional body or the service user. The moral imperative for educational professionals to 'serve the best interests of the students' might, in this case, be compromised. In this new climate of demanded accountability, professional ethics is often equated with and reduced to codes, rules and principles, rather than with internalised values (Shapiro and Stefkovich, 2011).

Ehrich et al. (2013) usefully distinguish between a moral accountability that is concerned with building and improving relationships and professional accountability that is concerned with upholding professional standards. Whilst these multiple forms of accountability might pull professionals in different directions (e.g. compliance with organisational requirements versus the specific needs of a child), they also hold competing demands in balance. For this reason, the recognition of moral accountability as one facet in the multiple accountabilities required of professionals is so very important.

---

### PAUSE FOR REFLECTION

- How important do you think professional ethics really is? Would you agree with the claims that it is fundamental to being a professional?

- Do you agree that moral accountability should be part of professional accountability? What would this look like?

---

Ethical principles are frequently translated into ethical codes in order to provide guidance on acceptable practice for individual professionals. This is done in a confusing array of codes of ethics, professional codes, professional standards and codes of professional practice. These codes address the circumstance that professionals are in positions of power (due to their specialist knowledge or their executive powers) over individuals, who depend on their competence and integrity for support. Codes define the overall aims of the profession (sometimes representing an idealistic goal and providing a sense of direction rather than describing practice), act as a quality assurance mechanism by outlining good practice, and are laying down minimum standards of conduct which may be used for disciplinary purposes (Schmit, 2006).

Whilst there is a dedicated ethical code for professionals working in special education in the USA (CEC, 2006), there is no comparable code for SEND professionals in England. Professionals engaged in SEND partnership working in England are guided by professional codes from their own professions, but this may contribute to conflicting priorities and challenge collaborations. For example, the professional code for social workers (BASW, 2011) highlights human dignity and the development of individual potential, social justice, and honesty and integrity, as well as competence in meeting the demands of the role. The code for nursing professionals (NMC, 2015) highlights the need to prioritise people, to practise effectively and safely, and to promote professionalism. The Teachers' Standards (DfE, 2011b: 14) emphasise that behaving ethically is a core component of the professional status of teachers and that teachers have a duty to 'maintain high standards of ethics and behaviour'. Whilst the Teachers' Standards document does not further define what it means by 'high standards of ethics', Knowles and Lander (2012: 2) describe them as 'those rules we use to guide us in knowing what correct or incorrect behaviour is, with regard to those things we believe to be important to us and feel are valuable for wider society too'. This interpretation highlights the difficulties professionals confront who may not always agree about what is important and valuable, what constitutes correct behaviour, or else whose personal 'rules' conflict with prescriptive guidance set out in professional codes. Teachers, for example, are required to maintain 'a rigorous focus on high standards, a determination to narrow attainment gaps, and a rigorous and stretching curriculum' (DfE, 2011b: 8), but also to 'adapt teaching to respond to the strengths and needs of all pupils' (DfE, 2011b: 11), and those respective expectations are not easily reconciled where children with SEND are concerned.

---

### PAUSE FOR REFLECTION

- What codes of ethics, professional standards and practice might be relevant for your current or future profession or place of work?

---

The attempt to codify professional activity in a prescriptive way may be unethical in itself, as it removes the responsibility for professional action from professionals. Dawson (1994) instead advocates an educational model of ethical conduct where professionals are always learning in response to given situations and so hone their practice as moral agents. This is the change from 'outside-in' professionalism which relies on codes of professional and ethical conduct, to 'inside-out' professionalism that relies on personal qualities of virtue, reflection and learning. The competent system discussed earlier fosters such an 'inside-out' professionalism.

Unlike some other professions, where graduate students take at least one ethics course as part of their training, this is not required in teaching, and this may result in a lack of 'competence in moral reasoning' (Shapiro and Stefkovich, 2011: 20). It may limit educationalists to resort to a professional ethics that simply equates with following codes, rules and principles, all of which may fit neatly into traditional concepts of justice, but often do not take sufficient account of complexities and individual need. Professional codes should, therefore, be seen as limited – and sometimes limiting – as they are 'unlikely to provide answers to a complex multi-layered situation where there are competing responsibilities at hand' (Ehrich et al., 2011: 175). Whilst professional codes may be valuable, it is likely that too much is expected of them with regard to daily moral professional decision making.

---

**PAUSE FOR REFLECTION**

- How necessary, useful or limiting are ethical codes and codes of practice in your view?

- Do you agree that adhering to codes could be unethical in some circumstances?

---

**ETHICS**

*Professional ethics*: are the norms and standards of behaviour of specific occupational groups, and the ethical issues and dilemmas that arise in their practice.

*Normative ethics*: concerns itself with standards of right conduct and with what it means to be a good or virtuous person. It is about what people ought to do or what they ought to be like and attempts to formulate moral principles.

*Situation ethics*: considers moral justifications in a specific context for a particular case.

*Beneficence*: is the action done for the benefit of others.

*Ethical reasoning*: applies specific moral principles to a particular dilemma where a distinction is made between a more general justification of ethical principles and the moral justification in a specific context for a particular case.

## Ethical Knowledge and Ethical Reasoning

In this section, we explore the role of ethics and moral theories in providing the basis for justifying professional decisions. We also consider the nature of ethical dilemmas and moral stress. Professional action is almost always moral action, as doing something that could harm or benefit someone else is a moral matter. Moral theories can provide moral guidance for decision making and offer criteria for a moral evaluation of human conduct. They can also provide individuals with tools to justify the decisions that they have made to others. Learning how to apply moral principles to specific problems produces ethical knowledge and enables moral reasoning (Driver, 2007; Strike et al., 2005).

### Traditional Moral Theories
*Consequentialism or Results-based Ethics: 'Maximising the Good'*
Consequentialism argues that determining what is right or wrong depends on the consequences of an act, and that the more good consequences are produced, the better the act is. One branch of this results-based ethics is utilitarianism, which claims that people should be concerned with maximising human welfare and wellbeing

('utility' is the old-fashioned word). When faced with a moral dilemma, a person should choose the action that maximises good consequences. Action is judged on the basis of how useful it is and the happiness it brings.

Alternative actions and their consequences also need to be considered, as the right action is the one that brings about the most overall good, not just the most good for the individual who carries out the act. Consideration also needs to be given to long-term consequences, rather than merely the immediate pleasure or good any action brings. This line of thinking encourages questioning and taking opposing positions seriously instead of silencing them. It encourages individuals to develop and articulate arguments in support of their own convictions and to allow others to question those taken-for-granted convictions in a climate of free speech (Driver, 2007).

### Deontology or Duty-based Ethics: 'Doing What Is Right and Your Duty'

Deontological (duty-based) ethics are concerned with what people actually do, not with the consequences of their actions. A wrong action in this view is not determined by the bad it produces, but rather by the kind of action that it is. Moral duties are seen as categorical and unconditional – predominantly based on reason rather than emotion. Moral worth consists in following the moral law, even if it is against personal inclinations.

One important aspect of this theory is the imperative to treat others with respect and never merely as a means to an end, due to the supreme moral worth of each individual. Another is to distinguish between perfect and imperfect duty. Whilst the duty to tell the truth is perfect and lying is always seen as impermissible in this moral theory, the duty to beneficence is imperfect and does not need to be adhered to at all times. Contemporary moderations of this view hold that there will be a hierarchy of duties and a recognition that duties might conflict with each other (Driver, 2007).

### Social Contract Theory: 'Failure to Follow Rules Would Result in Social Chaos'

Social contract theory holds that moral rules are agreed between rational individuals and that this agreement then authorises our actions. Humans will abide by those rules because they are self-interested and realise that not following those agreements would bring about social chaos. Social contract theory provides an explanation for the existence of and a justification for adhering to codes of conduct. It further argues that even if there is no compelling self-interest, individuals will not break social norms because they want to avoid being left out.

This view is moderated by suggesting that individuals recognise advantages gained from cooperation, as well as the threat of future withholding of benefits from those refusing to cooperate. Detractors would argue that people are not only motivated by self-interest, but also by sympathy for others.

### Virtue Ethics: 'What Would a Virtuous Person Do?'

Virtue ethics places character rather than action at the centre of its moral theory, and considers how we ought to be, rather than what we ought to do, first. It advocates emulating the actions of a virtuous person rather than following abstract principles. The claim is that the virtuous person will produce the right action, rather than that right action brings a virtuous person into being.

Practical wisdom enables individuals to work out how to act well, which is necessary for moral virtue and the possibility of wellbeing: 'the virtuous agent exhibits practical wisdom, knowledge of what he is doing and why it is good' (Driver, 2007: 139). This implies an awareness of the choices the individual has, rather than acting in ignorance; and a cultivation of virtues which demonstrates practical wisdom. Practical wisdom necessitates training and development of the capacity to see the rightness or wrongness of a particular action.

## The Limits of Traditional Moral Theories

Traditional moral theories have been challenged as being too bound to claims of universal moral certainty and as too focused on norms and rules for guiding decision making. In what follows we consider two alternative moral theories.

### Feminist Moral Theory: 'It Is about Relationships, Not Rules'

Feminist moral theory places an emphasis on relationships rather than rules. It questions theories that assume that agreements are made between autonomous individuals and argues that we are bound by relationships and the resulting moral responsibilities. Moral ways of thinking in this theory reflect an understanding of the self as relational rather than autonomous. Feminist moral theory also suggests that traditional moral theories are likely to overlook those who are not fully able to enter autonomous agreements, which may well include children and young people with SEND and their families. This interpretation does not reinforce a stereotypical view of women as emotional carers, but rather offers a critique of a 'rule-based, formalist system of morality that leaves no room for things such as exceptions – even reasoned exceptions' (Driver, 2007: 164). It argues that kind responses to the needs of others should be regulated by reason and offers a corrective to theories that have been developed by males and with male assumptions and prejudices.

### Postmodern Ethics: 'Uncertainty Is the Home Ground of the Moral Person'

Postmodern ethics argues that humans are often morally hesitant and conflicted and rejects the assumptions that it is possible to 'provide clear-cut rules for the choice between proper and improper and leave no grey area' (Bauman, 1993: 11). It embraces the moral self, constituted by responsibility rather than through learnable knowledge of rules, and places answerability to moral self-conscience over answerability to legislators and guardians. Bauman (1993 11) argues for a postmodern morality because 'the majority of moral choices are made between contradictory impulses, ... and is shot through with uncertainty'.

## Operationalising of Professional Ethics through Decision-making Models

Rather than viewing the various moral theories reviewed in the last two sections as mutually exclusive, attempts have been made to offer frameworks for drawing on various theories at appropriate times in support of professional ethical practice. Shapiro and Stefkovich's (2011) multiple ethical paradigm approach is one example. The model suggests four distinct ethical paradigms: an ethic of justice, an ethic of critique, an ethic of care and an ethic of the profession. They argue that this assists 'in grappling with complexities, uncertainty, and diversity' (p. 3) and suggest that by either focusing on one of the four particular paradigms, or by holding them in dynamic tension, professionals can be supported in their ethical decision-making processes and professional judgments.

An ethic of justice adopts an analytical and rational approach and focuses on rights and the law, looking for universal principles that can be impartial and verifiable. It draws on the range of traditional moral theories discussed above and particularly explores dilemmas around fairness and making exceptions, as well as the rights of the individual versus the greater good of the community. An ethic of critique determines whether a law or legal process is just and seeks to make the invisible visible: 'The intent is to awaken us to our own unstated values and make us realise how frequently our own morals may have been modified and possibly even corrupted over time' (Shapiro and Stefkovich, 2011: 13). It also asks hard questions regarding social class, race, gender and disability. An ethic of care rejects the idealised notion of the 'isolated individual' often implied in the previous perspectives, and focuses on relationships. It challenges patriarchal notions in the ethic of justice and draws attention to concepts such as loyalty, trust and empowerment. This requires 'leaders to consider multiple voices in the decision-making process' (p. 18) and individuals to learn how to be attentive and responsive. An ethic of care does value rational as well as relational and emotional responses such as empathy and compassion in decision-making processes. A fourth, and in their view most neglected paradigm, is an ethic of the profession which values professional judgement and decision making based on life stories and critical incidents, as well as the experiences and expectations of working lives.

In the case study about Travis later in this chapter, we will think about how to apply the moral theories and the suggested multiple ethical paradigm approach in a challenging professional situation.

## Moral dilemmas and moral stress

---

### PAUSE FOR REFLECTION

- How would you define a moral dilemma?
- Can you think of examples where moral dilemmas might arise for professionals working together and with parents in their joint endeavour to serve the best interests of a child?

---

Moral dilemmas can be 'a difficult choice between two or more equally defensible alternatives, between two equally indefensible alternatives, or a choice involving doing wrong in order to do right' (Campbell, 2008: 368). Dilemmas present them-selves in whether to openly voice moral opposition, quietly subvert expectations, or to live with the guilt of doing nothing. They are encountered in opposing views on what constitutes the best interests of the child, and the tensions between individual choice and the greater social good, where personal autonomy may undermine prin-ciples of justice and solidarity (Cribb and Gewirtz, 2012). There are three responses to moral dilemmas: defensive practice of following the rules; reflective practice which considers dilemmas for improved practice in future situations; and reflexive practice which implies a self-awareness and an understanding of how particular interactions influence a particular situation (Banks, 2006). Many moral dilemmas can't be solved or resolved, but rather must simply be somehow managed by profes-sionals (Ehrich et al., 2011).

The field of SEND 'is wrought with ethical dilemmas' (Fiedler and Van Haren, 2009: 160). Ethical issues arising for SEND professionals include: an individual's right to make decisions and choices and the professional's potentially conflicting responsibility to ensure their welfare; the conflicting responsibilities towards the service user, their family or advocate, the employer, the taxpayer and society at large; balancing equity, equality and diversity; resolving dilemmas between recom-mending 'appropriate' versus 'available' services; and boundaries between personal and professional values and identities (Banks, 2006; Helton et al., 2000). Norwich (2008) discusses the dilemmas of identification (at what point to label difference), curriculum (should this differ for different children?) and location (what justifies a separately located education?) as particular dilemmas arising for professionals working with children with SEND. These dilemmas result in deliberations and sometimes moral conflicts about whether to press for statutory assessment; what the most beneficial placement decision ranging from special to resource to main-stream provision might be, and whether to privilege local provision over 'best' provision; whether an entitlement to transportation is enabling or creates depend-encies; whether one-to-one support enhances capabilities or is disabling; and whether the curriculum should focus on academic or life skills (Hellawell, 2015). SEND professionals appear often to be caught between applying universalised judgments – outlined, for example, in the statutory Code of Practice – and provid-ing personalised care for individual children and their families. These moral dilemmas can lead to moral stress.

Moral stress is distinguished from merely experiencing moral uncertainty and from grappling with moral dilemmas where principles and values conflict. Moral stress implies a sensitivity to personal moral responsibility which gives rise to 'traditional negative stress symptoms that occur where [professionals] are not able to preserve all interests and values at stake' (Kälvemark et al., 2004: 1083). Initial distress may cause feelings of frustration, anger and anxiety but can result in active responses, whereas reactive stress turns these feelings into nightmares, headaches, thoughts of worthlessness or depression.

Rather than focusing on the psychological dimensions of moral stress, Cronqvist et al. (2006: 406) highlight the 'moral component of a stressor' in the tension between personal (moral) values and professional obligations, where it may be clear what is expected and 'should' be done, but not whether this 'ought' to be done. Deliberating the choice between 'should' and 'ought' leads to feelings of stress. Routine moral stress addresses the 'routine and pervasive nature of the burden' (Cribb, 2011: 124). The focus is on the everyday and unrelenting aspects of moral stress which do not constitute crisis points for individuals, because they realise that the potential harm or wrong done is quite small, and that the demands made on them appear legitimate, but are experienced as burdens nevertheless, and have a cumulative negative effect on motivation and wellbeing.

More significant dilemmas can be understood as critical moral incidents. They often highlight the conflict between an ethic of justice which demands consistent standards and an ethic of care requiring genuine sensitivity to individual need.

---

*An ethic of care*: focuses on our interconnectedness and obligations in relationships.

*An ethic of critique*: questions the accepted norms and challenges established practice.

*An ethic of justice*: draws on normative moral theories and is looking for universal principles.

*An ethic of the profession*: considers the dynamic relationship between personal values, professional codes and the ethics of the wider community and the practical wisdom gained from professional as well as life experiences.

*Consequentialism*: what is right or wrong depends on the consequences of an act; the more good consequences are produced, the better the act is.

*Critical moral incidents*: an incident which is highly significant for you because it makes you stop and think and raises questions and might leave you feeling quite distressed.

*Deontology*: considers moral duties to be categorical and unconditional.

*Ethical paradigms*: are sets of assumptions, concepts, values and practices that constitute a way of viewing reality. The four particular ethical paradigms discussed in this chapter are:

o   *Feminist moral theory*: argues that we are bound by relationships and their attending moral responsibilities and that context rather than general rules or reasons determine moral ways of thinking. Reasoned exceptions may be moral responses in particular situations.

o   *Moral dilemmas*: a difficult choice between two or more equally defensible alternatives, between two equally indefensible alternatives, or a choice involving doing wrong in order to do right.

---

○ *Moral stress*: sensitivity to personal moral responsibility which gives rise to traditional negative stress symptoms. This may be caused by conflicting moral virtues.

○ *Moral theories*: provide guidance for decision making, offer criteria for a moral evaluation of human conduct and contribute tools to justify decisions that have been made.

*Multiple ethical paradigm approach*: a particular model which aims to support professionals in deliberating ethical dilemmas. It draws on four distinct ethical paradigms.

*Post-modern ethics*: rejects universally applicable norms and accepts uncertainty and ambivalence as the starting point for moral action.

*Social contract theory*: holds that moral rules are agreed between rational individuals which they agree to out of self-interest and because they don't want to be left out.

*Utilitarianism*: a form of consequentialism which argues that people should be concerned with maximising human welfare and wellbeing.

*Virtue ethics*: places character rather than action at the centre of its moral theory.

## The Case of Travis

This extended case study of Travis will help us to further consider issues around professionalism and professional ethics that have been raised in the first part of this chapter. The insights that you have already gained from other chapters and the second part of this chapter will help you in formulating some of your responses.

Travis is five years old and profoundly deaf in one ear and severely deaf in another. He is a fairly recent arrival to this country and has had no experience of early years education in his country of origin. One local authority (LA) has legal responsibility for him because he first came to the attention of Social Care whilst living in this authority with his mother in temporary accommodation. He was identified as a child in need and allocated a social worker. The small family unit then moved to a different LA, where Travis started school in a local Reception class. Not long after starting school he was taken into care under a child protection order and, because his new foster family lived in a neighbouring borough to that of the school, the responsibility for statutory assessment of his educational needs transferred to this third authority. This administrative complexity and some confusion about particular professional responsibilities led to Travis being assessed by three separate teachers of the deaf who were all clearly saying he needed specialist provision either in a resource base in a mainstream school or else in a special school. However, almost three months later he is still in a mainstream school that has no specialist resources or experience. Additionally, his school is a long way from his foster placement.

---

### PAUSE FOR REFLECTION

- Who are the key professionals involved in this case and what are their particular roles?
- What are the complicating factors in this particular case?
- Which pieces of legislation and statutory guidance are relevant for this case?

---

Travis's social worker provides a vivid account of the complexities and frustrations of partnership working which has to be conducted within the constraints of statutory guidance: 'Travis has only been in the country for a year now and wasn't diagnosed as deaf until he came here. He was diagnosed, he was fitted with hearing aids, and he is now being assessed for a cochlear implant. A lot has happened in the last year. He was originally enrolled in a nursery class, but they didn't start any process for an EHC plan. Then he moved to his current school in a different LA. And actually, it's not been the school that have been difficult. The school were saying, "We don't think that we can meet his needs long-term, he very clearly needs a school with a hearing impaired provision, but we don't have a plan identifying that". So the school started doing observations to begin that process. And then he did end up in foster care.'

---

### PAUSE FOR REFLECTION

- What do you know about provision and support for children with hearing impairment (HI)?
- What is an EHC plan and who has responsibility for initiating assessments for this plan?
- Why do you think the nursery school had not started this process? Were they right not to do so? What are the arguments for and against early identification and labelling?
- What is your response to the school's claim that they can't meet Travis's need? Consider arguments around professional knowledge and inclusive values in your reflections.

---

Travis's social worker continues: 'When he was in his mum's care, he started at the mainstream school. Then about two weeks later he came into care, and it was taking him two and a half hours each way to school, and he's only five. So initially we stopped sending him to that school, thinking he's not statutory school age yet. And mum was calling me; she had brought her child here to have his health needs met, and for his educational needs to be met. So she was beside herself that he wasn't going to school. He'd been removed from her care and wasn't going to school. And I felt really ... because I totally agreed with her, could see why she was upset. But from a professional standpoint, you have to remain professional and not go against your ... you know. And I felt that really challenged me, because I thought, this mum was struggling and she did make some mistakes, but one thing she was doing was getting her child to school every day. And he's been removed from his mum's care, and we're not doing one of the things that she was doing. It just really challenged me, that. I found that really hard.'

---

### PAUSE FOR REFLECTION

- What is the key challenge for this social worker and how is this informed by her understanding of what it means to be a professional?
- Would you say this is an example of moral stress?
- What is your response to the social worker's account of the situation? Do you think an early years practitioner or teacher would have a slightly different perspective?
- What are some of the considerations around professional ethics?

---

The social worker adds: 'I think I might be partly to blame for some of the confusion because I don't think I completely understood the process. Travis is a LAC (looked after child) in my authority, so I got in touch with the SEN department here. And the teacher of the deaf is very, very passionate about what he does, and could see that this little boy wasn't getting the education that he needs and is entitled to, so started to try to get involved. But then that wasn't really his place to do that, so then the teacher of the deaf from the authority where his foster placement is became involved. And it just ... the child just got lost in it really, because it was all these sorts of processes, that because he technically lived in a different authority, it was this authority that needed to do the EHC plan. But it's not decided that he's going to stay there. Actually, it's looking very likely that he's going to move back to his mother's care, which would be here. So it would be another delay for him before he can move to the right school, because the authority where he is currently living will have to transfer the responsibility to write the EHC plan to us, it would be just another delay. For me, it just seemed simple. He is our LAC. Chances are, he's going to return to his mum's care. Make an exception on this occasion for the child; it's going to be better for him.

'This started at the end of September, and we're still no further in December. We had the assessment from the teacher of the deaf identifying that he thought, written on paper, that a hearing impaired provision would be right. I said, "Please, can Travis be sent to our provision here in case he gets sent back to mum, because I don't want him to have another change of school". And they did accept that. And then his assessment had to be presented at their SEN panel to say, "Yes, we agree with this assessment". Then they had to agree to ask our SEN panel to consider their request to place the child in the hearing impaired provision here in our LA. So then we had to hold our SEN panel, and they agreed with the proposal. So then the formal approach to the special school happened. And the school arranged to meet the little boy and consider what support he needed. And then they've written back to our SEN panel to get that agreed. So that's where we are, and we're still not in the right school.

He's still going to this mainstream school where, you know … it's a lovely school, and the teachers are all really committed to him, but it's not the right place for him.

'For me, it felt like this little boy got lost in all of it. The SEN panel leader from my authority was going to accept the assessment of the teacher of the deaf from his placement authority, so almost missing the step of having to go to their SEN panel first. She was going to accept that because she could see … And then her manager said, "No, we have to follow the process and it has to go to their panel first". And I just felt, we have processes, and maybe they look at our process and think, "Why do you do that?", but, for me … you know, he's a little boy, he's been taken away from his mother, he's in foster care. He's got hearing aids that he's not really used to yet. He's gone through so much, and we can't even just fast-track him into the school that he needs, because we have to follow these processes. And he's still not there and we're what, two and a half months later. It just seems that this child, everyone forgot about him and it was, "Well, no, we have to do this and this". That's how I felt. I felt really upset for him, that people couldn't just be a bit creative and flexible about how they worked, just to meet his needs.'

---

### PAUSE FOR REFLECTION

- Can you identify and outline the moral dilemmas in this scenario? How would different moral theories resolve these dilemmas?
- Should the professionals involved have made an exception as suggested by the social worker, or would this have been unethical, unlawful or unprofessional?
- Can you offer a response based on applying the multiple ethical paradigm approach discussed earlier on?
- What do you consider the role of the 2015 SEND Code of Practice to be in this case? Does it help or hinder?

---

'I know that I was annoying people because I had to take on the role as his parent really, a corporate parent. So I was emailing every single day, being like "When is the decision going to be made?", and I was hounding them. And the responses I got, I think maybe because I was coming from a professional side, they were getting a bit annoyed with me. And it might have been that I was asking questions that weren't …, but it's because I don't really understand it. It just seems a really, really complicated process for what could be quite simple.'

---

### PAUSE FOR REFLECTION

- What are some of the challenges for partnership working alluded to in this and the previous section?
- How can they be addressed?

'We get monthly supervision where we reflect on cases. And because it was such a hot topic within the team, I sounded off on a lot of people really, and particularly to those that were involved in it. And my supervisor was just as frustrated by it. And even when we went to the Courts, where we were very heavily criticised for not sending him to the school that he was at, even the judge stood up and said, "I know how hard this is, with SEN, the processes when different local authorities are involved". She said, "I imagine the social workers are very frustrated by this". So even someone at that level, and not necessarily directly involved in the process, knows and understands how difficult it can be.'

## PAUSE FOR REFLECTION

* What are the similarities and differences in terms of professional support for social workers and early years teachers?

*CiN (Child in Need) plan*: A child in need plan is put in place where there is no danger to the child, but where they have been identified by social care as needing extra support. The plan specifies what the family has to do to ensure that the child will not be removed from their care, as well as the support social care is putting in place for the family. Social workers are the lead professionals.

*Cochlear implant*: An electronic device that replaces the function of the damaged inner ear. Unlike hearing aids, which make sounds louder, cochlear implants do the work of damaged parts of the inner ear (cochlea) to provide sound signals to the brain.

*CP (Child Protection) plan*: A child protection plan follows the removal of a child from their family because they are considered to be at significant risk of harm. The plan put together at a child protection case conference details the ways in which the child is to be kept safe, how their health and development can be promoted and any ways in which professionals can support the child's family in promoting the child's welfare. Social workers are the lead professionals.

*EHC plan*: An EHC plan is a legal document that describes a child or young person's special educational, health and social care needs. It follows a statutory assessment and explains the extra help that will be given (either in a mainstream school, resource provision or special school) to meet those needs and how that help will support the child or young person to achieve what they want to in their life. The focus is on removing barriers to learning. SENCOs are usually the lead professionals for this plan.

*(Continued)*

*(Continued)*

*Profoundly deaf*: Deafness refers to the inability to understand speech through hearing even when sound is amplified. Profound deafness means the person cannot hear anything at all.

*Resource base*: A unit attached to a mainstream school that supports a group of children with a specific SEND, such as hearing impairment.

*SEN panel*: A panel of professionals convened by the LA where decisions about statutory assessments of SEN as well as decisions about provision and placements for children with SEND are made.

*Severely deaf*: Mild, moderate or severe hearing loss describes degrees of deafness.

*Teacher of the deaf*: A qualified teacher, who is additionally qualified to teach deaf children.

## CHAPTER SUMMARY

In this chapter we have explored different conceptions of professionalism and professional knowledge, as well as the role of professional ethics and ethical knowledge for supporting partnership working in the best interests of the child. Our extended case study in the form of an emotional first-person account has highlighted some of the challenges and complexities that hardworking and well-meaning professionals encounter and are expected to resolve. An over-riding question for you to consider has been whether the 2015 SEND Code of Practice helps or hinders in these professional (and often personal) deliberations.

## Suggested Further Reading

Banks, S. (2004) *Ethics, Accountability and the Social Professions*. Basingstoke: Palgrave Macmillan.

Campbell, E. (2003) *The Ethical Teacher*. Maidenhead: Open University Press.

Two excellent books on professional ethics for social and education professionals.

Driver, J. (2007) *Ethics: The Fundamentals*. Oxford: Blackwell.

A more general book about moral theories.

Shapiro, J.P. and Stefkovich, J.A. (2011) *Ethical Leadership and Decision Making in Education: Applying Theoretical Perspectives to Complex Dilemmas* (3rd edn). Abingdon: Routledge.

Investigating moral dilemmas and decision making.

## Recommended journal articles

Black-Hawkins, K. and Florian, L. (2012) 'Classroom teachers' craft knowledge of their inclusive practice', *Teacher and Teaching: Theory and Practice*, 18 (5): 567–84.

Fox, M. (2015) '"What sort of person ought I to be?" – Repositioning EPs in light of the Children and Families Bill', *Educational Psychology in Practice*, 31 (4): 382–96.

Hellawell, B. (2015) 'Ethical accountability and routine moral stress in special educational needs professionals', *Management in Education*, 29 (3): 119–24.

Mintz, J. and Wyse, D. (2015) 'Inclusive pedagogy and knowledge in special education: addressing the tension', *International Journal of Inclusive Education*, 19 (11) 1161–71.

Urban, M. (2008) 'Dealing with uncertainty: challenges and possibilities for the early childhood profession', *European Early Childhood Education Research Journal*, 16 (2): 135–52.

Urban, M., Vandenbroeck, M., Van Laere, K., Arianna Lazzari, A. and Peeters, J. (2012) 'Towards competent systems in early childhood education and care: implications for policy and practice', *European Journal of Education*, 47 (4): 508–26.

# 7

# EARLY INTERVENTION AND TRANSITION

## REBECCA CRUTCHLEY
## AND RUTH HUNT

### CHAPTER OBJECTIVES

- Discuss the evolution of the early intervention approach and its impact on early years provision.

- Consider models of best practice when implementing early intervention programmes.

- Explore some of the challenges involved in effective early intervention approaches.

It has long been recognised that timely and appropriate intervention to support children with SEND is the most effective approach to ensuring that children's needs are supported and provision is appropriate to their development and learning. Reference to early intervention was made as long ago as the Warnock report in 1978, who stated in her recommendations:

> The education of children with disabilities or significant difficulties must start as early as possible without any minimum age limit. In the earliest years parents rather than teachers should be regarded, wherever possible, as the main educators of their children. (Warnock, 1978, paras 5.2–3)

After being elected in 1997, the Labour Government embarked on an ambitious programme of investment in early years services aimed at increasing access to childcare for working parents, narrowing the gap between the highest- and lowest-attaining children before compulsory school age, safeguarding vulnerable children and addressing the needs of children with SEND (DfEE, 1998).

The legislative framework underpinning this investment has been discussed in Chapter 1. It is important to stress, however, that this investment represented a significant acknowledgement that effective and timely investment in services in the early years can mitigate social concerns and underachievement in later life. As mentioned in Chapter 1, much of the evidence for the benefits of early intervention came from the High/Scope Perry pre-school research in the USA (Schweinhart et al., 1993) and was later confirmed by the initial findings of the Effective Provision of Pre-School Education research (EPPE) conducted by Kathy Sylva and her team at the Institute of Education (Sylva et al., 2004, 2012). Sir Michael Marmot's report into the social determinants of health and education outcomes, entitled *Fair Society, Healthy Lives* (2010), reiterated the link between low income and poor educational outcomes. Evidence from the Children's Society suggests that children with a disability are considerably more likely to be living in a poorer household than typically developing children, which can affect their access to high-quality nutrition, appropriate resources and ability to access support services in their local area to support their needs (Children's Society, 2011). Attendance at repeated medical appointments can further compound their attendance at school, putting them at risk of falling further behind. More recently Labour MP Graham Allen wrote his influential report entitled *Early Intervention: The Next Steps* (2011), where the case for early intervention for children at risk of falling behind in their development and learning due to disadvantaged circumstances (including having a SEN or disability) was made.

Focusing on both the life chance outcomes and the economic benefits of early intervention, Allen called for an 'early intervention culture' whereby funding priorities would be targeted at improving the life chance outcomes of disadvantaged communities. Notably, and as reflected in the Children and Families Act 2014, he stressed the importance of evidence-based intervention programmes and criticised the costly duplication of services which could not fully demonstrate their impact on vulnerable children and families. The first part of this chapter will consider in more depth some of the key issues introduced in previous chapters in relation to the evolution and development of early intervention programmes for children with SEND, and the role of schools and settings in ensuring that children and their parents/carers are fully involved in this process, as stipulated in the Children and Families Act 2014 and the 2015 SEND Code of Practice. The second part of the chapter will focus on transitions for children with SEND in the early years, and the role that early intervention programmes can have in ensuring that children's needs continue to be met as they transition from home to nursery and from nursery to statutory schooling, whether this is in the mainstream or special school sector.

## How Has Early Intervention Evolved?

As noted above, the most significant attempt to introduce early intervention programmes to identify and address the needs of vulnerable children including those with SEND, arose from the unprecedented investment in early years provision by the Labour Government in office from 1997 to 2010. Sure Start local programmes and the Children Centre agenda and their role in establishing multi-agency support for children and families and the enhanced requirements for professionals from education, health and social care services to share information in relation to children and families receiving support have been discussed in previous chapters. Early intervention processes were thus facilitated by the increased cooperation and collaboration between professionals, in compliance with the Every Child Matters framework legally enshrined in the Children Act 2004 (amended in 2006 and 2009).

The evidence for the need for early intervention to support the needs of children with SEND between the ages of 0 and 5 arose to some extent from the increased number of children attending nursery provision before statutory school age, necessitated in part by the increase in women returning to the workforce (Blackburn, 2013), greater access to quality childcare (a result of the National Childcare Strategy), the expansion of free childcare provision from 12.5 hours per week to 15 hours per week in 2010, and the raft of schemes to support families with childcare costs via the nursery voucher scheme, initially introduced in 1989 and expanded alongside other benefits for families (e.g. working tax credits) in 2004, and also by the emerging evidence that attendance at a high-quality group-based educational setting would better prepare children for compulsory schooling, influenced by the EPPE research (Sylva et al., 2004) and it's evidence of the role of effective early education on the narrowing of the attainment gap. Children Centres met much of this demand, while there was also an increase in private nursery provision and childminders from the early 1990s to a more static position by 2006, all of whom, after 2008, were required to comply with the Statutory Framework of the EYFS (DCSF, 2007a). Blackburn (2013) recognises that the demand for childcare is predicated upon three factors: the birth rate, maternal employment creating a demand for childcare, and the ability of parents to pay. In more recent months, the proposed extension of the free nursery provision from 15 hours to 30 hours per week; although welcomed by parents, this has raised concerns in the daycare sector due to the anticipated costs to providers of subsidising these extra hours (NDNA, 2017).

Sure Start local programmes (SSLPs) and later Children Centres had a responsibility to identify children from disadvantaged families, including those who appeared to have a possible SEN, or who had a congenital disability in their local ward though pre- and post-natal support services and signpost them to appropriate provision. Thus one of the outcomes of the increased number of children attending pre-school provision was that their developmental and learning needs became more apparent and strategies were required to meet their needs at a much earlier age. Building on the 2-year-old pilot evaluated by Kazmirski et al. (2008), the expansion of the opportunity for 15 hours free nursery provision for vulnerable 2-year-olds has increased the number of under-3s attending some form of pre-school provision. One of the key criteria across LAs for accessing these 15 hours is if a child has a disability or complex need. Therefore children who may traditionally have experienced their pre-school years within the home were given increased opportunities to access pre-school education and care, and the wider services available via the multi-agency services provided by their nursery setting (discussed further in Chapter 9). Nevertheless, there have been concerns that the pace at which the 2-year-old offer was rolled out has led to some vulnerable 2-year-olds accessing services which are not fully prepared for the developmental needs of this age group, or for meeting the needs of children with severe or complex medical or health concerns or severe disabilities (Wolfson and King, 2008).

---

**PAUSE FOR REFLECTION**

- Consider how changes in legislation have increased opportunities for children with disabilities or complex needs to access provision to support their needs.

- What are some of the implications for schools and settings providing the 2-year-old offer?

---

## The Inclusion Development Programme

As has been noted earlier, the post-1997 Labour Government's commitment to reducing inequalities in the early years and addressing the needs of children with SEND brought about a raft of initiatives aimed at supporting parents and professionals in the early years and SEND field. Notable amongst these initiatives was the Inclusion Development Programme (IDP) (DCSF, 2007b), many of whose materials continue to be used to support practice by practitioners in early years settings and schools. The IDP provided resources for schools and settings on a range of SEN and disabilities, for example, speech, language and communication needs, and autistic spectrum disorders.

In addition to the IDP aimed specifically at children with a wide range of SEND, the National Strategies early years department at the DCSF (working in partnership with the National Literacy and National Numeracy Strategy teams) produced a series of materials aimed at improving literacy and numeracy from the early years sector through to secondary school age. Every Child a Talker (followed by Every Child a Reader and Every Child a Writer) (DSCF, 2008a) introduced the roles of Early Language Lead Practitioner and the Early Language Consultant, thus partnering speech and language therapists with teachers and early years practitioners to develop school- or setting-led intervention programmes, using an action research model to develop, improve and sustain best practice. LAs were funded to provide specialised training in children's language development in recognition both of the impact of language delay in early childhood upon later literacy outcomes, and in response to data collected for the Bercow Report (2008), which suggested that timely and appropriate interventions in the early years can overcome transitory language delays, recorded as making up 50 per cent of the total number of children identified as requiring additional interventions with 7 per cent of children under five having more persistent or long-term language disorders.

## The Early Support Programme

One of the key approaches for supporting children with severe and complex needs was the introduction of the Early Support programme (DCSF, 2003). Initially trialled with a selection of 'pathfinding' LAs, the programme was aimed at families whose children were supported by a range of professionals and for whom a key worker would be allocated to coordinate support, and crucially to act as an advocate for the family. It should be noted that the role of the Key Person can be adopted by any professional working with the family, and that their role, while similar, is not the same as the role of the Key Person in a nursery or early years setting. In terms of partnership with parents, the early support programme's ten principles demonstrate how partnership with parents was at the heart of the programme

---

### EARLY SUPPORT PRINCIPLES

1. The uniqueness of children and young people and families is valued and provided for.

2. Children, young people and families can be confident the people working with them have appropriate training, skills, knowledge and experience.

3. Multi-agency working practices and systems are integrated.

4. Children, young people and families are able to make informed choices.

5. Service delivery is holistic, coordinated, seamless and supported by key working.

6. An integrated assessment, planning and review process is provided in partnership with children, young people and families.

7. Children, young people and families are involved in shaping, developing and evaluating the services they use.

8. Children, young people and families are able to live ordinary lives.

9. Children and young people's learning and development is monitored and promoted.

10. Continuity of care is maintained through different stages of a child's life and through preparation for adulthood.

(adapted from the National Children's Bureau website, www.ncb.org.uk)

---

### PAUSE FOR REFLECTION

- Consider how the ten principles of the Early Support programme are reflected in the 2015 Code of Practice.

- What are the key skills and qualities required by key workers in order to work in effective partnership with children, young people and parents?

## Early Support and the Early Years Development Journal

When the Early Support programme was originally launched in 2003, it was accompanied by a range of support materials, initially aimed at parents but also accessed by practitioners. The journals were designed to enable parents to contribute to a formative record of their child's developmental milestones, which could be shared with professionals at review meetings. The idea that parents 'owned' this development journal was received positively by parents and carers, according to the Council for Disabled Children (2013). Guidance was provided throughout the journal to enable parents to clearly identify their child's strengths and areas for development. Initially, there were separate Early Support development journals focusing on specific areas of need; for example autism, babies and children with Down syndrome, children with multiple needs, children with visual impairment and children with hearing impairment. However, following the revision of the EYSF framework in 2012, these have been combined into one document and renamed the Early Years Development Journal (EYDJ), although the principles and design have remained unchanged.

The EYDJ supports parents to identify, monitor and assess their child's development according to four areas:

- Personal and social development.
- Communication and language.
- Physical development.
- Thinking.

For each of these four areas there are ten sequential steps, with clearly written jargon-free descriptors to enable parents to recognise the developmental progress their child has achieved. For each of these ten steps, parents can assess their child's progress according to three 'judgements': emerging, developing or achieved. The descriptors for each step are linked to the EYFS framework to ensure continuity and consistency and to avoid children with SEND being assessed according to a completely separate list of descriptors. In this way, the EYDJ follows the process of 'small steps' adopted by portage workers, many of whom work with parents to complete the journal in a collaborative manner.

## What Are the Key Processes of Early Support?

- The child is identified as having multiple or complex needs. This identification could be by their parent/carer, midwife (during ante- or post-natal care visits), their health visitor or their GP.
- The LA assigns a key worker whose role is to assess the child's immediate needs, and act as a single point of contact between the parents and education, health and social care professionals (where relevant) now and in the future.
- Families may be provided with a Family Pack to ensure that they understand what their involvement in the Early Support programme requires, and promoting their full engagement in the process.

## Portage Workers and SEND in the Early Years

Portage workers work with children with SEND and their families within the home to support development and learning. Through the provision of a home visiting service parents of children with developmental or learning difficulties, physical disabilities or other special needs are encouraged to support their children's development by suggesting activities and daily routines. Portage workers build on the parent's in-depth knowledge of their child and their existing parenting capacities to enable them to meet their development and learning outcomes. For children who also attend early years settings or schools, information about the portage support package is shared with other key professionals working with the child to ensure continuity and consistency.

---

### THE ROLE OF A PORTAGE WORKER

According to the National Careers Service the role involves:

- observing the child and talking to the parents to identify skills the child already has

- deciding with the parents which skills are most important for the child's future learning

- suggesting a programme of activities for the parents and child to practise together

- breaking down tasks that are difficult, or take a long time, into small steps

- showing parents how to use an activity chart or notebook to record their child's progress

- encouraging parents/carers to meet and offer each other support

- guiding parents in applying for disability benefits

- visiting weekly or fortnightly to check on progress and agree on new goals

- writing progress reports and working with the parents to develop long-term goals

- working in partnership with other professionals.

(www.nationalcareersservice.direct.gov.uk)

---

## Integrated Reviews and Early Health Assessments

The idea of an integrated review for 2-year-olds was originally proposed in the review of the EYSF framework in 2012, and many settings developed materials and resources to implement this requirement called the '2-year-old progress review'.

However, working alongside other professionals to complete the reviews was often problematic (CDC, 2013). Therefore the renewed commitment, in the 2014 revisions to the EYSF framework, to an integrated health review (see Figure 7.1) which combined the progress check from early years practitioners with health visitor assessments required by the Healthy Child Programme (DoH, 2009b) was welcomed by many in the field. Section (5) of the 2015 Code of Practice outlines the objectives of the integrated review thus:

- identify the child's progress, strengths and needs at this age in order to promote positive outcomes in health and wellbeing, learning and development
- enable appropriate intervention and support for children and their families, where progress is less than expected, and
- generate information which can be used to plan services and contribute to the reduction of inequalities in children's outcomes.

(DfE, 2015c: 83)

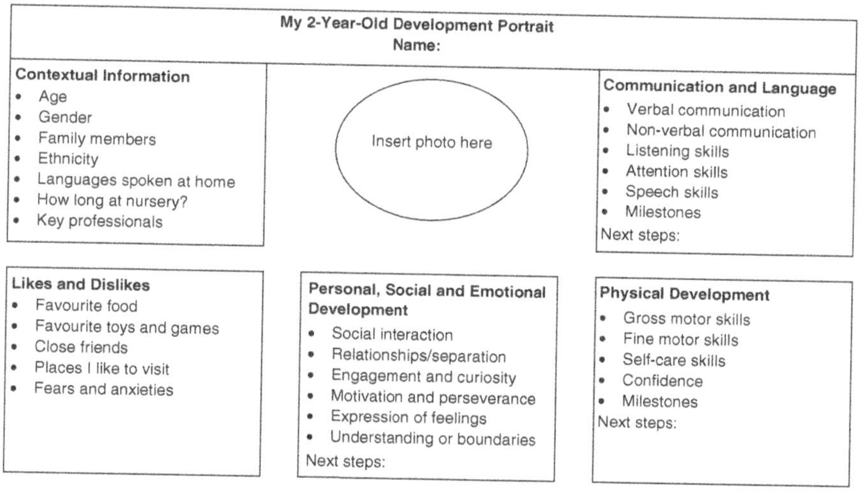

**My 2-Year-Old Development Portrait**
Name:

**Contextual Information**
- Age
- Gender
- Family members
- Ethnicity
- Languages spoken at home
- How long at nursery?
- Key professionals

Insert photo here

**Communication and Language**
- Verbal communication
- Non-verbal communication
- Listening skills
- Attention skills
- Speech skills
- Milestones

Next steps:

**Likes and Dislikes**
- Favourite food
- Favourite toys and games
- Close friends
- Places I like to visit
- Fears and anxieties

**Personal, Social and Emotional Development**
- Social interaction
- Relationships/separation
- Engagement and curiosity
- Motivation and perseverance
- Expression of feelings
- Understanding or boundaries

Next steps:

**Physical Development**
- Gross motor skills
- Fine motor skills
- Self-care skills
- Confidence
- Milestones

Next steps:

**Figure 7.1** An example of an integrated review

Working in partnership with parents and children is a key principle of the integrated review. Guidance from the National Children's Bureau, who commissioned research with two of the LA pathfinders, stresses the importance of remaining sensitive to the concerns and anxieties parents may have about their child's developing abilities. They encourage health visitors and early years practitioners to explore parents' understandings and enable them to engage emotionally and intellectually with the review process, presenting the review as an opportunity for parents to make an essential and valued contribution to their child's assessment. The importance of building relationships with parents before, during and after the review meeting was also acknowledged as key to effective practice.

Furthermore, the acknowledgement that children are at the heart of the assessment process during the integrated review is stressed in the Government guidance (DfE, 2014d). Health visitors and early years practitioners should ensure that they consider how the child is experiencing the review, and offer opportunities for the child to demonstrate their developing abilities in a relaxing and age appropriate environment. Any existing information held by the parents, or the professionals, about the child's interests and anxieties should be used to create an environment that elicits a positive response. For example, some reviews may take place in the child's home or nursery setting where the child is more comfortable, rather than in a new and unfamiliar clinic.

---

**PAUSE FOR REFLECTION**

- What skills and qualities are required by practitioners in order to ensure parents contribute positively to the integrated review process?

- What concerns and anxieties may parents have that practitioners need to be sensitive to?

---

## Evidence-based Interventions

The 2015 Code of Practice (DfE, 2015c) places greater emphasis on the role of teachers and early years professionals in monitoring the development progress of all children with SEND in their class. The graduated review process aims at supporting practitioners to evaluate the impact of interventions designed to allow children with SEND to meet their intended outcomes. There is reference in the Code of Practice to evidence-based interventions, support programmes which have been proven to be effective at improving outcomes for children and young people. Similarly, Allen, in his report *Early Intervention: The Next Steps* (2011: vii), reinforces the need for 'authoritative evidence about which forms of Early Intervention are most successful, and about their impact'.

In addition, interventions to support children with SEND must be specific to their individual needs and not their diagnosis (another message clearly stated in the 2015 Code of Practice), for while it is accepted that there are behavioural and cognitive characteristics associated with specific conditions (e.g. autistic spectrum disorders), it is equally crucial to recognise that children and young people experience their disability in unique and individual ways, thus interventions must be planned in response to this uniqueness and not to the child's assumed needs based on the label of disability assigned to them.

## When to Intervene

Parents and professionals working with children in the early years may be concerned about a child's development if they make the following observations over a period of time:

- There is little progress in the child's learning or development.
- During summative assessment periods the child continues to work at levels significantly below other children of the same age.

- Despite intervention strategies aimed at managing the child's behaviour, he/she continued to exhibit emotional or behavioural concerns.
- Children with physical or sensory needs make insufficient progress even after interventions using mobility aids or sensory enhancement resources have been applied over a sustained period.
- Specific support to assist the child with interaction or communication difficulties have not demonstrated progress for the child in these areas, and further support is thus required.
- After having been assessed in their home language, the child displays delays in their language and communication development.

(adapted from Wall, 2011)

## How to Intervene

Effective intervention may include the following strategies or combination of strategies relevant to the individual needs of the child. Examples may include:

- Introduction of focused activities in small groups or one-to-one (repeated throughout the week as necessary).
- Use of software.
- Following a programme from an external professional (e.g. speech and language therapist).
- Visual timetable.
- Augmented alternative communication approach (including sign language, voice activated communication output systems).
- Environmental adaptations (e.g. for children with physical disabilities).

Whatever the strategy chosen it is crucial that the practitioners have clear outcomes that lead the choice of intervention. For example, many schools and settings continue to use SMART targets (see Table 7.1) when identifying outcomes and planning interventions to address children's developmental needs. The 2015 Code of Practice is clear in its position in this respect and stipulates that interventions should be outcome focused. This emphasis aims at reducing the possibility of an intervention being planned that maintains the child's existing level of development and reinforces low expectations. As has been noted, the emphasis on high-quality teaching as an essential prerequisite for effective provision for children with SEND is stipulated explicitly in the Code of Practice: 'Special educational provision is underpinned by high quality teaching and is compromised by anything less' (DfE, 2015c: 25). Section 1.25 of the Code outlines what high-quality teaching might look like in practice:

- ensure decisions are informed by the insights of parents and those of children and young people themselves
- have high ambitions and set stretching targets for them
- track their progress towards these goals
- keep under review the additional or different provision that is made for them

- promote positive outcomes in the wider areas of personal and social development, and
- ensure that the approaches used are based on the best possible evidence and are having the required impact on progress.

(DfE, 2015c: 25)

Once again, the importance of engaging parents and children in the process is strongly affirmed.

**Table 7.1**  SMART targets

| SMART targets outline interventions which are: | |
| --- | --- |
| **Specific** | The outcomes are specified in such a way as to facilitate effective assessment and evaluation of the child's progress, e.g. specifying the number of minutes of increased engagement in a self-chosen activity and *not* 'X will spend more time in self-chosen tasks'. |
| **Measurable** | The outcomes are able to be easily measured and evaluated (see above). |
| **Achievable** | The outcomes set build sequentially upon the child's current stage of development and are pedagogically relevant. |
| **Realistic** | The outcomes are realistically capable of being met based on the resources available and the timescales allocated to the intervention. |
| **Time-bound** | The time allocated for the implementation of the strategy or intervention is clearly stated and appropriate, after which the outcomes will be reviewed. |

SMART targets can be used to plan a programme of support or an intervention strategy for children whose needs fall under the SEN support category – formerly Early Years (School) Action and Early Years (School) Action Plus. Intervention plans can take the form of an individual education plan (IEP) (see Figure 7.2), a provision map (see Figure 7.3) or, for children whose needs have been assessed as requiring provision which is additional too or different from that which is able to be provided within the school/early years setting context, an EHC plan (see Chapter 3).

| Name | | Date of birth | | |
| --- | --- | --- | --- | --- |
| Summary of strengths and needs | | | | |
| Long-term goal | | | | |
| Outcomes | What/Whom? | When/Where? | Success criteria | Evidence |
| Provide three outcomes which you would like the child to achieve. | What will the intervention programme(s) be and who will be involved? | How often will the intervention programme take place and where? | What criteria will be used to assess if the outcomes have been met? | What type of evidence will be provided to demonstrate that the outcomes have been met? |

**Figure 7.2**  Individual education plan

| Name and DOB | Area of need | Weekly provision | Other agencies |
| --- | --- | --- | --- |
| Tony, 2.2.15 | Speech and Language Delay | Language Group 10 mins daily | Parents<br><br>Speech Therapist |
| Gary, 29.8.14 | Autism | Nurture Group for 15 mins 3 × per week, visual timetable at child's level, Language Group 10 mins daily; Sensory Room 15 mins daily | Parents<br><br>Speech and Language Therapist<br><br>Educational Psychologist |

**Figure 7.3**  Provision map

## Challenges and Dilemmas

As clearly stated in the EYFS from its inception in 2008 and in subsequent reviews (DfE, 2012, 2014b), children develop in different ways and at different rates, hence the recognition of the 'Unique Child' (DCSF, 2007a). It can be challenging, therefore, for practitioners working with very young children to distinguish between an individual's unique developmental pattern and a special educational need. While the guidance regarding when to intervene can be useful (see above), there can be additional concerns faced by practitioners which may delay the support a child received. For example, communicating concerns with parents, particularly when working in diverse communities where there are different cultural expectations of children's development and learning. Often early years practitioners, especially those working with children under three, are the first professionals to raise a concern, so heightened sensitivity is essential when sharing concerns with parents and carers. In addition, as stated in the Bercow Report (2008), delays in language development, for example, may be transitory and short term, requiring a time-limited intervention. However, language which 'labels' a child as having a language delay can nevertheless cause concern and anxiety amongst parents and carers, reinforcing the point that the development of positive relationships with parents is essential. The issue of labelling is addressed in the *Support and Aspiration* green paper (DfE, 2011a), which preceded the Children and Families Act 2014. According to information gathered for Ofsted's *Special Educational Needs and Disability Review* (2010), too often a label is used an excuse for the acceptance of low expectations for children with SEND (p. 9). The review suggested that too many children were being identified as having SEN rather than schools addressing poor-quality teaching. It should be noted that teaching unions have disputed the implications of the Ofsted review, which was published ahead of reductions in SEN funding for schools (NASUWT, 2010). An additional concern raised about the process of early identification of additional needs for children with suspected SEND is that the intervention required may be dependent on staff knowledge and expertise (often from an external professional) or a specific resource, neither of which may be immediately available, thus heightening the concerns and anxieties of parents and carers and delaying the commencement of the intervention (DfE, 2011a: 93).

## CASE STUDY

Jim was diagnosed with delayed speech, language and communication at the age of three, following concerns raised by his parents about his poor verbal communication skills. After a series of assessments and a six-week speech therapy programme, he was discharged and his parents were advised that the issues with his communication would correct themselves over time. On entry to primary school the diagnosis was shared with his class teacher. During the regular meetings between the school and his parents, Jim's delayed communication skills were discussed and monitored. When he struggled to make progress with the school's synthetic phonics programme (for reading and spelling), the impact of his poor verbal communication was perceived to be responsible for this lack of progress. For example, Jim's disordered auditory processing skills (which contributed to his verbal pronunciation issues) were viewed as the main cause of his difficulties with phonics. While his parents could understand this relationship, they were frustrated that alternative approaches to the teaching of reading were not explored further.

## Transition in the Early Years

The next section of this chapter will focus on transition from home to early years settings and from these settings to Key Stage 1 (years 1 and 2 of primary school).

'Transition' refers to a change, and specifically within education and care settings to a change of class, year or setting. Thus, moving from a PVI nursery to a maintained nursery is a transition, equally moving from Reception to year 1 within the same setting is also classed as a transition. Some transitions necessarily involve more change and potential disruption, for example a change of setting which for the child potentially entails a new route to school; new uniform; different key person and teaching staff; a new SENCO; different boundaries and expectations; different routines; and a lack of familiar faces. Other transitions, which might appear to an outsider to be more minor, such as a change of year within a school, may also have a significant effect on a child: a move from year 2 to year 3 may involve the loss of a playtime (in many schools Key Stage 2 do not have an afternoon break), a different lunchtime, different furniture, lack of a fruit snack, more homework and new staff.

### Transition Impact on Children

The work of American psychologists McDermott et al. (2013) charting potential impact of transitions within the early years for children identified as having emotional and social difficulties in the USA pinpoints a range of socio-emotional outcomes of transition, including aggression and withdrawal. This indicates that transitions can have a measurable negative effect on children, who may require additional support at times of transition as they adjust to new situations, people and routines. In a UK study (Sanders et al., 2005), children transitioning from Reception to year 1 expressed concerns about diminished opportunities for play and child-led activities. There are other timetabling changes which can impact on children: a move from Reception to Key Stage 1 involves the introduction of specific playtimes, and as Fabian's (2005) study demonstrates, this may be a cause of significant stress for children.

The limited studies of early years children's experience of transition do indicate that children are aware of transition, although it should be noted that children were also mindful, in Sanders et al.'s study (2005), of possible benefits in terms of new experiences and feeling more mature. There is clear need for considerable research into how children with SEN and those who receive tailored support are informed of and supported through transitions.

## Transition: Impact on Parents

Potter et al.'s (2012) innovative work on involving fathers in transition in the early years in the UK indicates that transition impacts on and is impacted by the whole family. They highlight that transition strategies are unlikely to explicitly target fathers, with the term 'parent' often defaulting to 'mother'. There is perhaps room to reflect on how the mechanics of transition might impact family dynamics and family cohesion, particularly for families involved with early support. The Sanders et al. (2005) NFER report highlights school–family communication as a key issue raised by parents in terms of transition, and indicates that during transition from a setting into Reception communication of change was not viewed as positively as communication during the Reception/Key Stage 1 transition. This is perhaps inevitable, with between-setting communication likely to be less developed than within-setting links. For families whose children are working at a different curriculum level, including those with SEN, generic transition information may not provide full information on how the new year will affect their child's daily learning (Scanlon et al., 2016). The standard information may also serve, unwittingly, to create a feeling of distance as parents are present with 'normal' expectations that their child may or may not be in a position to meet. This, understandably, could cause tensions and create barriers to effective communication.

For parents whose children receive input from a range of services or agencies, transition involves additional changes to ensure that services now include the new setting or new staff. Long-standing regular appointments may need to be re-arranged around the school day, and different access arrangements discussed for visiting professionals. Moving between settings can involve moving between different ratios of staff (DfE, 2014b), and parents may find a new setting unable to dedicate staff time to a particular intervention at a particular time, and here negotiation will be necessary. An Irish study of primary to post-primary transitions (Scanlon et al., 2016) indicates that parents are alive to the particular tensions between wanting to raise issues with a new school to ensure provision, and not wanting to be perceived as difficult or demanding. Figure 7.4 presents various transition considerations.

## Transition impact on staff

Staff working in different settings, year groups and Key Stages work to different organisational patterns and demands. Research on experiences of staff and

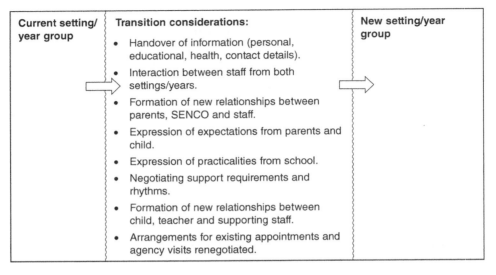

| Current setting/year group | Transition considerations: | New setting/year group |
|---|---|---|
| | • Handover of information (personal, educational, health, contact details). | |
| | • Interaction between staff from both settings/years. | |
| | • Formation of new relationships between parents, SENCO and staff. | |
| | • Expression of expectations from parents and child. | |
| | • Expression of practicalities from school. | |
| | • Negotiating support requirements and rhythms. | |
| | • Formation of new relationships between child, teacher and supporting staff. | |
| | • Arrangements for existing appointments and agency visits renegotiated. | |

**Figure 7.4** Transition for children, parents and staff

children (Orlandi, 2012) indicates that tensions between staff from different Key Stages can arise around transition, with differences in assessment and data being highlighted. This difficulty was seen to arise within a school, indicating that in addition to between-setting challenges, within-setting difficulties of assessment and administration do exist. Transition is therefore, as yet, imperfect, and requires considerable effort from all parties to ensure effective transfer of information and practice.

Sanders et al.'s (2005) study looking at experiences of parents, teachers and children around transition also highlights teachers' concerns around moving too soon from play-based learning in the early years to formal learning in Key Stage 1. The same study (Sanders et al., 2005) identified teacher beliefs that this move from play-based learning to formal learning could pose particular problems for children whose SEN meant a shorter attention span or less ability to sit quietly. This assumption of deficit should be critiqued, however the recognition that different skills and strengths are valued in different Key Stages/settings indicates a potential challenge for children who may have other strengths.

## Supporting Transition

From the brief survey of experiences of transition above, it is clear that communication is at the heart of good transition. For families with a TAC group in place, the lead professional can be a key driver in sharing information and ensuring continuity of services where possible. A sense of isolation was evident for parents in Scanlon's 2016 study, with parents reluctant to be seen as demanding, and therefore unsure of how to best advocate for their child. With this in mind, settings should create clear channels of information with parents and seek to be involved in multi-agency working groups for the child as soon as practicably possible. Each child's experience of transition is unique, and all children may experience hopes and fears around the experience of changing setting or class. Children and their families with identified educational needs may have an additional layer of concern, and the onus is surely on settings and schools to proactively seek joint working to ensure the continuation of appropriate educational provision.

## CASE STUDY   PRIVATE NURSERY

*Times*: 8 am – 6 pm

*Staffing*: According to ratios for under-4s, large and rotating staff team to cover the full day. Children assigned to key workers who are parents' first point of contact.

*Routines*: Play, food and changing according to Nursery schedule, with use of small group work and key worker groups.

*Children*: Aged 0–4, child may know all other children by site, may spend time with siblings during the course of the day.

*Links with parents and professionals*: Daily diaries go home with information on food and activities, children visited by professionals at any point in the day, parents able to speak to staff at drop off or pick up, and by telephone where appropriate during the day.

## CASE STUDY   MAINTAINED RECEPTION CLASS

*Times*: 9 am – 3.30 pm (with variations between 8.30 and 3)

*Staffing*: A teacher and teaching assistant within the class, large numbers of other school staff who may not be linked to Reception. Key worker groups are half the class per adult, teacher retains ultimate responsibility.

*Routines*: In-class routines decided by teacher, within the whole-school routines of assemblies, PE lessons, lunch times, library visits and events.

*Children*: Within the school, aged 4–11, children in Reception may be youngest and smallest, with potentially hundreds of older children at lunch and in playgrounds.

*Links with parents and professionals*: Whole class/phase newsletters may go out termly or weekly, depending on school policy. Staff may briefly comment in weekly reading diaries. Main casual contact with staff is at drop-off and pick-up, which may not be parents if their work schedules do not allow this. Key worker teaching assistant may not be available, depending on working hours. Teacher will need to wait for all children to be collected before talking to parents, and may have meetings scheduled immediately after the school day. Professionals from agencies visit at any point, this may cause children to miss specific timetabled activities (e.g. PE or use of ICT suite). Staff available by phone when arranged in advance, scheduled around teaching and meetings.

## PAUSE FOR REFLECTION

- Based on the above scenario, how might any child or parent respond to the changes in setting and routine? How might that influence their feelings towards the school?

- What considerations do staff in the new setting need to take for the children arriving? What pressures and demands does that place on staff? How might staff see these?

- What additional challenges might there be for a child and family who are involved in early support?

## CHAPTER SUMMARY

This chapter has focused on two significant issues affecting practice for children with SEND in the early years, early intervention and transition. Each section has provided a short summary of the development of practice alongside relevant legislation, discussed effective practice and considered some of the key challenges and concerns. Cases studies have been provided to illustrate some of the key tensions.

## Suggested Further Reading

Dubiel, J. (2016) *Effective Assessment in the EYFS*. London: Sage.
Written by a former National Strategies assessment consultant, this book addresses some of the key challenges faced by practitioners when assessing children's needs in the early years, and provides useful and practical strategies for meeting the diverse needs of children aged 0–5.

Mathieson, K. (2015) *Inclusion in the Early Years Foundation Stage*. Maidenhead: OUP.
Another accessible and authoritative guide to working with children with SEND, and from other diverse communities in the early years foundation stage.

Brooker, E. (2008) *Supporting Transitions in the Early Years*. London: McGraw-Hill.
Highly interesting and relevant discussion of the key themes and challenges associated with transition within and beyond early years settings.

# 8

## CPD OPPORTUNITIES FOR STAFF WORKING WITH CHILDREN WITH SEND IN THE EARLY YEARS

### RUTH HUNT AND ANNA NEWBOLD

**CHAPTER OBJECTIVES**

- How have on-entry to profession qualifications of a range of staff working with children with SEN in early childhood education and care settings changed over time?

- What are current continuing professional development opportunities for different staff roles?

- What factors influence settings and schools when allocating continuing professional development amongst staff?

This chapter will discuss continuing professional development (CPD) for staff in schools and settings working with children with SEND. The range of entry-level qualifications for staff working with children with SEND are highlighted through an exploration of how these roles, and the qualifications required for them, have changed over time. An exploration of current CPD opportunities available is then followed by discussion of how training needs and priorities are determined by schools and settings. The case studies in this chapter are fictional accounts to support the reader in applying their understanding to practical situations.

## What Is Continuing Professional Development?

Currently in the UK the majority (97 per cent) (DfE, 2016a) of teachers have a degree and an initial teacher training qualification on entry to service. Throughout their teaching time, staff are entitled to a continuing programme of professional development in the form of in-service training days (INSET days – non-contact training days within the school year), courses, qualifications and weekly staff meetings. Many of these opportunities should be available to all staff working with children, including teaching assistants. PVI education and childcare settings also offer ongoing training to all staff, which may include early years teachers, room leaders and nursery managers. These training cycles should include training for staff on specific inclusion-related topics, and particular SEN needs. CPD might include in-setting staff meetings, courses leading to a certificate of completion, work leading to a recognised and tariffed qualification, post-graduate qualifications, and observing practice in other settings.

CPD is designed to enhance staff skills and ensure good teaching and learning opportunities for all children. At the same time, CPD for staff can be a way of developing their career and future employment opportunities. For some, additional qualifications can improve their earning potential and expand the areas they can work in. When negotiating CPD needs with senior leaders or managers, staff may have requests which are not immediate school or setting priorities, and which the settings may be reluctant to fund. Similarly, training required for particular additional needs may not be seen as a personal priority for staff members. CPD may not always be welcomed by staff, and hoped for CPD may not be within the school priorities.

Essential CPD is funded by the school from their notional training budget. Essential training, such as safeguarding refresher training and SENCO qualifications, will be prioritised in times of falling budgets. All training is therefore assessed with regard to value for money and necessity. Settings may offer training that is desirable to staff in order to improve staff retention, for example offering the chance to train as a SENCO in return for an agreement of an extended contract. Teaching staff are required to undergo yearly performance management, in which their targets are discussed and set for the coming year. Teachers must indicate in these sessions the impact of any specific CPD they have received, and in this way schools can gain some sense of the effectiveness of some CPD training.

## Staff Groups – Qualifications and Training Needs

In schools, nurseries and childcare provision there are a range of staff members, whose roles have changed dramatically over the last 50 years. This change in expectation of both qualification, experience and skill has had an impact on the initial and ongoing training that staff receive. The following sections discuss the genesis of current roles for staff working with children with SEND, and highlight the changing nature of personnel and skills required, particularly in light of the changes in the inclusion agenda over time. In line with current Ofsted parlance, this chapter refers to teaching assistants for staff who are not teachers or holders of higher qualified roles who work with children in an educational capacity in schools. This section explores the complexity of the current early childhood workforce in terms of training and qualifications, to set CPD needs within a robust context.

## Teaching Assistants

The role of the teaching assistant (TA) and other support staff has changed a great deal in recent years. Those at school in the 1970s and 1980s would remember the welfare lady who washed paintbrushes and heard children read for a couple of afternoons a week. TAs are now expected to deliver parts of the curriculum, manage behaviour, mark work and give feedback, and teach whole classes across a school or a Key Stage. Many work full time and take responsibility for after school clubs, displays and first aid. This dramatic change in role has necessarily led to a change in expectation, qualification and ongoing training.

In the 1990s, a number of initiatives led to an increase in teacher workload. The government introduced the National Curriculum in 1998 along with end of Key Stage SATS, a new regime of inspections carried out by Ofsted and resulting league tables in 1992, and the National Literacy and Numeracy Strategies in 1998 (Blatchford et al., 2012). In order to relieve some of the workload of the teacher, a large number of support staff were recruited. The number of TAs has tripled since 1999, and 26 per cent of the education workforce are now TAs (DfE, 2014b). The key moves towards mainstream inclusion of the majority of children has precipitated a key change in TA roles. TAs have been called upon to meet the needs of children with SEN. It should be noted that this role devolved to the existing TAs, who previously had taken on more general tasks in the school. Staff with no specialised training had been given a new and complex role.

From 1991 to 2000 there was a significant rise in the numbers of children with SEND being taught within mainstream settings. The number of statemented children in mainstream schools rose by 95,000 (Blatchford et al., 2012), which meant that more than 90 per cent of statemented children were now not being educated in special schools or settings. In 1991, half of all statemented children were educated in special schools and by 2000 this had dropped to one-third (House of Commons, 2006). At the same time there was also an increase in the number of children on School Action or School Action Plus, the then term for children with SEN who did not qualify for a statement or who had not been awarded one yet (now known as SEN Support).

Schools and teachers felt unprepared and ill-equipped to manage this number of SEN children in the classroom. As a result, schools with high proportions of children with SEN were noted to employ a correspondingly high number of TAs (Ofsted, 2004). Large numbers of TAs having been recruited, by 2006 Ofsted reported that SEN children who received the majority of their instruction and support from TAs were less likely to make good progress than SEN children who had access to specialist teaching (Ofsted, 2006).

The National Agreement on Pay and Conditions of Service in 2003 (NJCLGS, 2003) was designed to tackle the problems of teacher workload and retention within the profession. It included the proposal that TAs should perform some of the time-consuming yet non-teaching tasks which had started to take up a lot of teachers' time, such as collecting dinner money, thus enabling the teacher to focus on the teaching. This had an indirect effect on pupil standards as it allowed teachers to focus on teaching, preparations and assessment. However, there were suggestions that TAs should also have more impact on pupil attainment through activities and teaching sessions that required higher levels of skills and experience (Blatchford et al., 2012; Ofsted, 2004). This created a clear gap between the actual qualifications of TAs and the target skills and qualifications that schools began to require. This mismatch of skills may go some way to explaining the 2004 Ofsted review of reading in which it commented unfavourably on some TA interventions.

In many school settings, a child with SEN often receives much of their instruction from a member of support staff. Giangreco et al. (2011) suggested that many children with SEN get the majority of their learning through a TA and have less interaction with a teacher as a result. This is echoed by Blatchford et al.'s (2009) research, which found that increased support from a TA can lead to a decrease in interaction with the teacher for those children. Children who are entitled to support via their EHC plan are often supported by a TA within the classroom, meaning the TA is required to deliver a modified version of the curriculum to the child and support them throughout the day, often including at playtimes and lunchtimes. Whilst this model of inclusion should be questioned, this also indicates that a TA should be highly skilled to avoid a child being taught for the majority of their school day by an unqualified adult.

In contrast to the model of majority one-to-one support, Giangreco et al. (2006), Groom (2006), Lee (2003) and Moran and Abbott (2002) all found that it was more beneficial for a class academically and socially if the TA works with a range of students across the class rather than just one student all the time. This indicates that the need for the TA to have good subject knowledge in order to support all mainstream learning is increasing. This has implications for CPD, as to perform this role effectively TAs would require curriculum knowledge, specific SEN-related skills, and whole classroom management skills. This might be seen as an ambitious request for a low-paid and traditionally lower-skilled workforce.

As levels of training and experience may vary a great deal between schools and individual TAs (Blatchford et al., 2009), these staff may not always be used to their full potential, as they may have certain skills which are not fully recognised or utilised by the school (Devlin, 2008). Another aggravating factor in the unsuccessful deployment of TAs might be found in Giangreco's (2013) study, which suggests the teacher can sometimes find the provision for children with SEN overwhelming and leave many or all of the decisions about what SEN children are learning to TAs, who may not have the skills required to perform these tasks. This indicates that ongoing training needs might be very different for teachers and TAs, and that whilst both need a firm understanding of how to support children's needs, teachers also require additional skills in managing staff and delegating tasks appropriately.

Despite these caveats, there is also research which highlights the positive benefits of TAs, and this could guide schools towards the type of CPD they offer to TAs. Muijs and Reynolds (2003) found using TAs to support children in small groups to be effective. The role of the TA has also been found to increase individualisation of attention and overall teaching, increased classroom control, and leads to pupils showing more engagement and a more active role when interacting with adults (Blatchford et al., 2009). If TAs have the qualifications and skills to work with the whole class, as Moran and Abbott (2002) suggest, there could be great benefits to all children.

The current situation for TAs' training and qualifications, however, is piecemeal. In contrast to teachers, there is no national requirement for TAs' qualification. There are recommended Level 2 (GCSE equivalent level) and HLTA (Level 3, A-level equivalent) qualifications. TAs today in schools may have no qualifications, level 2 or 3 vocational qualifications, or may be graduates. Pay still varies between locations (NCS, 2016a), and there is a strong history of local people, particularly mothers, taking TA roles. As has been discussed in this chapter, these roles tend to have been low-paid and historically seen as low-skilled and low-accountability roles. This may have meant that less priority was given to their training needs in the past, and there is not yet a nationally recognised pathway of progression in training and skills for all TAs.

## Other Non-teacher Roles

In addition to the general TAs, there is the position of nursery nurses, qualified with the now sadly defunct NNEB qualification and the Early Years Educators (CACHE, 2016) working within early years settings. These specialised support staff have a wealth of knowledge around health and development. Like TAs, all of these 'assistant' roles have changed over time. Schools expect more skills, more learning support and a higher level of qualification (UNISON, 2016). Amongst support staff now it is more likely to find graduates: in London those who are not teacher-qualified and would like to be, or who want a flexible day-time job; outside of London, anecdotal evidence tells of qualified teachers who have not been able to find teaching work taking employment as TAs. This mixture of initial skills and training means that any training aimed at non-teacher assistants in mainstream schools is aimed at a diversely qualified and experienced group of people. As Nye et al. (2016) highlight, TAs are asked to perform roles with regard to inclusion which assume a high level of skills and specific experience. The training that these staff are offered in schools therefore also needs to be high-level and relevant.

## Teachers

Teachers, at the time of writing, require an undergraduate degree, a post-graduate teacher training qualification, and to complete a post-qualification year (NQT year), with constant assessment by certified bodies within this time (DfE, 2015a). In line with many other graduate jobs, teachers may be willing to commute or relocate for work; however, more remote schools (Weale, 2016) or those who have a poor Ofsted outcome may struggle to recruit teachers. Before the widespread introduction of academies and the subsequent removal of statutory pay scales in September 2013 (DfE, 2013a), to be replaced by minimum and maximum pay awards (DfE, 2015b), there was a guaranteed graduate salary for teachers (DfE, 2013a), with matching expectations and accountability. The complex and often costly pre-service training could be justified, and staff expected commensurate in-service training.

This highly-skilled professional body has, like TA roles, developed over time, and again, as for support staff, the initial qualification and ongoing training they require has dramatically increased over time. Prior to 1998, when under Tony Blair the (DfEE, 1998) set out plans to increase professionalisation for teachers, teaching qualifications had gradually evolved. Teachers initially required either a Certificate of Education, or a degree (DfEE, 1998), a post-graduate teacher training certificate was first introduced in 1974. In 1998 (DfEE, 1998) there came a change in qualification content, with a requirement for prospective teachers to spend more time in schools and for a one-year post-certification qualifying period, known as the Newly Qualified Teacher (NQT) year, which ultimately leads to Qualified Teacher Status (QTS). Following the New Labour White Paper (HMSO, 1997), teacher qualifying and professional standards were updated in 1998 (DfEE), 2002 (NUT), 2007 (TDA) and 2013 (DfE, 2013a). These rapid changes in expectation and qualification content mean that within schools, teachers holding the same qualifications may have significantly different experiences and knowledge, dependent on the year that they trained in. Figure 8.1 shows a timeline of teacher qualifications.

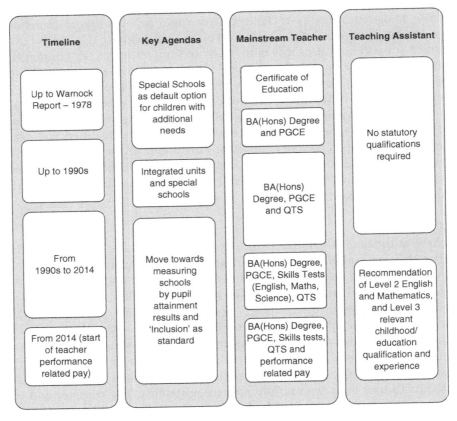

**Figure 8.1** Timeline of qualifications

In an education climate with the seemingly constant change in curriculum and assessment, with, for example, the DfE (2015a) listing 15 time points of major change in five years, many of these changes affecting whole curriculums or suites of qualifications and implemented within a short time-frame, teachers re-entering the profession may have gaps in their knowledge of current practice, and particularly current inclusion practice. These myriad factors in how teachers are perceived, trained and resourced have a knock-on effect on the CPD they expect and require: teachers must not be seen as a homogenous group, especially not with regard to training needs. They are required to deal with change, assimilation of new standards, curriculum and advice, and a growing role managing TAs, to whom they are not line-managers yet are held accountable for the outcomes of children given TA support.

## Special School Staff

In addition to teachers with post-graduate qualifications, and mainstream support staff with a range of experience and qualifications, there are teachers and support staff from special schools. Although serving a relatively small percentage of the population, and despite numbers of specials schools falling consistently from 1,597 schools in 1980 to 1,197 in 2000 (DfEE, 2000) the numbers stabilised, with the 1,039 in 2016 (DfE, 2016a) echoing those of the previous four years, with 1,039 schools in 2012 (DfE, 2012) and 1,040 schools in 2015 (DfE, 2015a). Staff working within special schools may have long specialised experience working with children with additional needs, and may have received specific medical training, alongside social and communication training. These staff have benefited from courses and in-school training in an environment which is solely focussed on supporting children with high levels of social and communication, health and educational needs. In terms of supporting children with SEN, this might be seen as positive; however, Ofsted (2004) has noted that some special schools lack emphasis on curriculum skills, with Science being seen as particularly poor. This assessment, whilst open to challenge around what a suitable curriculum is for a child with profound and multiple learning needs, implies that in contrast to mainstream staff, special school staff are given higher levels of specific-need training, with less emphasis on curriculum knowledge training.

## Early Year Teachers

Early years teacher (EYT) status is a professional status originally designed for those working in the PVI nursery sector. It is a graduate qualification, which can be completed whilst employed in a nursery, or undertaken as a college or university based course over one year or six months. For those with relevant experience and a relevant degree these routes can be shortened (Skills Funding Agency, 2016). The early years teacher status is a much contested qualification. Its origin, as Early Years Professional status (EYP status) in 2007 (Teaching Agency, 2012), was designed to improve educational opportunities in PVI nurseries, which had few graduate staff members, in response to research that suggested that graduate level staff were a major factor in children's attainment and progress (Siraj-Blatchford et al., 2002).

The then government initially posited this qualification as equivalent to teacher status, but without QTS, which was seen by some unions as an attack on the professional status of QTS qualified teachers (NUT, 2008). The role was originally positioned as leading practice in settings, with less emphasis on direct work with children (NUT, 2008), in contrast with traditional teacher roles.

The prospect of making these qualifications directly interchangeable created an economic difficulty: PVIs pay less than maintained schools to their teaching staff, and their hours of business are longer and often anti-social, so a closer link between PVI and maintained qualifications would have expensive ramifications for the PVI sector if they were to bring their working conditions into line with maintained settings. Creating a truly equivalent qualification would bring with it an expectation of a teacher salary, which many PVIs would be reluctant or struggle to pay. As a compromise, the Government pressed its proposal for more graduates in the PVI nursery sector, but omitted any claims for parity of pay and conditions. As a by-product this instantly created a two-tier view, with maintained school teacher status attracting a higher salary than early years teacher status, and with few early years teachers being employed in school nurseries as sole teachers of a nursery class. Further comparisons between these two statuses was caused by the renaming of EYP status as early years teacher status (EYT status) in 2013 (DfE, 2013b). The shift to being called a teacher both down-played the original role of coordinating good practice and causes uncomfortable comparisons with QTS teachers who have more specified duties but an equivalently higher wage.

The use of teachers and early years teachers in maintained nursery classes has caused particular tensions: schools have a statutory duty (DfE, 2014c) to employ a qualified teacher, which also gives the school flexibility of workforce (they could be utilised anywhere between Nursery and year 6), whereas early years teachers' specialisation can be seen as a limiting factor, and schools interpret them as not counting within the published ratios for teachers in maintained schools (DfE, 2014c). Hence, schools that employ early years teachers may tend to employ them in addition to a teacher. This creates a mismatch of pay within a setting: EYT salaries at the time of writing are between £18,000 and £23,000 (Skills Funding Agency, 2016), whereas outside of London recommended teacher pay scales for maintained schools start at £23,000 and range up to circa £33,000 (NASUWT, 2015). This has the potential for EYTs to feel under-valued, or for teachers, whose pay is linked to performance a large part of which is pupil attainment, to see EYTs as having fewer responsibilities and as being less pressured.

EYTs' predominant placement in PVI settings also raised the issue of funding. As noted previously, funding budgets in PVIs may be more precarious than in maintained settings, as these are dependent either on fees, donations or grants. This may cause CPD budgets to be reduced dependent on circumstance. Since 2014 teachers' pay has been notionally linked to performance (individual schools decide what expected performance is), whereas EYT pay is set by each individual setting and may or may not be performance linked. With a lesser emphasis on performance related pay, there may also be a weaker culture of professional development meetings and targets which the school supports with funding. There may be, dependent on the setting, more of a reliance on cost-effective whole-setting training, rather than personalised training. As for maintained settings, there is then a balance between curriculum subject knowledge, assessment and inclusion/SEND training. The ratio of this balance is determined according to each setting's particular staff and pupil demographic, and may be reactive (e.g. specific training when a child with an additional need joins the setting). For EYTs employed within the maintained sector, their presence as an additional adult (DfE, 2014c) rather than as main class teacher, brings with it the complications of hierarchy and the potential school prioritisation of training for teachers.

Regardless of the ethical and financial morass around the positioning of EYTs within the workforce, it is clear that EYTs are skilled and focussed individuals. As with any training that is on-the-job, EYTs' experiences of inclusive strategies and working with children with SEN are likely to be highly influenced by the settings in which they trained. As with teacher training, this creates a likely range of experience and understanding of inclusion and SEND. Similarly to teachers, EYTs can be expected to have diverse CPD needs. The change in focus from EYP to EYT also indicates that when the staff member was trained has a significant impact on the content and focus of the course, with possible changes from coordinating inclusive practices to actually delivering them with children, which creates an additional layer of complexity when organising training for this group.

## Private Nursery Staff

PVI nursery settings are subject to different staffing requirements to maintained schools, with a similar diversity in on-entry staff qualifications. Staff working in these settings may not have any recognised qualifications. The Statutory Framework for the Early Years Foundation Stage (DfE, 2014b) highlights the impact trained and skilled staff have on outcomes for children. With this in mind, a nursery manager must hold a full and relevant level 3 qualification (DfE, 2014c) and at least half of other staff must hold a level 2 qualification. Induction training must be provided to new staff, although this covers emergency procedures, safeguarding and policies and does not always include pedagogical content. There is a requirement for a member of staff with a paediatric first aid certificate to be present at all times (DfE, 2014c). Ratios must be adhered to depending on the age of the children; in order to be included in ratios practitioners must be over the age of 17, and there are regulations concerning the ratio of qualified and experienced adults to children, depending on the age of the children. However, while there are strict guidelines about the suitability of adults to work with children, including DBS checks, it is possible to work as an unqualified practitioner in a private childcare setting. Settings may choose whether to employ qualified or unqualified members of staff at the discretion of the management. In independent schools, child to adult ratios can be lower, but the requirement to have at least half of the staff with a level 2 qualification remains the same. In settings which provide before or after school care only, the ratios for Reception age children or older are the same as in school, although it is up to the provider to satisfy themselves that their staff have sufficient qualifications, experience and skills. This cohort of staff therefore may have diverse training needs, and as new staff join, basic skills and practices may need to be re-visited.

## Childminders

A childminder is a person providing childcare for payment in a non-commercial setting, most likely a home setting. Formal qualifications are not required prior to registration. However, depending on the age of the children, childminders must enrol on the Early Years Register or the Childcare Register. When registering, Ofsted will carry out a DBS check, a health check and other checks such as a 'Known to Ofsted' check, to ensure the applicant is entitled to work in the UK and is not barred from working with children or has not previously been disqualified as a childcare provider. The childminder will be visited to ensure that the home is safe for children, and interviewed to assess their ability to deliver the EYFS curriculum, if applying for the Early Years Register (Ofsted, 2016). Childminders wishing to work with children aged 0–5 must have completed training, which helps them to understand and implement the EYFS before they can register with Ofsted or a childminder agency (DfE, 2014c). Applicants are required to undertake first aid training and an introductory course provided by their LA (where these still exist). Childminders are advised to work towards a unit from the Level 3 Diploma for the Children and Young People's Workforce, which covers childcare legislation, developing business procedures, setting up play and learning activities and working alongside parents (NCS, 2016b). Childminders have the opportunity to attend training provided by their LA, where this still exists. The Professional Association for Childcare and Early Years (PACEY) also offer courses to their members. These include training around learning through play, first aid, child protection and the EYFS curriculum. However, these courses are optional and there is no formal requirement to attend any training.

## Summary

This overview of the potential range of staff qualification, experience and role within the early years childcare and education sector indicates that any training must take into account the diverse possible backgrounds of the participants, the different responsibilities they might hold and their working hours and contracted duties.

# Continuing Professional Development: Types of Training

For teaching staff within early years settings (PVI and maintained) and primary schools, training can take different forms, each with their own benefits and challenges. In this chapter the focus is on the professional qualification for the SENCO, specific support for TAs working with children with an identified SEN, externally run courses, INSET days and staff meetings.

## NASENCO Course

In line with the SEN Code of Practice (DfE, 2015c), all maintained schools and academies are required to have a qualified SENCO. Unless the SENCO has been in post for more than three years or was appointed before 2008, the National Award for Special Educational Needs coordinators (NASENCO) is compulsory and must be completed within three years of appointment. SENCOs in maintained schools and academies are required to be a qualified teacher with QTS, therefore the NASENCO is an additional post-graduate qualification. The course is part time; participants usually attend one day per week for a year. It is a Masters-level qualification worth 60 credits, and must be awarded from a recognised higher education provider. Practitioners who have undertaken the NASENCO, or work with those who have, report that it improves subject knowledge and knowledge of current practice, and that participants develop strategies for implementing an improved whole-school approach to SEN provision and inclusion. They develop a wider understanding of their roles, and provision across the school improves as they are empowered to deploy staff and engage parents more effectively (Griffiths and Dubsky, 2012). Parallel to the extensive benefits for the school, the NASENCO is also highly beneficial for the individual practitioner in that participants have frequent opportunity to reflect on practice and reflect with colleagues. Pearson and Gathercole (2011) also found that those who had completed the NASENCO had a deeper understanding of their roles and felt that their status had increased among colleagues.

## Teaching Assistant – Specific Continuing Professional Development

As we have seen, there are often gaps between the skills that TAs have and the tasks required of them. Certainly there are situations in which the TA has greater skills which are not being effectively used by the school, but there are also often TAs who, whether due to the demands of the role having changed since they were first employed or some other reason, do not have the skills they need to have a positive impact on pupil progress even though they are working with some of the most vulnerable children. The NFER (2005) found that TAs held a large variety of qualifications between them, but only a few held each of the different types. Furthermore, it was reported that one-quarter of respondents had not completed any accredited courses and were not taking part in any at the time of the survey. Again, this highlights the range of skills and qualifications held by support staff, compared with teaching staff who nearly all a hold a degree plus a postgraduate qualification (96.6 per cent) (DfE, 2014c).

## CASE STUDY

A school in North London took the step of restructuring their support staff, as it was felt many were not deployed effectively or lacked relevant skills. As part of this, the TAs' working day was extended by 30 minutes at the beginning and end of each day. Teachers and TAs reported increased satisfaction that they had time to communicate with each other about the teaching and learning as well as about day-to-day issues. The attainment of some children supported by TAs was easier to track and the data was more reliable as staff could check in with each other about it more easily. This had a positive effect on progress for children with identified SEN.

**PAUSE FOR REFLECTION**

- What challenges do you think this restructure posed for the school and the staff?
- How might this restructure impact positively on the CPD available for TAs?

CPD is a key factor in closing this gap, and schools have to decide where to prioritise their resources when deciding what CPD to offer. With this in mind, just over half of head teachers reported that their school had a policy for the professional development of TAs (Webber et al., 2013). The introduction of the new National Curriculum in 2014 was quickly discovered to have a significant emphasis on, among other things, grammatical and mathematical terms, and teachers had to adapt swiftly in order to keep abreast of the new content. Many found it a challenge. Schools responded by providing training in staff meetings or INSET days, in which subject leaders, who had usually attended external training on the new curriculum, shared what they had learned with teaching colleagues and senior leaders. However, TAs do not always attend staff meetings – in fact only 45 per cent of TAs said that they were always included in CPD on INSET days (NFER, 2005) – but were still required to impart the knowledge and use the same terms as teachers when working with their one-to-one child or small groups. TAs have also reported feeling underprepared when going in to support a teacher in a lesson. They felt that this was due to not always having time before the lesson to consult the teacher about what the objectives or approach is, but also due to training needs not having been met (Webber et al., 2013). Teachers spend a significant portion of their time (albeit before or after school or in PPA time) planning and preparing lessons, yet research would suggest that TAs' working time often does not allow any time for preparation.

**CASE STUDY   WHEN CPD SYSTEMS WORK**

Sara works with autistic children in a large mainstream primary school in an inner-city area. Although she did not have any formal training, Sara shows aptitude for working with autistic children and enjoys helping them make progress. All TAs in Sara's school attend weekly 30-minute training sessions after school, which are led by subject specialists from the teaching staff. Sara has therefore had training around phonics, maths, outdoor provision, reading and supporting writing, as well as training pertinent to working with ASD and SEND. Sara's school has a culture of staff taking responsibility for their own training requirements; as part of this, staff are regularly asked what training they feel they need. Training needs are also identified by teaching staff and the SLT as part of routine termly observations. Sara has attended day courses around ASD, managing behaviour and supporting writing as these were identified by her and her line manager as priorities. As a result, Sara feels valued by the school, and in her performance review she was able to show evidence of her practice having improved.

## Specialised Training for Teaching Assistants Working Predominantly with Children with SEND

Schools should provide sufficient time for TA training (Sharples et al., 2015). How they choose to provide this training is up to the individual school. In schools, staff who manage TAs can arrange for peer observations of more experienced or qualified colleagues, which can be done in an informal way and has minimal financial implications. Staff can also attend training from the LA, although as highlighted above, there are often financial or time constraints. TAs working with specific children with SEND should also be able to access training around mainstream teaching methods and current practice. For example, it was found that TAs were more likely to focus on task completion and often supplied answers, whereas teachers used more open-ended questions to promote thinking and learning, gave more feedback and spent more time explaining concepts (Webber et al., 2013). This kind of skill should be developed in all staff, as well as encouraging development in specific skills relevant to the child/children the TA works with. It has been recommended that TAs receive CPD alongside teachers (Giangreco et al., 2012), and this would certainly go some way towards ensuring consistency among practitioners in the same setting.

## Implications of SEND-specific Training for Teaching Assistants

Teaching assistants do clearly need training around working with whole groups of children with SEND, such as children with ASD, deaf children or children with global developmental delay, as they do not necessarily enter the profession with any experience or qualifications at all. They may also need training on specific health needs for one child, as with EpiPen training or knowing how to support a child who suffers from convulsions. The limits of this are that skills such as these, while essential for one or a small number of children, do not equip the TA with any transferable skills which will develop their subject knowledge in the long term. There has also been a great deal of research showing that TAs should not be used solely to support one or more children all the time, and that this actually hinders progress for these children, which would suggest that while TAs need to be upskilled in their work with SEND children, they also need a range of skills and knowledge which would allow them to work with any child, for example being able to deliver quick and effective interventions to several groups.

## Continuing Professional Development: Common Formats
### External courses

One option for CPD delivery is whole- or part-day training during term time, provided by either external companies or a cluster/network of local schools. These courses have a cost to them, typically between £100 and £400 for a one-day course. In addition to the course cost, the school must arrange a cover teacher or TA. If the school goes through a teaching agency, they are likely to be charged anything between £120 and £280 per day per supply teacher (of which sometimes only half goes to the supply teacher). In times of austerity the cover teacher is likely to be an existing member of staff who is not normally a class teacher, often a TA, who as

Roffey-Barentsen and Watt Brunel's (2014) study suggests, may or may not feel happy or confident about doing so, or a member of the SLT. This inevitably causes a shortfall of staffing elsewhere within the school and requires careful planning to avoid disruption to other classes. For the teacher going on the course there is also a time cost; they are required to leave work for the substitute professional, and may also be expected to mark any work done in their absence. The classes that are covered by substitute teaching on that day will also experience disruption, however minor, which may have an impact on their learning. Children who struggle with change or uncertainty may find the day without their usual teacher, and that teacher's return difficult to process, often resulting in displays of behaviour which are seen as negative. To even attend a daytime course, there is a cost for all involved. Schools must therefore be confident that the training they are paying for is worth the financial, administrative and time costs.

## EXAMPLES OF SEN/INCLUSION FOCUSSED EXTERNAL TRAINING COURSES

TEACCH – Structured teaching system for individuals with ASD.

PECS Communication – Using symbols to support English language development.

Makaton – Sign system supporting English spoken grammar.

Manual handling – Safe and dignified lifting/moving/personal care for individuals with mobility needs.

EpiPen training – Safe administration of EpiPens used when individuals have allergic reactions.

Social Stories – Using and creating simple stories about events to enable individuals to understand what might happen when, and what to do in certain situations (e.g. greeting strangers, using a bus, how to express feelings appropriately).

### In-service training days (INSET)

In light of the cost of day-courses run by external agencies, and the very real need for staff who are confident and equipped to meet the needs of a range of learners, other training routes are often considered. Whole-school INSET (in-service training) may be an attractive option. These are days when the school is closed to children, but staff meet for training. This may be delivered by an external company or by colleagues who have particular specialisms or training. INSET days can be used to ensure that all staff receive the same training, and may be seen as effective in creating a whole-school vision or agreement on inclusion, inclusive practices or anti-discriminatory practices. However, earlier in this chapter we considered the wide range of possible experiences, qualifications and responsibility of staff within mainstream schools. Therefore delivering training to a school staff has some similarities to teaching a widely mixed ability class. We may question how different staff members will receive and engage with the same materials. In addition, there are only a limited number of INSET days within a school year, and specialist inclusion training is only one of many topics that a school management will need to cover. Essential safeguarding training, curriculum changes, literacy and numeracy all crowd out INSET schedules. Training on specific strategies for specific children, or in medical or personal care handling, may not be either possible in large groups or gain a place in the limited INSET timetable.

## Staff meetings

Staff meetings tend to happen more regularly, but while for TAs these may be within teaching hours (removing them from working with children), teachers meetings are almost universally out of teaching hours. This creates a two-track system, where skills that are passed on to TAs in terms of administering medication or working with key children with additional needs may not be shared with teachers. Equally teaching staff may be given more information about curriculum and teaching. Over the course of a year there might be 35 staff meetings, which in addition to specific SEND training or inclusion skills, will also need to include safeguarding, curriculum updates, core subject practice sharing (Literacy, Numeracy, Science and other areas), assessment and moderation meetings. Specific sessions on SEND issues are therefore simply one part of the training that takes place, and have to justify their inclusion in the timetable. Scheduling staff meetings around SEND can be seen to be a response to both school priorities and circumstance: how far SLTs value SEND and inclusion priorities, and what particular SEND training is essential given the cohort of students.

---

**PAUSE FOR REFLECTION**

- Consider the range of training required throughout the school year. How much time should a setting/school dedicate to SEND training in staff meetings?

---

Whether the staff meetings are led by an external company or by school staff, there are again complications. Buying in training incurs costs and requires careful coordination of dates. Beyond the practicalities of securing outside trainers, using existing staff members can create significant difficulties. If we look beyond the basic requirements of time for those staff members to carefully prepare materials, and for the need for they themselves to be appropriately trained, there is an issue which has wide implications. Schools and settings exist within social and cultural networks (Bronfenbrenner, 1976) and staff experiences of social and cultural aspects in settings can raise a potential barrier to effective training. Within any workplace there will be professional relationships that are more successful or trusted than others. A staff member leading training brings themselves to the session – if colleagues do not professionally respect or trust the trainer, then their message becomes diluted, and may even be rejected. Effective training, of any sort, relies upon a workplace culture of respect and trust. It could be argued that this is the case for all training. It seems to be particularly pertinent for training around particular strategies for working with children with complex needs, as a partial grasp of training content could have a profound effect on the children being supported. If a communication system, medicine regime or feeding procedure is not fully understood or accepted by a staff member, the impact could be much more damaging than, say, an incorrect grasp of a PE concept.

## Discussion of Current CPD

This chapter has noted the disparity in initial qualification of the varied staff within the early years workforce, and Chambers (2015) draws attention to a similar inequality of ongoing training between teachers and support staff. When thinking about why this might be the case, we need to consider the wider educational culture. Drawing on Bronfenbrenner's (1976) ideas of ecological systems in education, it seems certain that school culture is affected by wider political and values systems. How training is apportioned is affected by how children, staff and inclusion are valued in the wider political and cultural system. It should be noted that Bronfenbrenner (1976) highlights that time is a factor, attitudes towards training and education change over time, and so CPD priorities may change within and between governments. Just as inclusion in schools is itself part of a wider system, so is the training of staff within schools. CPD must continually be monitored and evolve to meet new requirements and training needs over time.

Part of a school's assessment of whether training is viable centres upon how this information will impact wider school life. A school is a structure which exists within a wider educational and political structure, and any change within schools is affected by myriad factors, as a result of both external to the school and internal school structure and culture (Hopkins, 2007). Research by Matthews (2009) indicates that whatever the political landscape and policy requirements, SLT interpretation of Ofsted criteria may be the key driver to school priorities. Any sustainable change in inclusive practice or specialist SEN knowledge will therefore need to be approved and championed by the setting manager or school head teacher. Changes driven by individual teachers may well flounder, unless grounded in a culture of collaborative professional practice (Harris, 2003). If there is a strong lead of prioritising resourcing for inclusion, and providing appropriate resources and time to plan additional support, then it is far more likely that effective training can be disseminated in the educational work place. This embedded collaboration is seen in Little's (1993) research as vital to effective CPD. A strategic arrangement for sharing of training, through staff meetings, briefings and co-teaching, is needed to ensure that CPD makes real impact on children's experiences and schools' cultures. An important factor for senior leaders and budget holders is how the information will be disseminated.

To share the knowledge or skills gained from training, staff need to be able to facilitate training within their setting. Anecdotal accounts suggest that not all staff feel confident to train other professionals, and therefore may be reluctant to share the result of their training. Different staff members may have different levels of teaching experience and may therefore struggle to effectively share the key points of their training. Another factor to be considered is the nature of different staff groups. Despite the Deployment and Impact of Support Staff project (DISS) (Blatchford et al., 2009) findings about support assistants seeming to have a negative effect on student progress, it is still the case that in mainstream schools any additional support for children with additional needs is delivered by TAs. As noted earlier, there may be wide disparity in the skills and experience of this diverse group of staff, and whilst some TAs will be confident and capable of sharing knowledge in staff meetings, this cannot be taken for granted, especially not within schools where the disparity between experience and responsibilities may be especially marked. An additional consideration is when the knowledge is to be disseminated, with many schools operating separate TA and teacher staff meetings or training. A further complication is that during times of austerity and shrinking budgets there is a rise in using agency TAs to fill posts. Whilst in the short term this can be more expensive, it allows schools to have the flexibility to terminate employment if budgets suddenly become strained, for example if the school roll (and therefore funding) falls or if the school has to cover long-term sickness of permanent staff. Schools are unlikely to send temporary staff on these courses, even if it is these staff who work most closely with the children with the most complex needs. When choosing who to send on expensive school-time training, managers therefore have to balance who needs the specific training with who will be able to disperse that information to the school community (see Table 8.1).

**Table 8.1**  Types of training typically funded by a school or setting, according to staff role

| | SENCO | Teacher | Teaching Assistant | Early Years Teacher in Nursery | Room Leader | Level 3 Nursery Worker |
|---|---|---|---|---|---|---|
| INSET training | / | / | Dependent on school | / | / | / |
| Weekly evening Staff Meetings | / | / | Dependent on school | / | Dependent on setting | Dependent on setting |
| Staff Meetings within the school day | x | x | / | Dependent on setting | Dependent on setting | Dependent on setting |
| External Short Courses – Curriculum | x | / | Dependent on school – less common | / | / | Dependent on setting |
| External Short Courses – SEN/Medical | / | X | / | / | / | Dependent on setting |
| SENCO Masters level module | / | X | X | X | X | X |

---

**PAUSE FOR REFLECTION**

- How does your experience reflect or challenge this?

---

Within current education systems with the rise of academisation and a change in necessary qualifications, the spread of experience of staff is likely to be ever-widening. The CPD required by staff will therefore be more fragmented and need to be highly targeted. This is further impacted by the ongoing changes in pupil needs and educational levels, linked with external factors of increased neo-natal care and survival rates of children who are then more likely to have an ongoing severe health need. This increases the complexity of skills required by staff, again increasing the likelihood of needing rigorous regular CPD, particularly around medical and social communication strategies. With fewer staff employed by schools, and not all of these on permanent contracts, there is a need for staff to be multi-skilled and flexible, with a wide range of knowledge about potential life-threatening health conditions and practices. These multi-skilled workers will require a range of ongoing CPD in order to safely and practically support children with additional needs and other complex medical needs. Inevitably when there are staff absences, staff are directed to cover, and therefore there needs to be a pool of workers with overlapping skills to minimise the potential for a child not having a trained and effective worker. This indicates that all staff need to have training on health needs and communication strategies for the children with the most challenging needs, and this poses questions about non-teaching time for CPD training. Schools therefore have to balance requirements for training effectively with budgetary concerns and the need to minimise adult time away from children.

## CASE STUDY   CONTINUING PROFESSIONAL DEVELOPMENT

*Denise*: 48 years old

*Highest qualification*: Took O-level exams in 1980s, grades awarded were not equivalent to current day GCSE C grade or above.

*Experience*: 25 years as TA (General and 1:1) in one school

*Current role*: 1:1 support for a child with an EHC plan for a diagnosis of ASD, but would prefer general class TA work, has always enjoyed teaching art. The year 3 child, James, that they work with is currently working within P-Levels [P-Levels assess achievement below National Curriculum Level]. James uses signs and symbols to communicate, particularly likes buses and timetables, and requires support with toileting. His EHC plan highlights that he has a short attention span and one of his targets is to complete a one-step task to receive a reward.

*Type of contract*: Permanent part-time contract.

*School-identified training needs*: Functional skills English and Maths, Supporting children with ASD with communication.

*Charlie*: 21 years old

*Highest qualification*: Degree in French and Spanish

*Experience*: 6 months agency TA work in a variety of schools (Secondary and Primary and Special School).

*Current role*: Small-group work with children identified at SEN Support level or as low attainers in year 5. Group includes: Sally, Ahmed, Javeenah and Timmy. Sally is partially deaf and often struggles to hear the teacher's input and finds group work challenging but is high-attaining in Maths. Ahmed has global development delay and requires all curriculum input to be modified to enable him to access it. Javeenah has missed large amounts of school due to illness and is currently working at year 3 expectations. Timmy has pathological demand avoidance syndrome and so finds it very challenging to follow instructions and stay on task.

*Type of contract*: Temporary through an agency, has been verbally offered a long-term placement up to the end of the academic year.

*School-identified training needs*: Differentiation of work.

---

### PAUSE FOR REFLECTION

You are the senior management in the school:

- Based on the children's needs, what training would you recommend?

- Based on the adult profile, what professional training would you recommend?

- What type of training would have the most impact on the children?

- What type of training might be most attractive to staff?

- With a limited budget for training, what would you prioritise?

- Are there more efficient/inclusive ways you could use these staff? What training would that require?

---

In light of changes of contract type, schools may have to prioritise training for staff who are employed on permanent/long-term contracts, and who have the skills to be able to disseminate information from their training. This may mean that those sent on the training may never use the skills within their own role. This raises two issues: first, the motivation for the person going on the course may be lower if they are not personally invested in the skills and can see no personal benefit to attending training; second, they may not have an understanding of the day-to-day practicalities of the duties that the training is designed to aid. Without an in-depth knowledge of the practicalities for the children/adult, they may not be attuned to essential details of information or may not retain what others might consider key details. A similar scenario would be to perhaps imagine a non-driver going to a training session about rally driving. There would be a knowledge gap in terms of everyday experience, vocabulary and awareness of hazards and possibilities. Whilst a practitioner may be able to convey the information effectively, they may not have the insight or experience to know what the key information or nuances are.

The issue of who gets which type of training is therefore highly complex, and sometimes appears only tangentially related to the specific needs of children. The training is decided through the lens of cost, political funding cuts, contract types, staff motivation and aspiration, and prevalence of children with this particular need. In contrast to what we might hope, from this review it seems naïve to assume that children's needs and the added value to individuals' lives and learning are the driving force behind the decision to train staff.

## CHAPTER SUMMARY

Schools and settings use CPD to ensure that staff have the skills and qualifications necessary to provide high-quality education and care for all pupils, and specifically those with SEND. Decisions around CPD are complex, and involve budgets, career aspirations, staff contract types and the needs of children. Staff within early childhood education and care have a diverse range of qualifications and experience, and therefore pitching training at appropriate levels can be extremely challenging.

## Suggested Further Reading

The list below offers some further information and guidance on the key points raised in this chapter.

Blatchford, P., Bassett, P., Brown, P., Martin, C., Russell, A. and Webster, R. (2009) *Deployment and Impact of Support Staff Project: Research Brief.* London: Department for Children, Schools and Families.
This report offers an overview of the extensive research into the roles and effects of support staff in schools, and valuable links to other reports from the project. Although this research is not specifically focussed around SEND or the early years, the widespread use of teaching assistants to support children with SEND make the studies from this research an invaluable source of information and prompts for discussion.

Blatchford, P., Russell, A. and Webster, R. (2012) *Reassessing the Impact of Teaching Assistants: How Research Challenges Practice and Policy.* London: Routledge.
Discussion of the role of teaching assistants, useful as a starting point for discussion of what the training needs are for this group with relation to both their individual skills and the demands of their changing role.

Chambers, D. (2015) *Working with Teaching Assistants and Other Support Staff for Inclusive Education.* Bingley: Emerald Group.
This book explores the role, deployment and training needs of teaching assistants and others, considering effective and practical use of these roles.

Pearson, S. and Gathercole, K. (2011) *National Award for SENCOs: Transforming SENCOs.* Tamworth: NASEN.
A consideration of the SENCO National Award, and how this qualification was intended to remodel the work and role of SENCOs, with potential impact on the training and deployment of staff within schools and settings.

# 9

# MULTI-AGENCY WORKING: PARTNERSHIP AND COLLABORATION

## ESTELLE MARTIN

### CHAPTER OBJECTIVES

- To outline aspects of models of multi-agency collaboration and services for children and families.

- To consider the importance of the range of disciplines that may be involved in the support of children with SEND to come together in collaboration to provide integrated services.

- To consider the policy and practice regarding the expression and voice of children with SEND to contribute to their own review and developmental process within a person-centred approach.

## Definitions of Multi-agency Working

Multi-agency working can be defined in many different ways. The Wigfall and Moss definition below particularly recognises the importance of shared objectives from a variety of service providers when meeting the needs of children with SEND and their families.

> A range of different services which have some overlapping or shared interests and objectives, brought together to work collaboratively towards some common purposes.
>
> (Wigfall and Moss, 2001: 71)

Other definitions focus on the integrated systems and the importance of effective processes for communication and information sharing. Thus you may see multi-agency working labelled as 'integrated approaches' or 'multi-professional practice'. Despite these differences in definition, the main aim of the multi-agency approach is for all professionals working with a child with SEND to work towards shared goals, collaboratively and in partnership, in order to achieve positive outcomes for children and families. As will be seen later in the chapter when we look at some of the challenges of multi-agency working, this overarching aim of the multi-agency approach is not necessarily straightforward.

## A Brief History of Multi-agency Working

Section 25 of the Children and Families Act 2014 places a legal duty on local authorities to ensure that education, training, health and social care provision are integrated around the needs of the child with SEND and are outcome led. As such, the Children and Families Act 2014 is the last in a long line of legislation aimed at improving integration of services for children with SEND and from other vulnerable groups. The Laming report into the death of Victoria Climbié (Laming, 2003) addressed the impact of inadequate communication and information sharing between service providers and its 108 recommendations were enshrined in the Children Act 2004 (DCSF, 2004: 31) and further reiterated in the 2006 Act (DfES, 2006). The Every Child Matters framework (DfES, 2004b) further emphasised the importance of integrated working, and processes such as the Common Assessment Framework and the introduction of the Integrated Workforce further strengthened opportunities for multi-professional collaboration. It is important to recognise the limits of terms such as 'multi-agency' approaches. It could be suggested that 'trans-agency' working more accurately reflects the complexity and variation of children's services.

It is often assumed that words such as 'partnership' and 'collaboration' are universally understood, and as such do not require specific definition. However, as has been seen in the Lamb Inquiry (2009), parents' experiences of working in partnership with professionals vary enormously, suggesting that conceptualisations of partnership and collaboration may differ.

For the purpose of clarification, whilst the authors of this publication recognise that partnership between professionals, children and parents involves cooperation, coordination and collaboration, this has to be achieved through respectful acknowledgement of the equal, yet different, contribution that all parties are able to make to the development of shared aims and outcomes for a child with SEND. This is of particular relevance when accessing specialist services, as the holistic needs of the child (medical, social, educational) will be best understood by actively listening and respecting the child and parent's experiences and perspectives.

As discussed in Chapter 2, the Pen Green model of parental partnership and community engagement, which our definition above echoes, has been influential in the early years sector as an example of 'best practice', reflected in its Beacon status award as a national training forum for early childhood practitioners pursuing a multi-agency approach.

Some of the beneficial impacts of multi-agency working for children with SEND and their families have been documented in a series of evaluative reports.

For example, Oliver et al.'s (2010) review of the impact of integrated approaches, although citing mixed responses from professionals across a range of professional disciplines, noted that for children with disabilities, the health needs of children were improved through greater access to a wider range of services. For children with severe or complex needs, who qualified for the early support programme, the findings were similarly positive. Young et al. (2006, cited in Oliver et al., 2010) noted that these families reported reduced stress, increased confidence and greater opportunities to be involved in decision making. Finally, Pettit (2003) recognised that for older children with mental health concerns, integrated working within the Child and Adult Mental Health service (CAMHS) led to improved behaviour, better educational outcomes and enhanced peer relationships.

Historically, examples of multi-agency teams working with a range of children and young people have included:

- Sure Start multi-disciplinary teams.
- Education Professionals (SENCOs).
- Behaviour Support teams.
- Health Visitors and Paediatric Health specialists.
- Speech and Language Therapists.
- Social Workers and Family Outreach teams.
- Educational Psychologists.
- Portage Workers.
- Educational Welfare Officers.
- Local Authority Children's Services teams.
- Midwives.

During the first phase of the Children Centre programme (2006–2008), many of these professionals were co-located in Children Centre hubs, enabling parents and carers to access a range of services simultaneously and facilitating greater communication and information sharing between professional teams. Since 2010, however, the removal of ring-fencing for Children Centre services and successive cuts to early intervention grant funding (discussed in more depth in Chapter 1) has meant that key specialist services have been removed from Children Centres, and their role increasingly focused on targeted provision for the most vulnerable children and families rather than on universal preventative support strategies. Despite these recent policy and funding developments, commitment to multi-agency working remains strong at policy and practice level as evidenced in section 25 of the Children and Families Act 2014.

It should be noted that cuts to Children Centre services (NCB, 2015) have gone ahead across LAs in England, despite evidence of positive responses to the services that the centres provided. For example, the 2015 4Children Children Centre Census revealed that:

- 55.2 per cent of parents said they used their local Children Centre at least once a week.
- 90.5 per cent of parents said that attending a Children Centre has had a positive impact on their child.
- 79.4 per cent of parents said that if they were unable to use their local Children Centre this would make life harder for them and their family.
- 34.4 per cent of parents said it would make a 'big difference' and life would become 'a lot more difficult'.
- More than one million children and families are regularly using Children Centres, with a majority of centre managers saying that numbers have gone up in the past 12 months.
- 57.5 per cent of managers who have experienced a budget reduction say they will have to cut back services as a result and 32 per cent say they will be unable to reach as many families as before.
- 24.5 per cent of managers know changes will be made to the way their Children Centres are run in the next year, but do not know what this will involve.

## Models of Multi-agency Working

Atkinson et al.'s study (2007), which involved professionals working together from education, social services and health sectors of LAs, highlighted five different models of multi-agency activity which were evident within the sample: decision-making groups; consultation and training; centre-based delivery; coordinated delivery; and operational delivery. So some models focused on direct delivery to a range of target groups, whilst in others the primary aim or purpose was decision making or providing consultation and training to other agencies. Agencies came together for different reasons and, for each of the different models, different levels of engagement with professionals from other agencies were evident. Thus, a continuum may be described from decision-making groups, where professionals from different agencies maintained their distinct role, to operational teams, where professionals worked in close proximity and therefore the merging of roles was more likely.

Overall, reports such as the Atkinson et al. example can offer useful evidence of what may need to be improved and developed for early childhood communities at a particular time in history and at policy level. This may include changes to policy (see Chapter 1), for example the introduction of the Integrated Review (see Chapter 7), and the development of EHC plan (see Chapter 3) as part of the reforms in the Children and Families Act 2014 and 2015 SEND Code of Practice.

Furthermore, the Atkinson et al. report identified a range of key issues for professionals and families when working towards an integrated or multi-agency approach and claims to have revealed a new 'hybrid' professional type who have personal experience and knowledge of other agencies, including, importantly, these services' cultures, structures, discourse and priorities. These so-called 'hybrid' professionals can be seen to be the beneficiaries of multi-professional information sharing practices, for example the early years practitioner who has been trained by a speech and language therapist to deliver language intervention programmes. The professional benefits of multi-agency working are discussed below. However, the report also intimates the enormous variation in initiatives and practice that are operating as 'multi-agency'.

## Challenges Affecting Multi-agency Working

As discussed above, multi-agency working offers children with SEND and their families the opportunity to receive streamlined, outcome-led interventions and provision, emanating from collaboration and shared decision making between specialist professionals, and in the best examples, in response to active and valued participation from children and parents themselves (see Chapter 2).

However, the approach does not come without its challenges. Anning et al. (2010), for example, identify four categories of dilemma for teams working in multi-professional ways:

- Structural.
- Ideological.
- Procedural.
- Inter-professional.

*Structural* dilemmas can arise as a result of the complexities of leading and managing professionals from a range of disciplines with varied codes of conduct and contractual arrangements, the allocation of funding, deployment of roles and the challenge of monitoring and evaluating the services not located on site; *ideological* dilemmas may include the impact of 'value-led' approaches to working with parents and children and the extent to which different professionals respect the role that these contributors can make to the decision-making process; *procedural* dilemmas can include alignment of documentation, use of professional language and jargon, and diverse understandings of issues such as confidentiality; and *inter-professional* dilemmas may include challenges associated with the different value afforded to key professional roles within the multi-professional team, and the impact this may have upon hierarchical relationships, for example the perspective of a portage worker may not be accepted as equally valid as that of the educational psychologist due to the latter's perceived enhanced professional status.

Similarly, Aubrey (2011) acknowledges the impact on leadership roles and responsibilities when managing a multi-agency team, for example when leading teams of professionals with diverse polices and priorities for practice, with different salaries, career progression and professional status or with divergent understandings of professional team working. Even where multi-agency teams are co-located, differences in funding allocations and threats to the sustainability of funded secondments (e.g. the deployment of a speech and language therapist from the local health trust to a Children Centre) combined with the varying needs of inter-professional training, can result in significant challenges for integrated centre leaders.

---

## PAUSE FOR REFLECTION

- How might some of the challenges to multi-agency approaches listed above be effectively overcome?

- How can a shared language between professionals be successfully developed?

- What are your experiences of working in partnership with parents and with other professionals?

---

## Professional Benefits of Multi-agency Approaches

Although the professional responses to multi-agency approaches have been mixed (Oliver et al., 2010), there have been some indications that working alongside professionals from different disciplines has had a beneficial impact on the knowledge and skills of staff within the fields of early childhood and SEND. In 2008, the now disbanded Children's Workforce Development Council (CWDC) introduced the Integrated Qualifications Framework aimed at training professionals from mixed backgrounds in a set of common core skills, which would reduce cross-sector misunderstandings and facilitate shared constructions about the most effective strategies for supporting children with SEND and their families.

---

## COMMON CORE SKILLS

- Effective communication and engagement

- Child and young person's development

- Safeguarding and child protection

- Supporting transitions

- Multi-agency working

- Sharing information

---

Unfortunately, despite some initial positive outcomes for integrated approaches, particularly in Sure Start local programmes (later known as Children Centres), in regard to enhanced attitudes and perceptions, knowledge and skills (Frost et al., 2004), there remains limited national data on the impact of multi-agency working on professional development.

At a local level, however, the impact of joint professional working has been more forthcoming. For example, an evaluation project from Worcestershire County Council into the impact of the Every Child a Talker programme (DCSF, 2008a) identified improved practitioner knowledge and confidence about the stages of children's language development as a key outcome indicator. Evaluations with early years practitioners involved in this programme (aimed at supporting early language development through collaborative intervention strategies designed jointly by speech and language therapists and early years key workers) suggested that their knowledge of the stages of early language development increased by 73 per cent following their involvement in the initiative (Worcestershire NHS Trust, 2013).

The perspectives of different professionals towards multi-agency working were further researched by Lindqvist et al. (2011), who looked at the views of different occupational groups on special needs education within the Swedish context of multi-agency approaches. Professionals involved in the study included:

- Teacher assistants.
- Pre-school teachers.
- Special educational needs coordinators (SENCOs) (in Swedish *specialpedagoger*, literally special pedagogues).
- Special needs teachers.

The summary of findings from Lindqvist et al.'s research acknowledges the significance of value-led approaches (also identified by Anning et al., 2010), whereby different occupational groups construct an understanding of support for children with SEND based on their construction of the children's abilities, rights or deficits.

Lindqvist et al. argue that it is important to continue the 'discussions between different occupational groups regarding what inclusive education amounts to and the role of different occupational groups within a process of making education more inclusive'. They suggest that 'decisions about special needs education should involve political levels, administrators, teachers, resource staff, parents and children' (2011: 156).

## Professional Training

The Lindqvist et al. study is particularly relevant to the current UK context due to the reforms of the role of the SENCO in the Children and Families Act 2014 (see Chapter 1) and the introduction in 2009 of the National SENCO award which raised the status and qualification of the SENCO role (although, as discussed in Chapter 1, this Master's level training is only available to qualified teachers, and as such leaves SEND provision within the PVI sector the 'poorer cousin' in terms of access to knowledge and expertise). Nevertheless the introduction of the National SENCO award has been perceived favourably in the field as recognition of the role's complexity. Perhaps more relevant as a reflection of the findings from the Lindqvist et al. study is the clear move towards a 'rights-based' approach to provision for children with SEND and a greater emphasis on the legal duty of LAs to ensure integrated working and information sharing with parents and carers through the publication of the local offer (DfE, 2015c).

---

**PAUSE FOR REFLECTION**

- What types of multi-disciplinary training for practitioners can benefit children and families?

- How does the integration of services support inclusion for children and their parents/carers?

- What strategies may support greater parental involvement for multi-professional teams?

---

## Communities of Practice When Working with Children with SEND

The five Cs (Figure 9.1) can assist our concept of what may be needed in multi-agency services within and across the different specialist fields that practitioners and parents have to navigate, across the range of landscapes whether it be health services, social care or education.

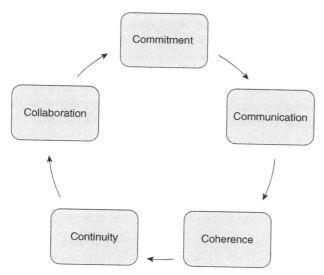

**Figure 9.1**   Multi-agency and trans-disciplinary approaches and opportunities

*Commitment* – which is underpinned by values and beliefs that all children are to be respected and to enable children with SEND to have a voice and to express their individual ways of being. This can be achieved by looking through a 'child-rights-based' lens moving forwards from a needs-led approach. This will help practitioners involved with the children and families to include the whole child, hence having a holistic view of the child and not just seeing the additional need or disability. This is also about the ethos of the setting reflecting the principles that underpin your practice and the attitudes of other practitioners alongside.

The ethos of a school, nursery or Children Centre may be seen as the culture that demonstrates the emotional climate for staff and children and the ways in which goals can be achieved.

*Communication* – the communication process is at every level an essential part of the co-construction of trust that supports the quality of relations between practitioner and child or parent and practitioner as a continuous flow of conversations to construct and clarify what aspects of assessment, diagnosis and type of intervention are required and to review the process as an ongoing aspect of sharing information. This can be effective practice with observations, for example audio and visual accounts of the child's developmental progress and next steps. Effective practice is realised in this way through sharing information in a confidential context, following boundaries for safeguarding children and putting professional policy into practice. So in this way communication should be a democratic process that enables participation and collaboration between people including children.

*Coherence* – the communication within the professional agencies is one strand of many that needs to be linked to other strands so the coherence of how the intervention for the child is taken forwards and carried out is clear for all practitioners within agencies. This is also effective practice across agency boundaries so that each agency can behave as a coherent service contributing to the benefit of the family and child. This reflects the key theme above in that high-quality communication creates the conditions for overall coherence within, between and amongst practitioners and, with parents, and inclusion for the child. Creating the conditions for coherence means including all staff, showing respect, creating a community that values listening, and promotes consultation between and within staff teams. Early childhood practitioners may find themselves part of several teams working with children and their families within their centre, and also in collaboration with other settings and agencies.

*Continuity* – the continuity of care is another strand of quality for children's experience in early childhood and influences their potential beyond the EYFS as practitioners and parents can have a shared understanding of how and what interventions will be supported over time as the child and family circumstances change. This may be due to developmental change that has implications for practice or resources the child may need to communicate or be enabled to express their perspectives and knowledge. For example, a child may have a physical disability that restricts their movements or speech, although they have age appropriate cognitive skills and knowledge and understanding. How children's needs can be planned for includes involving the child in the process to reflect the child's views and concerns that may be different to the concerns of adults. This can be a challenge for all professional groups so that they can develop more accurate insights into the roles and responsibilities of other disciplines who may assess and observe children from different perspectives and use different methodologies which may include the child to a lesser or greater extent.

*Collaboration* – the collaboration process is part of multi-agency systems and ways of working. When practitioners and researchers collaborate it means that a partnership approach is not only adopted but can reinforce the existing participation of parents, children and specialist practitioners for effective outcomes for the child and family. There are examples of collaboration in the integrated services model of how some projects work in an integrated way, bringing together the different disciplines to work collaboratively to meet the holistic needs of the child and family. This is reflected in the 2015 SEND Code of Practice.

The Team Around the Child (TAC) is an approach that has supported the improvement of multi-agency working and the Common Assessment Framework (CAF) has led to enhanced outcomes for children and families through the pre-assessment checklist to identify unmet needs at an early stage, which is used by all agencies. The opportunities are about providing benefits and relevant outcomes for the child within a person-centred approach.

## Solution-focused Approaches for Goal Setting with Children in Education

The literature about children and the deficit model (Booth and Ainscow, 2004; Cousins, 2006) shows that self-esteem plays a huge part in how children see themselves as people and as learners. When children and young people are enabled to experience an inclusive education this can be supported by the use of solution-focused strategies which are essentially person-centred.

## CASE STUDY   UNDERPINNING PRINCIPLES

As part of a school's counselling service a school counsellor, funded by the local National Health Service Trust, was able to visit a local primary school regularly and offer counselling support to children with anxiety issues. During the therapeutic process children could decide how they would put into practice their changes by setting goals for themselves. This person-centred approach advocates the trust and belief that children can express their preferred ways of being and make changes towards improving their experience, behaviour and in most cases reducing anxieties. For children with SEND it may not be possible to change their disability; however, they can be empowered to find solutions to manage problems associated with their disability toward a solution rather than focusing on the problems. This is also the set of strategies that can be adopted in trans-disciplinary teams to reduce the historical dominant discourses of certain disciplines influencing attitudes of

*(Continued)*

*(Continued)*

practitioners viewing and categorising children within a deficit frame. This can assist practitioners in progressing towards their professional commitment and ethics in recognising children's strengths and cultural identities as individuals in a holistic way. Nutbrown et al. (2005: 27) emphasise that unless all cultural and personal strengths of the child are valued a deficit model of the child's capabilities will be assumed, which may threaten the child's perception of their competencies and damage their self-esteem.

Meighan and Siraj-Blatchford (2003: 374) concur that 'society generates certain definitions of what the normal individual should be like, and those who fail to meet these definitions may become stigmatised'.

Looking and listening to researchers and practitioners helps us reflect on our practice to understand the importance of seeing the whole child and not to reinforce the limitations children may be faced with in their developmental journey.

The triangle of trust and relationships in integrated services can be a transformative process for adults as well as children. The triangle of trust is a shared experience that evolves through relationships and can be more significant when the mental health and emotional wellbeing of a child is affected. Children's mental health can be enhanced through the trust between parents, practitioners and children; this in turn can influence children's improved development and their learning process – when children are trusted to learn and achieve at their own level they become more confident learners towards realising their potential, having a sense of belonging and being in a learning environment that feels like they are loved (Martin, 2013).

Roberts' (2010) study also reflects the emphasis of relationships in aspects of wellbeing, especially for children under three years old. Four aspects are necessary to realise wellbeing:

*Agency*: a state of wellbeing is achieved through being able to make a difference, which influences how a person learns, how confident they are, whilst nurturing their self-esteem.

*Belonging and boundaries*: also a state of wellbeing that is indicated through how safe someone feels, feeling special and wanted, being part of what is going on around them.

*Communication*: a central process of wellbeing that relies on talking, listening, understanding and communicating with other people.

*Physical wellbeing*: which, together with communication, is a determinant of wellbeing and the basis of the other aspects.

(adapted from Roberts, 2010: 32)

The EYFS 2012 was revised in order to represent an enhanced curriculum framework with guidance for practitioners following the Tickell Review (2011).

This included the shift towards prime and specific areas of learning and development in order to assist the realisation of early learning goals and outcomes. The prime areas are the underpinning and overarching framework from which the specific areas of learning and development can be built. Children will achieve those outcomes during the foundation stage at their own level and potential is not always realised in a linear sequence. This is particularly so for some children with SEND and for children who are in disadvantaged circumstances who may have additional learning needs as a result, although for some the circumstances are not permanent and with the appropriate assessment and professional support children may realise their potential within a time-limited period.

## Goal Setting for Change

It is more useful to assist children to build a detailed picture of their goals and their preferred future rather than focusing on the past or the problems that give rise to automatic thinking that the same problems of the past will still exist and never change.

The child can be helped to identify their strengths and skills and assist them in identifying how they have used those strengths and skills to find solutions to their worries or problems. For children, sometimes it is the worry that is the problem rather than an actual problem that exists; however, some children can become convinced and 'overthink' their worry and so their anxiety increases to a level that may be influencing their mental health and interrupts the learning process. Solution-focused approaches to supporting young children's mental health will include looking for the abilities of the child and not for the deficits and problems. A solution-focused approach will look and listen for what is going well. This includes the detail of how the child has managed to cope and find ways to build on their skills and strengths.

Families and parents have also some aspects that may need more support or recognition, and again the parents can be respected and helped to build on their strengths and skills, and recognise their own resources to increase their confidence and enhance their family relations, which in turn can influence the children.

De Shazer and Molnar (1987) advocate the acceptance and understanding that people do not want to be unhappy or be dependent on others for their own wellbeing, and so in this way the solution-focused theory underpins applications that practitioners (educational psychologists, counsellors, teachers and teaching assistants, health practitioners), may use with children in schools, to support them to manage change and enhance their emotional wellbeing.

Multi-agency training and CPD linked to a reflective process can increase the understanding of other professional roles and responsibilities. So in this way, training across boundaries and mixed disciplines can reduce the barriers to joint working in a meaningful way as advocates for the child with SEND and their family.

Multi-disciplinary training can provide the skills and understanding of the solution-focused approaches and applications in schools and Children Centres in future development of more integrated ways of working together. Goals must be clear, realistic and manageable; children are capable of working towards their own goals and to identify what needs to change (see Chapter 3).

## Family Conference Model

The family conference model is associated with children who may be seen as at risk or have already been identified as being at risk or having been exposed to harmful experiences. Children in some circumstances will be taken into care and are referred to as looked after children (LAC). The family conference model is used by LAs and organisations like the Children and Family Court Advisory and Support Service (CAFCASS) to take forwards what may be best for the child, with family involvement alongside multi-agency practitioners coming to meet together to be advocates for the child and also consider what the most appropriate action is for the child and family.

Family group conferences are decision-making meetings that bring children and families and their wider support networks together. The process is designed to bring about solutions to the difficulties the family are experiencing by negotiation and discussion together. In principle it is to support the child and empower the child to express their voice and opinions, and the family to make decisions together that are in the best interests of the child.

The Family Rights Group (n.d.) refers to the New Zealand model for family group conferencing which has influenced the development of the models in England and Wales. Professionals from multi-agency teams in New Zealand initiated a solution-focused approach to enable and empower communities and multi-agency support services to work together and find solutions with families and children in social and culturally sensitive and responsive ways. This reflects the Maori culture, and is a strengths-based model. A range of health, education, psychology and social work practitioners may also attend these family group conferences to be advocates in the process, especially where the progress of the future child and family is emergent and positive outcomes and decisions can be made together.

---

### PAUSE FOR REFLECTION

- What may be the impact of multi-agency working on your future work as a practitioner in your particular discipline?

- In what ways could you contribute to multi-agency working in the future, within a school or with other agencies or professionals?

---

## Creating a Listening Culture

Multi-agency work with children and young people is positioned within a person-centred framework which is promoted through the assessment and review processes described earlier. Person-centred approaches reflect the theory base of Carla Rinaldi (2006) and Loris Malaguzzi (1993), educationalists and advocates of the child-centred Italian preschools of Reggio Emilia which advocate creative and experiential approaches, focusing on children's rights to an inclusive educational experience rather than a needs-based or compensatory model. This right-based approach is emerging within the UK legislative context (see Chapter 1), although the embedding of such child-centred philosophies requires professional commitment alongside legislative requirements. Creating an authentic, multi-modal listening culture is also relevant to ensure that children with complex needs are supported and when advocating for their voice to be heard.

## Ways of Seeing – Social Constructions of Children

Children that attend more than one setting or are in transition between home-based care with child-minders, nursery or a child development centre, for example, was a focus of research by Nind et al. (2011). This identified the social constructions of individual children and their identities in that there were shared perceptions by different staff across settings about the children, although some elements about the role of the learning environment and the culture of inclusion influenced the ways in which children can be socially constructed in the categorisation of special needs in English early years provision. Boggis (2016: 1) argues:

> If we are to work towards a more inclusive society, cultural changes are necessary. It is therefore essential that early years practitioners take time to challenge existing practice, critically consider opportunities for change and develop practice in order that the outcomes and life chances for young children with SEN and or disabilities can be improved.

Learning through empirical evidence of how children are experiencing their childhoods is challenging how we conceptualise childhood. Children are not simply learning and practising to exist for the future, they are also socially active members of their families, communities and societies in the here and now.

Valuing young children's varied language repertoire is part of the listening to young children approach through RAMPS, a set of principles for valuing young children's perspectives in research and participation (Lancaster and Kirby, 2010), challenging the deficit model.

---

### RAMPS PRINCIPLES

- **R**ecognising children's rich language repertoire
- **A**llocating spaces that enable children to articulate their perspectives of their experiences
- **M**aking time so children can participate fully
- **P**roviding children with genuine choices
- **S**ubscribing to reflexivity

---

Goleman (1995) identifies seven 'ingredients' that are essential for children to become confident learners and which will underpin their capacities to learn across a range of cross-curricular areas through opportunities to practise:

- Confidence.
- Curiosity.
- Intentionality.
- Self-control.
- Relatedness.
- Capacity to communicate.
- Cooperativeness.

## CASE STUDY   USING DRAWINGS TO ARTICULATE FEELINGS

An effective strategy to support children to explore their feelings is through annotated drawings. These can be a useful way for children to articulate their frustrations and anxieties and make these 'visible' to adults. For example during a CAMHS session with a multi-agency team, Child A explored his feelings of anger towards his sister. His drawings reflected that he was aware that he could reduce his anger through 'ignoring my sister', then telling an adult like his Mum or Teacher; so an alternative to hitting was found and an appropriate solution considered. Child A's drawings of him counting to 10 demonstrated his realisation that he could do something other than wait or continue to feel aggravated when his sister teased him. In other words, his drawings of his responses to the teasing from his sister suggested that he knew that if he was able to wait long enough to manage the impulse to hit his sister; it will eventually disappear. Furthermore, the drawings suggested that Child A understood the concept of the inner and outer self and awareness of several perspectives of others in one situation, and several sources of information at the same time. So in this way Child A was able to de-centre which revealed his emotion knowledge and self-regulation. Child A was able to identify strategies to help himself make the changes and use scaling exercises to monitor his own experience and map it visually on a scale from 0 to 10 which is often used in solution-focused approaches. In this way Child A could select and make choices about how he would take his next step and this increased his abilities to reflect on his own learning, leading to changes in his behaviour, therefore enhancing his self-regulation and benefits to his sister and peers. Child A was able to reflect upon the drawings in his sessions to talk about how he would reduce his aggressive outbursts and explore 'what if?' in a safe place where he was confident to share his perspectives and take risks without judgement or criticism. The scaling exercises and goal setting were helpful and he was able to understand how these could support his progress. At the end of the term, again using the medium of drawing, Child A showed his delight at being with his family on a day out with all happy moments with his sister and the rest of the family so he was able to create positive memories with his sister as a result of his enhanced self-regulation.

---

## PAUSE FOR REFLECTION

- Who might be the multi-agency professionals working to support Child A and his family?

- How might different professionals have divergent views on the child's participation in the assessment process?

- What might be some of the challenges presented by these divergent perspectives?

---

## Child and Adolescent Mental Health

Children's mental health is of increasing concern, even within the early years sector. Data from Young Minds (2016) suggests that 1 in 10 children and young people aged 5–16 suffer from a diagnosable mental health disorder (i.e. around three children in every class), so child and adolescent mental health services are often vital contributors to multi-agency teams. In addition, the link between poverty and health inequalities (Marmot, 2010) has been well-established, as has the increased likelihood of families with a child with a special educational need or disability living in low-income families (Children's Society, 2012). Therefore multi-agency teams may consist of more than health and education professionals, and may include family outreach workers or social workers who are concerned with the impact and influence of external economic and structural factors on positive health and education outcomes for children with SEND.

It can be seen from the discussions above that within any multi-agency team, the importance of having shared values and a common commitment to achieving positive outcomes for children with SEND and their families is of paramount importance, regardless of the individual professional disciplines of the contributors. Increasingly, the relationship between health, disability, social inequality and educational outcomes is being recognised, and it is no longer possible for these outcomes to be disassociated from other external and structural influences upon children's lived experiences.

---

## PAUSE FOR REFLECTION

- In what ways do children represent their feelings and thoughts?

- Consider how you can enable children's voices in different modes and symbolic representations.

- Children with SEND may need to 'speak' and make their representations in different modes. What may be helpful to support children's voices through a range of electronic media in addition to paintings and drawings?

---

## CHAPTER SUMMARY

In this chapter we have considered some of the opportunities and challenges for multi-agency working and recognised the complexities and barriers to learning for children with SEND. We have also considered how policy and practice change to meet the requirements for provision for children with SEND in the early years, for example the recent SEND Code of Practice (DfE, 2015c). A key focus for this chapter was the importance of creating a listening culture with solution-focused ways of working to support children and their families. Finally, we have considered how children can take responsibility for their learning through child-centred approaches.

---

## Suggested Further Reading

Anning, A., Cottrell, D., Frost, N., Green, J. and Robinson, M. (2010) *Developing Multi-professional Teamwork for Integrated Children's Services* (2nd edn). Maidenhead: Open University Press.
This book offers a clear and precise summary of some of the key opportunities and challenges associated with multi-professional approaches across a range of professional disciplines.

Gasper, M. (2010) *Multi-agency Working in the Early Years: Challenges and Opportunities*. London: Sage.
As the title suggests, the key factors affecting the effectiveness of multi-agency approaches in the early years context are discussed and considered in this book.

Aubrey, C. (2014) *Leading and Managing in the Early Years*. London: Sage.
Chapter 8 of this book provides a particularly useful account of some of the complexities and challenges faced by leaders of integrated centres (Children Centres) striving to lead and manage multi-agency teams.

# REFERENCES

4Children (n. d.) 'SEN and disability in the early years: A toolkit'. London: Council for Disabled Children. Available at https://councilfordisabledchildren.org.uk/sites/default/files/uploads/documents/import/early-years-toolkit-merged.pdf (accessed 16.6.16).

4Children (2015) 'Children's Centre Census 2015'. Available at http://cdn.basw.co.uk/upload/basw_23838-9.pdf (accessed 25.4.17).

Agbenyega, I.S. and Sharma, U. (2014) 'Leading inclusive education: measuring effective leadership for inclusive education through a Bourdieunian lens', in Forlin, C. and Loreman, R. (eds), *Measuring Inclusive Education*. Bingley: Emerald Group. pp. 115–32.

Ainscow, M., Booth, T. and Dyson, A. (2006) *Improving Schools, Developing Inclusion*. London: Routledge.

Ainscow, M., Dyson, A., Goldrick, S. and West, M. (2011) *Developing Equitable Education Systems*. Abingdon: Routledge.

Allen, G. (2011) *Early Intervention: The Next Steps*. London: Cabinet Office and Department for Work and Pensions. Available at dwp.gov.uk/docs/early-intervention-next-steps.pdf (accessed 3.1.16).

Anastasiou, D. and Kaufman, J.M. (2011) 'A social constructionist approach to disability: implications for special education', *Exceptional Children*, 77 (3): 78–92.

Ang, L. (2013) *The Early Years Curriculum: The UK Context and Beyond*. London: Routledge.

Angelides, P. (2012) 'Forms of leadership that promote inclusive education in Cypriot schools', *Educational Management Administration & Leadership*, 40 (1): 21–36.

Angelides, P., Antoniou, E. and Charalambous, C. (2010) 'Making sense of inclusion for leadership and schooling: a case study from Cyprus', *International Journal of Leadership in Education*, 13 (3): 319–34.

Angus, L. (2015) 'School choice: neoliberal education policy and imagined futures', *British Journal of Sociology of Education*, 36 (3): 395–413.

Anning, A., Cottrell, D., Frost, N., Green, J. and Robinson, M. (2010) *Developing Multi-professional Teamwork for Integrated Children's Services* (2nd edn). Maidenhead: Open University Press.

Apsland, D. (2014) *Children and Families Act: The Concerns*. Available at www.special needsjungle.com/children-families-act-concerns/ (accessed 1.7.16).

Artiles, A., Harris-Murri, N. and Rostenberg, D. (2006) 'Inclusion as social justice: critical notes on discourses, assumptions, and the road ahead', *Theory into Practice*, 45 (3): 260–8.

Atkinson, M., Jones, M. and Lamont, E. (2007) *Multi-agency Working and Its Implications for Practice: A Review of the Literature*. Reading: CfBT Educational Trust. Available at www.nfer.ac.uk/publications/MAD01/MAD01.pdf (accessed 12.10.16).

Attwood, L. (2013) 'The real implication of "benevolent" SEN reform', *Support for Learning*, 28 (4): 181–7.

Aubrey, C. (2014) *Leading and Managing in the Early Years*. London: Sage.

Audit Commission (2002) *Special Educational Needs: A Mainstream Issue*. London: Audit Commission.

Audit Commission (2003) *Services for Disabled Children*. London: Audit Commission.

Bailey, J. and du Plessis, D. (1997) 'Understanding principals' attitudes towards inclusive schooling', *Journal of Educational Administration*, 35 (5): 428–38.

Baker, C. and Martin, B. (2008) 'An examination of stakeholders' perceptions of the collaborative process utilized within a school-linked integrated partnership', *Journal of School Public Relations*, 29 (1): 15–43.

Banks, S. (2004) *Ethics, Accountability and the Social Professions*. Basingstoke: Palgrave Macmillan.

Banks, S. (2006) *Ethics and Values in Social Work* (3rd edn). Basingstoke: Palgrave Macmillan.

Barnes, P. (2008) 'Multi-agency working: what are the perspectives of SENCOs and parents regarding its development and implementation?', *British Journal of Special Education*, 35 (4): 230–40.

Bauman, Z. (1993) *Postmodern Ethics*. Oxford: Blackwell.

Benedict, A.E., Brownell, M.T., Park, Y., Bettini, E.A. and Lauterbach, A. (2014) 'Taking charge of your professional learning: tips for cultivating special educator expertise', *Teaching Exceptional Children*, 46: 147–57.

Bercow, J. (2008) *The Bercow Report: A review of services for children and young people (0–19) with speech, language and communication needs*. London: Department for Children, Schools and Families.

Blackburn, P. (2013) 'Future directions for a mature UK childcare market', in Lloyd, E. and Penn, H. (eds), *Childcare Markets, Can They Deliver an Equitable Service*? Bristol: Polity Press. pp. 43–63.

Black-Hawkins, K. and Florian, L. (2012) 'Classroom teachers' craft knowledge of their inclusive practice', *Teacher and Teaching: Theory and Practice*, 18 (5): 567–84.

Blandford, S. and Knowles, C. (2013) *Achievement for All: Raising Aspirations, Access and Achievement*. London: Bloomsbury Education.

Blatchford, P., Bassett, P., Brown, P., Martin, C., Russell, A. and Webster, R. (2009) *Deployment and Impact of Support Staff Project: Research Brief*. London: Department for Children, Schools and Families.

Blatchford, P., Russell, A. and Webster, R. (2012) *Reassessing the Impact of Teaching Assistants: How Research Challenges Practice and Policy*. London: Routledge.

Boggis, A. (2016) 'Special educational needs and disability (SEND) in the early years', in Trodd, L. (ed.), *The Early Years Handbook for Students and Practitioners: An Essential Guide for the Foundation Degree and Levels 4 & 5*. London: Fulton. pp. 125–40.

Booth, T. and Ainscow, M. (1998) *From Them to Us: An International Study of Inclusion in Education*. London: Routledge.

Booth, T. and Ainscow, M. (2002) *The Index for Inclusion* (2nd edn). Bristol: International Centre for Innovation in Education.

Booth, T. and Ainscow, M. (2004) *Index for Inclusion: Early Years and Childcare*. Bristol: Centre for Studies on Inclusive Education.

British Association of Social Workers (BASW) (2011) *The Code of Ethics for Social Work*. Available at http://cdn.basw.co.uk/upload/basw_112315-7.pdf (accessed 10.5.14).

Brodie, K. and Savage, K. (eds) (2015) *Inclusion and Early Years Practice*. Abingdon: Routledge.

Bronfenbrenner, U. (1976) 'The experimental ecology of education', *Educational Researcher*, 5 (9): 5–15.

Brooker, E. (2008) *Supporting Transitions in the Early Years*. London: McGraw-Hill.

Brunton, P. and Thornton, L. (2010) *The Parent Partnership Toolkit for Early Years*. London: Optimus Education.

Bullen, P. (2015) 'Transfer news', *Nasen Special*, September: 38–40.

Burello, L., Lashley, C. and Beatty, E. (2001) *Educating All Students Together: How School Leaders Create Unified Systems*. Thousand Oaks, CA: Corwin Press.

Burstow, B. and Winch, C. (2014) 'Providing for the professional development of teachers in England: a contemporary account of a government-led intervention', *Professional Development in England*, 40 (2): 190–206.

Busher, H. (2000) 'The subject leader as a middle manager', in Busher, H. and Harris, A. with Wise, G. (eds), *Subject Leadership and School Improvement*. London: Chapman. pp. 92–103.

Butler, P. (2013) 'Hundreds of Sure Start centres have closed since election says Labour', *Guardian*, 28 January. Available at www.theguardian.com/society/2013/jan/28/sure-start-centres-closed-labour (accessed 3.1.17).

Butler, R.A. (1944) *The Education Act*. London: HMSO.

Callan, S. and Morrall, A. (2009) 'Working with families and parent groups', in Robins, A. and Callan, S. (eds), *Managing Early Years Settings*. London: Sage. pp. 125–50.

Campbell, E. (2003) *The Ethical Teacher*. Maidenhead: Open University Press.

Campbell, E. (2008) 'The ethics of teaching as a moral profession', *Curriculum Inquiry*, 38 (4): 357–85.

Carnie, F. (2011) *The Parent Participation Handbook*. London: Optimus Education.

Carr, D. (2000) *Professionalism and Ethics in Teaching*. London: Routledge.

Centre for Studies on Inclusive Education (CSIE) (2015) 'Including disabled children in mainstream schools'. Available at www.csie.org.uk/inclusion/disabled-children.shtml (accessed 25.4.17).

Chambers, D. (2015) *Working with Teaching Assistants and Other Support Staff for Inclusive Education*. Bingley: Emerald Group.

Cheminais, R. (2006) *Every Child Matters: A Practical Guide for Teachers*. London: Routledge.

Children's Society (2011) *4 in 10: Disabled Children Living in Poverty*. London: Children's Society.

Children's Society (2012) *Holes in the Safety Net: The Impact of Universal Credit on Disabled Children and their Families*. London: Children's Society. Available at www.childrenssociety.org.uk/sites/default/files/tcs/holes_in_the_safety_net_disability_and_universal_credit_full_report.pdf (accessed 3.3.16).

Children's Workforce Development Council (CWDC) (2008) 'Integrated working explained'. Leeds: CWDC. Available at www.gov.uk/government/uploads/system/uploads/attachment_data/file/182200/integrated_working_explained.pdf (accessed 26.6.16).

Children's Workforce Development Council (CWDC) (2009) 'The Team Around the Child (TAC) and the lead professional'. Leeds: CWDC. Available at http://webarchive.national archives.gov.uk/20130401151715/www.education.gov.uk/publications/eOrdering Download/LeadPro_Managers-Guide.pdf (accessed 21.7.16).

Clarke, A. and Moss, P. (2001) *Listening to Young Children: The Mosaic Approach*. London: National Children's Bureau.

Clyde, M. (1995) *Child Care Directors' Perceptions of Their Roles and Attitudes Needed to Contribute to Those Roles*. Melbourne: Department of Early Childhood Studies.

Contact a Family (2012) *Counting the Cost: The Financial Reality for Families with Disabled Children across the UK*. London: Contact a Family. Available at www.cafamily.org.uk/media/381221/counting_the_costs_2012_full_report.pdf (accessed 8.1.17).

Cook, J. (2013) *Leadership and Management in the Early Years*. London: Practical Pre-School Books.

Cornwall, J. and Graham-Matheson, L. (eds) (2012) *Leading on Inclusion: Dilemmas, Debates and New Perspectives*. London: Routledge.

Council for Awards in Care Health and Education (CACHE) (2016) 'We are the leading sector specialist in Health and Social Care. Find out why.' St. Albans: CACHE. Available at www.cache.org.uk (accessed 12.12.16).

Council for Disabled Children (CDC) (2013) *Early Years Development Journal*. Available at https://councilfordisabledchildren.org.uk/help-resources/resources/early-years-developmental-journal (accessed 3.3.16).

Council for Exceptional Children (CEC) (2006) 'Special education professional ethical principles'. Available at www.cec.sped.org/Standards/Ethical-Principles-and-Practice-Standards (accessed 10.5.15).

Court, S.D.M. (1976) *Fit for the Future: The Report of the Committee on Child Health Services*, Volume 1 (Court Report). London: HMSO.

Cousins, J. (2006) 'Self-esteem in young children', *Early Years Update*. July. Available at www.teachingexpertise.com/articles/self-esteem-in-young-children-1119 (accessed 1.7.16).

Cribb, A. (2011) 'Integrity at work: managing routine moral stress in professional roles', *Nursing Philosophy*, 12: 119–27.

Cribb, A. and Gewirtz, S. (2012) 'New welfare ethics and the remaking of moral identities in an era of user involvement', *Globalisation, Societies and Education*, 10 (4): 507–17.

Cronqvist, A., Lutzen, K. and Nystrom, M. (2006) 'Nurses' lived experiences of moral stress support in the intensive care context', *Journal of Nursing Management*, 14: 405–13.

Crowley, M. and Wheeler, H. (2014) 'Working with parents in the early years', in Pugh, G. and Duffy, B. (eds), *Contemporary Issues in the Early Years* (6th edn). London: Sage. pp. 217–35.

Daly, M., Byers, E. and Taylor, W. (2009) *Early Years Management in Practice*. London: Heinemann.

Dawson, A. J. (1994) 'Professional codes of practice and ethical conduct', *Journal of Applied Philosophy*, 11 (2): 145–53.

de Camargo, O.K. (2011) 'Systems of care: transition from the bio-psycho-social perspective of the International Classification of Functioning, Disability and Health', *Child: Care Health and Development*, 37 (6): 757–899.

De Shazer, S. and Molnar, A. (1987) 'Solution focused therapy: toward the identification of therapeutic tasks', *Journal of Marital and Family Therapy*, 13 (4): 349–58.

Department for Children, Schools and Families (DCSF) (2003) *Green Paper: Every Child Matters*. Nottingham: HMSO.

Department for Children, Schools and Families (DCSF) (2004) *Children Act*. Nottingham: HMSO.

Department for Children, Schools and Families (DCSF) (2007a) *The Early Years Foundation Stage*. London: DCSF.

Department for Children, Schools and Families (DCSF) (2007b) *The Inclusion Development Programme*. London: DSCF.

Department for Children, Schools and Families (DCSF) (2008a) *Every Child a Talker*. London: DSCF.

Department for Children, Schools and Families (DCSF) (2008b) *Raising Standards, Improving Outcomes*. London: DCSF.

Department for Children, Schools and Families (DCSF) (2008c) *The Early Years Foundation Stage, Setting the Standards for Care, Learning and Development for Children aged Birth to Five*. London: DCSF.

Department for Children, Schools and Families (DCSF) (2009a) *Healthy Lives, Brighter Futures*. London: DSCF.

Department for Children, Schools and Families (DCSF) (2009b) *Learning, Playing and Interacting*. London: HMSO.

Department for Children, Schools and Families (DCSF) (2009c) *Inclusion Development Programme*. Available at www.idponline.org.uk/ (accessed 12.1.17).

Department for Children, Schools and Families (DCSF) (2010) *Salt Review: Independent Review of Teacher Supply for Pupils with Severe, Profound and Multiple Learning Difficulties (SLD and PMLD)*. London: DSCF.

Department for Education (DfE) (2010a) *Review of Best Practice in Parental Engagement*. London: HMSO. Available at www.gov.uk/government/uploads/system/uploads/attachment_data/file/182508/DFE-RR156.pdf (accessed 21.7.16).

Department for Education (DfE) (2010b) *The Equality Act*. London: HMSO.

Department for Education (DfE) (2011a) *Support and Aspiration: A New Approach to Special Needs and Disability – A Consultation*. London: HMSO.

Department for Education (DfE) (2011b) *Teachers' Standards*. Available at www.gov.uk/government/uploads/system/uploads/attachment_data/file/301107/Teachers__Standards.pdf (accessed 20.10.15).

Department for Education (DfE) (2012) *Statutory Framework for the Early Years Foundation Stage: Setting the Standards for Learning, Development and Care for Children from Birth to Five*. London: HMSO.

Department for Education (DfE) (2013a) *Teachers' Standards: Guidance for School Leaders, School Staff and Governing Bodies*. London: DfE.

Department for Education (DfE) (2013b) *Consultation on Teachers' Standards (Early Years)*. London: DfE. Available at www.gov.uk/government/consultations/consultation-on-teachers-standards-early-years (accessed 12.1.17).

Department for Education (DfE) (2014a) *Children and Families Act*. London: HMSO.

Department for Education (DfE) (2014b) *Statutory Framework for the Early Years Foundation Stage: Setting the Standards for Learning, Development and Care for Children from Birth to Five*. London: DfE.

Department for Education (DfE) (2014c) *Early Years: Guide to the 0–25 SEND Code of Practice*. London: HMSO.

Department for Education (DfE) (2014d) *Implementation Study: Integrated Review at 2–2$^1/_2$ Years – Integrating the Early Years Foundation Stage Progress Check and the Healthy Child Programme Health and Development Review*. London: National Children's Bureau & ICF GHK. Available at www.foundationyears.org.uk/files/2014/11/DFE-RR350_Integrated_review_at_age_two_implementation_study.pdf (accessed 12.10.16).

Department for Education (DfE) (2015a) *Induction for Newly Qualified Teachers (England): Statutory Guidance for Appropriate Bodies, Headteachers, School Staff and Governing Bodies*. London: DfE.

Department for Education (DfE) (2015b) *School Teachers' Pay and Conditions Document 2015 and Guidance on School Teachers' Pay and Conditions*. London: DfE.

Department for Education (DfE) (2015c) *Special Educational Needs and Disability Code of Practice: 0–25 Years*. London: HMSO.

Department for Education (DfE) (2016a) *School Workforce in England: 2015 National Statistics*. London: DfE.

Department for Education (DfE) (2016b) *Special Educational Needs in England*. London: DfE.

Department for Education (DfE) (2017) *Survey of Childcare and Early Years Providers, England*. London: HMSO. Available at www.gov.uk/government/uploads/system/uploads/attachment_data/file/593646/SFR09_2017_Main_Text.pdf (accessed 28.2.17).

Department for Education (DfE) and Department of Health (DoH) (2011) *Supporting Families in the Foundation Years*. London: DfE.

Department for Education (DfE) and Department of Health (DoH) (2015) *Special Educational Needs and Disability Code of Practice: 0 to 25 Years*. Available at www.gov.uk/government/uploads/system/uploads/attachment_data/file/398815/SEND_Code_of_Practice_January_2015.pdf (accessed 17.7.16).

Department for Education and Employment (DfEE) (1998) *Teachers: Meeting the Challenge of Change*. London: HMSO.

Department for Education and Employment (DfEE) (2000) *Statistics of Education: Schools in England*. London: HMSO.

Department for Education and Skills (DfES) (1970) *The Education (Handicapped Children) Act*. London: HMSO.

Department for Education and Skills (DfES) (1981) *The Education Act*. London: HMSO.

Department for Education and Skills (DfES) (1994) *The Code of Practice for the Identification and Assessment of Special Educational Needs*. London: DfES.

Department for Education and Skills (DfES) (2000) *Curriculum Guidance for the Foundation Stage*. Nottingham: DfES.

Department for Education and Skills (DfES) (2001) *Special Educational Needs: Code of Practice*. Nottingham. DfES.

Department for Education and Skills (DfES) (2002) *Birth to 3 Matters: A Framework to Support Children in Their Earliest Years*. Nottingham: DfES.

Department for Education and Skills (DfES) (2003) *Together from the Start: Practical Guidance for Professionals Working with Disabled Children (Birth to Third Birthday) and Their Families*. London: DfES.

Department for Education and Skills (DfES) (2004a) *Removing Barriers to Achievement: The Government's Strategy for SEN*. London: DfES.

Department for Education and Skills (DfES) (2004b) *Every Child Matters: Change for Children*. London: DfES.

Department for Education and Skills (DfES) (2005) *Improving the Life Chances of Disabled People*. London: DfES.

Department for Education and Skills (DfES) (2006) *The Childcare Act*. London: DfES.

Department for Education and Skills (DfES) (2007b) *Children's Workforce Strategy: Building a World-class Workforce for Children, Young People and Families*. London: DfES. Available at www.education.gov.uk/consultations/downloadableDocs/CWS%20update%20PDF%20version.pdf (accessed 5.1.17).

Department for Education and Skills (DfES) (2007a) *Every Parent Matters*. London: HMSO.

Department of Education and Science (DES) (1970) *Education (Handicapped Children) Act*. London: HMSO.

Department of Health (DoH) (2001) *Valuing People: A New Strategy for Learning Disability for the 21st Century*. London: DoH.

Department of Health (DoH) (2003) *National Service Framework for Children*. London: DoH.

Department of Health (DoH) (2009a) *Valuing People Now*. London: DoH.

Department of Health (DoH) (2009b) *Healthy Child Programme: Pregnancy and the First 5 Years of Life*. Available at www.gov.uk/government/publications/healthy-child-programme-pregnancy-and-the-first-5-years-of-life (accessed 3.3.16).

Desforges, C. and Abouchaar, A. (2003) *The Impact of Parental Involvement, Parental Support and Family Education on Pupil Achievement and Adjustment: A Literature Review*. London: Department for Education and Skills.

Devlin, P. (2008) 'Create effective teacher – paraprofessional teams', *Intervention in School and Clinic*, 44 (1): 41–4.

Dickins, M. (2011) 'Listening as a way of life: leadership for listening', in Dickins, M. (ed.), *A–Z of Inclusion in Early Childhood*. London: National Children's Bureau.

Dickins, M. (2014) *A–Z of Inclusion in Early Childhood*. London: McGraw-Hill Education.

Dobson, B. and Middleton, S. (1998) *Paying to Care: The Cost of Childhood Disability*. York: Joseph Rowntree Foundation.

Driver, J. (2007) *Ethics: The Fundamentals*. Oxford: Blackwell.

Dubiel, J. (2012) 'How children learn: in the process', *Nursery World*, 3 February: 9–11.

Dubiel, J. (2016) *Effective Assessment in the EYFS*. London: Sage.

Durrant, I. and Twyman, A. (2015) 'Understanding leadership', in Ekins, A. (ed.), *The Changing Face of Special Educational Needs* (2nd edn). London: Routledge. pp. 74–90.

Early Childhood Action (n. d.) 'Fearlessly speaking truth to political power: Manifesto'. Available at www.earlychildhoodaction.com/manifesto.html (accessed 17.7.16).

Early Education (2012) 'Development matters'. London: Early Education. Available at www.early-education.org.uk (accessed 21.7.16).

Ehrich, L.C., Kimber, M., Millwater, J. and Cranston, N. (2011) 'Ethical dilemmas: a model to understand teacher practice', *Teachers and Teaching: Theory and Practice*, 17 (2): 173–85.

Ehrich, L.C., Klenowski, V., Harris, J., Smeed, J., Carrington, S. and Ainscow, M. (2013) 'Ethical leadership in a time of increasing accountability'. Conference Paper, BERA, 3–5 September.

Eisenstadt, N. (2011) *Providing a Sure Start: How Government Discovered Early Childhood*. Bristol: Polity Press.

Eisenstadt, N. (2012) 'Sure Start can work – don't let it die', *Guardian*, 12 July, p. 7.

Ekins, A. (2015) *The Changing Face of Special Educational Needs* (2nd edn). London: Routledge.

Ellis, C. and Beauchamp, G. (2012) 'Ethics in researching children with special educational needs', in Palaiologou, L. (ed.), *Ethical Practice in Early Childhood*. London: Sage. pp. 53–66.

Engel, G.L. (1977) 'The need for a new medical model. A challenge for biomedicine', *Science*, 196: 129–36.

Eraut, M. (2000) 'Non-formal learning and tacit knowledge in professional work', *British Journal of Educational Psychology*, 70 (1): 113–36.

Fabian, H. (2005) 'Outdoor learning environments: easing the transition from the Foundation Stage to Key Stage One', *Education, 3–13*, 33(2): 4–8.

Fabian, H. and Dunlop, A. (2006) *Outcomes of Good Practice in Transition Processes for Children Entering Primary School*. Paper commissioned for the EFA Global Monitoring Report 2007, *Strong Foundations: Early Childhood Care and Education*. Geneva: United Nations Educational, Scientific and Cultural Organization.

Family Rights Group (n. d.) *Family Group Conferences and Lifelong Links*. London: Family Rights Group. Available at: www.frg.org.uk/involving-families/family-group-conferences (accessed 2.12.16).

Ferguson, D. (2008) 'International trends in inclusive education: the continuing challenge to teach each one and everyone', *European Journal of Special Needs Education*, 23: 109–120.

Ferri, B.A. (2015) 'Integrazione scholastica: on not having all of the answers – a response to Anastasiou, Kauffman and Di Nuovo', *European Journal of Special Needs Education*, 30 (4): 444–7.

Fiedler, C.R. and Van Haren, B. (2009) 'A comparison of special education administrators' and teachers' knowledge and application of ethics and professional standards', *The Journal of Special Education*, 43 (3): 160–73.

Fisher, H. (2012) 'Progressing towards a model of intrinsic inclusion in a mainstream primary school: a SENCo's experience', *International Journal of Inclusive Education*, 16 (12): 1273–93.

Florian, L. and Black-Hawkins, K. (2011) 'Exploring inclusive pedagogy', *British Educational Research Journal*, 37 (5): 813–28.

Forlin, C. and Hopewell, T. (2006) 'Inclusion – the heart of the matter: trainee teachers' perceptions of a parent's journey', *British Journal of Special Education*, 33 (2): 55–61.

Forlin, C. and Loreman, T. (2014) *Measuring Inclusive Education*. Bingley: Emerald Group.

Fox, M. (2015) '"What sort of person ought I to be?" – Repositioning EPs in light of the Children and Families Bill', *Educational Psychology in Practice*, 31 (4): 382–96.

Frederickson, N., Dunsmuir, S., Lang, J. and Monsen, J.J. (2004) 'Mainstream–special school inclusion partnerships: pupil, parent and teacher perspectives', *International Journal of Inclusive Education*, 8 (1): 37–57.

Frost, N., Robinson, M. and Anning, A. (2004) 'Social workers in multi-disciplinary teams: issues and dilemmas for professional practice', *Child and Family Social Work*, 10: 187–96.

Fuchs, D. and Fuchs, L.S. (1994) 'Inclusive schools movement and the radicalization of special education reform', *Exceptional Children*, 60: 294–309.

Gallagher, D.J., Connor, D.J. and Ferri, B.A. (2014) 'Beyond the far too incessant schism: special education and the social model of disability', *International Journal of Inclusive Education*, 18 (11): 1120–42.

Gasper, M. (2010) *Multi-agency Working in the Early Years: Challenges and Opportunities*. London: Sage.

Giangreco, M.F. (2013) 'Teacher assistant supports in inclusive schools: research, practices and alternatives', *Australasian Journal of Special Education*, 37 (2): 93–106.

Giangreco, M.F., Broer, S.M. and Suter, J.C. (2011) 'Guidelines for selecting alternatives to overreliance on paraprofessionals: field-testing in inclusion-oriented schools', *Remedial and Special Education*, 32 (1): 22–38.

Giangreco, M.F., Doyle, M.B. and Suter, J.C. (2012) 'Constructively responding to requests for paraprofessionals: we keep asking the wrong questions', *Remedial and Special Education*, 33: 362–73.

Giangreco, M.F., Smith, C.S. and Pinckney, E. (2006) 'Addressing the paraprofessional dilemma in an inclusive school: a program description', *Research and Practice for Persons with Severe Disabilities*, 31 (3): 215–29.

Giddens, A. and Sutton, P. (2013) *Sociology*. Cambridge: Polity Press.

Glasby, J. and Littlechild, R. (2016) *Direct Payments and Personal Budgets: Putting Personalisation into Practice*. Bristol: Policy Press.

Golder, G., Jones, N. and Quinn, E.E. (2009) 'Strengthening the special educational needs element of initial teacher training and education', *British Journal of Special Education*, 36 (4): 183–90.

Goleman, D. (1995) *Emotional Intelligence*. New York: Bantam Books.

Goleman, D., Boyatzis, R. and McKee, A. (2002) *The New Leaders*. London: Sphere.

Griffiths, D. and Dubsky, R. (2012) 'Evaluating the impact of the new National Award for SENCos: transforming landscapes or gardening in a gale', *British Journal of Special Education*, 39 (4): 164–72.

Groom, B. (2006) 'Building relationships for learning: the developing role of the teaching assistant', *Support for Learning*, 21 (4): 199–203.

Guzman, N. (1997) 'Leadership for successful inclusive schools: a study of principals' behaviours', *Journal of Educational Administration*, 35 (5): 439–50.

Hargreaves, A. and Ainscow, M. (2015) 'The top and bottom of leadership and change', *Phi Delta Kappan*, 97 (3): 42–8.

Harris, A. (2003) 'Behind the classroom door: the challenge of organisational and pedagogical change', *Journal of Educational Change*, 4 (4): 369–82.

Harris, J. (2015) 'The new special needs maze, where parents go back to the start', *Guardian*, 17 February, p. 11.

Hellawell, B. (2015) 'Ethical accountability and routine moral stress in special educational needs professionals', *Management in Education*, 29 (3): 119–24.

Helton, G.G., Ray, B.A. and Biderman, M.D. (2000) 'Responses of school psychologists and special education teachers to administrative pressures to practice unethically: a national survey', *Special Services in the Schools*, 16 (1): 111–34.

Hillman, J. and Williams, T. (2015) *Early Years Education and Childcare: Lessons from Evidence and Future Priorities*. London: Nuffield Foundation.

HM Treasury (2007) *Aiming High for Disabled Children*. London: HM Treasury.

HMSO (1997) *Excellence in Schools*. London: HMSO.

Hopkins, D. (2007) *Every School a Great School: Realizing the Potential of System Leadership*. New York: McGraw-Hill.

House of Commons (2006) *Special Educational Needs: Education Select Committee Report*. London: House of Commons.

Hughes, A.M. and Read, V. (2012) *Building Positive Relationships with Parents of Young Children*. London: Fulton.

Hunt, P. (ed.) (1966) *Stigma: The Experience of Disability*. London: Geoffrey Chapman.

Independent Parental Special Education Advice (IPSEA) (2005) *Inquiry into Special Educational Needs*. Saffron Waldon: IPSEA.

Independent Parental Special Education Advice (IPSEA) (2014) 'IPSEA Responds to the draft SEN Code of Practice'. Available at www.ipsea.org.uk/file-manager/news/News2014/ipsea-april-2014-sen-code_of_practice_draft-final-1.pdf (accessed 05.01.17)

Ingram, P.D. (1997) 'Leadership behaviours of principals in inclusive educational settings', *Journal of Educational Administration*, 35 (5): 411–27.

Jean-Marie, G., Normore, H.A. and Brook, S.J. (2009) 'Leadership for social justice: preparing 21st-century school leaders for a new social order', *Journal of Research on Leadership Education*, 4 (1): 1–3.

Jones, A. and Pound, L. (2008) *Leadership and Management in the Early Years: From Principles to Practice*. Maidenhead: Open University Press.

Jorde-Bloom, P. (1992) 'The child care director: a critical component of program quality', *Educational Horizons*, 70 (3): 138–45.

Kälvemark, S., Höglund, A.T., Hansson, M.G., Westerholm, P. and Arnetz, B. (2004) 'Living with conflicts – ethical dilemmas and moral distress in the health care system', *Social Science & Medicine*, 58: 1075–84.

Kaweski, W. (2014) *Teaching Adolescents with Autism Practical Strategies for the Inclusive Classroom*. New York: Skyhorse.

Kazmirski, A., Dickens, S. and White, C. (2008) *Pilot Scheme for Two Year Old Children: Evaluation of Outreach Approaches*. London: NCSR.

Kearney, P.M. and Griffin, T. (2001) 'Between joy and sorrow', *Journal of Advanced Nursing*, 34 (5): 582–92.

Keen, D. and Rodger, S. (2012) *Working with Parents of a Newly Diagnosed Child with an Autism Spectrum Disorder: A Guide for Professionals*. London: Jessica Kingsley.

Knowles, G. and Lander, V. (2012) *Thinking through Ethics and Values in Primary Education*. London: Learning Matters.

Ko, B. (2015) 'Education, health and care plans: a new scheme for special educational needs and disability provisions in England from 2014', *Paediatrics and Child Health*, 25 (10): 443–9.

Kubler-Ross, E. (1969) *On Death and Dying*. London: Routledge.

Kugelmass, J. and Ainscow, M. (2004) 'Leadership for inclusion: a comparison of international practices', *Journal of Research in Special Educational Needs*, 4 (3): 133–41.

Kurniawati, F., De Boer, A.A., Minnaert, A.E.M.G. and Mangunsong, F. (2014) 'Characteristics of primary teacher training programmes on inclusion: a literature focus', *Educational Research*, 56 (3): 310–26.

Lamb, B. (2009) *Lamb Inquiry: Special Educational Needs and Parental Confidence.* London: DCSF.

Laming, Lord W. (2003) *The Victoria Climbié Inquiry.* London: DoH.

Laming, Lord W. (2009) *The Protection of Children in England: A Progress Report.* London: HMSO.

Lancaster, P.Y. and Kirby, P. (2010) *Listening to Young Children.* Maidenhead: Open University Press and Coram.

Lee, B. (2003) *Teaching Assistants in Schools: The Current State of Play.* London: Local Government Association.

Leko, M.M. and Brownell, M.T. (2009) 'Crafting quality professional development for special educators: what school leaders should know', *Teaching Exceptional Children*, 42 (1): 64–70.

Lendrum, A., Barlow, A. and Humphrey, N. (2015) 'Developing positive school–home relationships through structured conversations with parents of learners with special educational needs and disabilities (SEND)', *Journal of Research in Special Educational Needs*, 15 (2): 87–96.

Liasidou, A. and Antoniou, A. (2015) 'Head teacher's leadership for social justice and inclusion', *School Leadership and Management*, 35 (4): 347–64.

Lindqvist, G., Nilholm, C., Almqvist, L. and Wetso, G.M. (2011) 'Different agendas? The views of different occupational groups on special needs education', *European Journal of Special Needs Education*, 26 (2): 143–57.

Lipsky, D.K. (1994) 'National survey gives insight into inclusive education', *Inclusive Education Programs*, 1 (3): 4–7.

Little, J.W. (1993) 'Teachers' professional development in a climate of educational reform', *Educational Evaluation and Policy Analysis*, 15 (2): 129–51.

Lloyd, E. and Penn, H. (2013) *Childcare Markets: Can They Deliver an Equitable Service?* Bristol: Polity Press.

London Borough of Waltham Forest (n. d.) *Person-centred Review - Guidance for Schools and Other Services.* Available at www.walthamforest.gov.uk/content/person-centred-planning (accessed 12.12.16).

Lunt, I. and Norwich, B. (1999) *Can Effective Schools Be Inclusive Schools?* London: Institute of Education.

MacBeath, J. (2006) 'The talent enigma', *International Journal of Leadership in Education*, 9 (3): 183–204.

MacBlain, S. and Purdy, N. (2011) 'Confidence or confusion: how well are today's newly qualified teachers in England prepared to meet the additional needs of children in schools?', *Teacher Development*, 15 (3): 381–94.

Macintyre, C. (2014) *Identifying Additional Learning Needs in the Early Years.* London: Routledge.

Mackenzie, S. (2012) '"It's been a bit of a rollercoaster": special educational needs, emotional labour and emotion work', *International Journal of Inclusive Education*, 16 (10): 1067–82.

Malaguzzi, L. (1993) 'History, ideas and basic philosophy', in Edwards, C., Gandini, L. and Forman, G. (eds), *The Hundred Languages of Children*. Norwood, NJ: Ablex. pp. 49–99.

Male, D. (2000) 'Target setting in schools for children with severe learning difficulties: headteachers' perceptions', *British Journal of Special Education*, 27 (1): 6–12.

Marmot, M. (2010) *Fair Society, Healthy Lives: Strategic Review of Health Inequalities in England Post-2010.* London: Department for International Development.

Marrs-Grant, K. (2015) 'Impact of SEN reforms', *Nasen Special*, March.

Martin, E. (2013) 'Emotional development and learning in early childhood: exploring a pedagogy of emotion.' Unpublished PhD thesis, University of Kent, Canterbury.

Mathieson, K. (2015) *Inclusion in the Early Years Foundation Stage*. Maidenhead: OUP.

Matthews, P. (2009) *How Do School Leaders Successfully Lead Learning?* Nottingham: National College for School Leadership.

McCoy, S. and Banks, J. (2012) 'Simply academic? Why children with special educational needs don't like school', *European Journal of Special Needs Education*, 27 (1): 81–97.

McDermott, P.A., Watkins, M.W., Rovine, M.J. and Rikoon, S.H. (2013) 'Assessing changes in socioemotional adjustment across early school transitions – new national scales for children at risk', *Journal of School Psychology*, 51 (1): 97–115.

Meighan, R. and Siraj-Blatchford, I. (2003) *A Sociology of Educating*. London: Continuum.

Ministry of Education (1944) *Education Act*. London: HMSO.

Mintz, J. and Wyse, D. (2015) 'Inclusive pedagogy and knowledge in special education: addressing the tension', *International Journal of Inclusive Education*, 19 (11): 1161–71.

Mistry, M. and Sood, K. (2012) 'Challenges of early years leadership preparation: a comparison between early and experienced early years practitioners in England', *Management in Education*, 26 (1): 28–37.

Mittler, P. (2012) *Overcoming Exclusion: Social Justice through Education*. London: Routledge.

Moran, A. and Abbot, L. (2002) 'Developing inclusive schools: the pivotal role of teaching assistants in promoting inclusion in special and mainstream schools in Northern Ireland', *European Journal of Special Educational Needs*, 17 (2): 161–73.

Moylett, H. (2014) *Characteristics of Effective Early Learning: Helping Young Children Become Learners for Life*. Maidenhead: OUP.

Muijs, D. and Reynolds, D. (2003) 'The effectiveness of the use of learning support assistants in improving mathematics achievement of low achieving pupils in primary school', *Educational Research*, 45 (3): 219–30.

Murray, D. (2015) 'Working in partnership with families, parents and carers', in Martin-Denham, S. (ed.), *Teaching Children and Young People with Special Educational Needs and Disabilities*. London: Sage. pp. 70–78.

Nangah, Z. and Mills, G. (2015) 'Re-thinking children's well-being and inclusion in practice', in Brodie, K. and Savage, K. (eds), *Inclusion and Early Years Practice*. London: Fulton.

National Academy for Parenting Practitioners (NAPP) (2009a) 'Good practice in working with parents of disabled children: workshop summary'. London: King's College.

National Academy for Parenting Practitioners (NAPP) (2009b) 'What is evidence based practice? Workshop briefing paper'. London: King's College.

National Association of Schoolmasters/Union of Women Teachers (NASUWT) (2010) 'Teachers are not to blame for varying special needs provision'. Available at www.politics.co.uk/opinion-formers/nasuwt-the-teachers-union/article/nasuwt-teachers-are-not-to-blame-for-varying-special-needs-p (accessed 25.4.17).

National Association of Schoolmasters/Union of Women Teachers (NASUWT) (2015) 'Teachers' payscales (England and Wales) 2015–17'. Available at www.nasuwt.org.uk/advice/pay-pensions/pay-scales.html (accessed 12.12.16).

National Careers Service (NCS) (2016a) 'Job profiles: teaching assistant'. Available at: https://nationalcareersservice.direct.gov.uk/advice/planning/jobprofiles/Pages/teaching assistant.aspx (accessed 1.7.16).

National Careers Service (NCS) (2016b) 'Job profiles: childminder'. Available at https://nationalcareersservice.direct.gov.uk/job-profiles/childminder (accessed 12.12.16).

National Children's Bureau (NCB) (2006) *Parents, Early Years and Learning*. London: NCB.

National Children's Bureau (NCB) (2010) *Principles for Engaging with Families*. London: National Quality Improvement Network.

National Children's Bureau (NCB) (2015) *Cuts that Cost: Trends in Funding for Early Intervention Services*. London: NCB.

National Day Nurseries Association (NDNA) (2017) 'One fifth of providers won't provide 30 hours'. Huddersfield: NDNA. Available at www.ndna.org.uk/NDNA/News/Latest_news/2017/One_fifth_of_providers_won_t_provide_30_hours__DfE_survey.aspx (accessed 2.3.17).

National Foundation for Educational Research (NFER) (2005) 'The employment and deployment of teaching assistants'. Slough: NFER. Available at www.nfer.ac.uk/publica tions/TAD01 (accessed 15.8.17).

National Foundation for Educational Research (NFER) (2013) 'Compulsory age of starting school in European countries'. Slough: NFER. Available at www.nfer.ac.uk/eurydice/compulsory-age-of-starting-school (accessed 15.8.17).

National Joint Council for Local Government Services (NJCLGS) (2003) *School Support Staff: The Way Forward*. London: Employers Organisation.

National Union of Teachers (NUT) (2002) 'NUT briefing on "Qualifying to Teach": Professional standards for qualified teacher status and requirements for initial teacher training 2002', NUT circular. London: NUT.

National Union of Teachers (NUT) (2008) 'Early years professional status: advice and guidance for NUT members'. Available at www.teachers.org.uk/education-policies/early-years (accessed 12.12.16).

Nind, M., Flewitt, R. and Payler, J. (2011) 'Social constructions of young children in "special", "inclusive" and home environments', *Children & Society*, 25: 359–70.

Norbury, C.F. and Gooch, P. (2015) 'Too much, too soon? What should we be teaching four-year-olds?'. London: The Conversation Trust. Available at https://theconversation.com/too-much-too-soon-what-should-we-be-teaching-four-year-olds-43210 (accessed 25.4.17).

Norwich, B. (2008) *Dilemmas of Difference, Inclusion and Disability*. London: Routledge.

Norwich, B. (2014) 'Changing policy and legislation and its effects on inclusive and special education: a perspective from England', *British Journal of Special Education*, 41 (4): 403–25.

Norwich, B. and Lewis, A. (2001) 'Mapping a pedagogy for special educational needs', *British Educational Research Journal*, 27 (3): 313–29.

Nottinghamshire County Council (n. d.) Available at www.nottinghamshire.gov.uk/education/special-educational-needs-and-disabilities-send (accessed 12.12.16).

Nursing and Midwifery Council (NMC) (2015) *The Code for Nurses and Midwifes*. Available at: www.nmc.org.uk/standards/code/read-the-code-online (accessed 10.5.14).

Nutbrown, C. and Clough, P. (2013) *Inclusion in the Early Years*, 2nd edn. London: Sage.

Nutbrown, C., Hannon, P. and Morgan, A. (2005) *Early Literacy Work with Families*. London: Sage.

Nye, E., Gardner, F., Hansford, L., Edwards, V., Hayes, R. and Ford, T. (2016) 'Classroom behaviour management strategies in response to problematic behaviours of primary school children with special educational needs: views of special educational needs coordinators', *Emotional and Behavioural Difficulties*, 21 (1): 43–60.

Office for National Statistics (ONS) (2001) *National Census Data*. Available at www.ons.gov.uk/census/2011census/2011censusdata/2001censusdata (accessed 8.1.17).

Office for Standards in Education (Ofsted) (2004) *Special Educational Needs and Disabilities: Towards Inclusive Schools*. London: Ofsted.

Office for Standards in Education (Ofsted) (2006) *Inclusion: Does It Matter Where Pupils Are Taught? Provision and Outcomes in Different Settings for Pupils with Learning Difficulties and Disabilities*. London: Ofsted.

Office for Standards in Education (Ofsted) (2010) *The Special Educational Needs and Disability Review: A Statement Is Not Enough*. Manchester: Ofsted.

Office for Standards in Education (Ofsted) (2016) Available at www.gov.uk/government/organisations/ofsted (accessed 12.12.16).

Oliver, C., Mooney, A. and Statham, J. (2010) *Integrated Working: A Review of the Evidence.* Leeds: Children's Workforce Development Council. Available at http://dera.ioe.ac.uk/3674/1/Integrated_Working_A_Review_of_the_Evidence_report.pdf (accessed 21.6.16).

Oliver, M. (1983) *Social Work with Disabled People.* Basingstoke: Macmillan.

Oliver, M. (1990) *The Politics of Disablement.* Basingstoke: Macmillan.

Olshansky, S. (1962) 'Chronic sorrow: a response to having a mentally defective child', *Social Casework*, 43: 190–93.

Orlandi, K. (2012) *Onwards and Upwards: Supporting the Transition to Key Stage 1.* London: Routledge.

Packer, N. (2016) *The Teacher's Guide to SEN.* Camarthen: Crown House.

Pazey, B.L. and Cole, H.A. (2013) 'The role of special education training in the development of socially just leaders: building an equity consciousness in educational leadership programs', *Educational Administration Quarterly*, 49 (2): 243–71.

Pearson, S. and Gathercole, K. (2011) *National Award for SENCOs: Transforming SENCOs.* Tamworth: NASEN.

Pettit, B. (2003) *Effective Joint Working between CAMHS and Schools.* London: DfES.

Philpott, F.D., Furey, E. and Penney, S.C. (2010) 'Promoting leadership in the ongoing professional development of teachers: responding to globalization and inclusion', *Exceptionality Education International*, 20 (2): 38–54.

Picket, A., Gerlach, K., Morgan, R., Likins, M. and Wallace, T. (2007) *Paraeducators in Schools: Strengthening Educational Teams.* Austin, TX: Pro-Ed.

Plowden, B. (1967) *Children and Their Primary Schools.* London: HMSO.

Powers, S., Rayner, S. and Gunter, H. (2001) 'Leadership in inclusive education: a professional development agenda for special education', *British Journal of Special Education*, 28 (3): 108–112.

Potter, C., Walker, G. and Keen, B. (2012) 'Engaging fathers from disadvantaged areas in children's early educational transitions: a UK perspective', *Journal of Early Childhood Research*, 10 (2): 209–225.

Praisner, C. (2003) 'Attitudes of elementary school principals towards the inclusion of students with disabilities', *Exceptional Children*, 69 (2): 135–45.

Prizant, B.M. (2015) *Uniquely Human: A Different Way of Seeing Autism.* New York: Simon and Schuster.

Proctor, P. (1984) 'Teacher expectations: a model for school improvement', *The Elementary School Journal*, 84 (4): 468–81.

Pugh, G. (1980) *Preparation for Parenthood: Some Current Initiatives and Thinking.* London: National Children's Bureau.

Qualifications and Curriculum Development Authority (QCDA) (2009) 'P Scales'. Available at www.qcda.org.uk (accessed 25.7.16).

Ravet, J. (2011) 'Inclusive/exclusive? Contradictory perspectives on autism and inclusion: the case for an integrative position', *International Journal of Inclusive Education*, 15 (6): 667–82.

Riehl, C.J. (2000) 'The principal's role in creating inclusive schools for diverse students: a review of normative, empirical, and critical literature on the practice of educational administration', *Review of Educational Research*, 70 (1): 55–81.

Rinaldi, C. (2006) *In Dialogue with Reggio Emilia: Listening, Researching and Learning.* Abingdon: Routledge.

Rioux, M.H. and Pinto, P.C. (2010) 'A time for the universal right to education: back to basics', *British Journal of Sociology of Education*, 31: 621–42.

Rix, J., Sheehy, K., Fletcher-Campbell, F., Crisp, M. and Harper, A. (2013) 'Exploring provision for children identified with special educational needs: an international review of policy and practice', *European Journal of Special Needs Education*, 28 (4): 375–91.

Roberts, R. (2010) *Wellbeing from Birth*. London: Sage.

Rodd, J. (1994) *Leadership in Early Childhood: The Pathway to Professionalism*. Melbourne: Allen and Unwin.

Rodd, J. (1997) 'Learning to be leaders: perceptions of early childhood professionals about leadership roles and responsibilities', *Early Years*, 18 (1): 40–6.

Roffey-Barentsen, J. and Watt Brunel, M. (2014) 'The voices of teaching assistants (are we value for money?)', *Research in Education*, 92 (1): 18–31.

Ross, D.D. and Blanton, L. (2004) 'Inquiry communities in special education teacher education', *Teacher Education and Special Education*, 27 (1): 15–23.

Ryan, J. (2006) *Inclusive Leadership*. San Francisco, CA: Jossey-Bass.

Salend, S.J. (2005) *Creating Inclusive Classrooms: Effective and Reflective Practices for All Students* (5th edn). Upper Saddle River, NJ: Pearson.

Sanders, D., White, G., Burge, B., Sharp, C., Eames, A., McEure, R. and Grayson, H. (2005) *A Study of the Transition from Foundation Stage to Key Stage 1: National Foundation for Educational Research*. Nottingham: DfES. Available at www.nfer.ac.uk/publications/FKT01/FKT01.pdf (accessed 20.1.17).

Scanlon, G., Barnes-Holmes, Y., Enteggart, C., Desmond, D. and Vahey, N. (2016) 'The experience of pupils with SEN and their parents at the stage of pre-transition from primary to post-primary school', *European Journal of Special Needs Education*, 31 (1): 44–58.

Schmit, C. (2006) 'A code of ethics for people working with children and young people'. Available at www.ances.lu/index.php/fice/sarajevo-2006/69-a-code-of-ethics-for-people-working-with-children-and-young-people (accessed 10/5/14).

Schweinhart, L.J., Barnes, H. and Weikhart, D. (1993) *Significant Benefits: The High/Scope Perry Pre-School Study through Age 27*. Ypsilanti, MI: High/Scope Press.

SE7 (2011) 'Pathfinder Case Study: Personal budgets and direct payments'. Available at https://se7pathfinder.files.wordpress.com/2013/10/se7pathfindercasestudy-personal budgets.pdf (accessed 25.4.17).

Shakespeare, T. (2014) *Disability Rights and Wrongs Revisited* (2nd edn). London: Routledge.

Shapiro, J.P. and Stefkovich, J.A. (2011) *Ethical Leadership and Decision Making in Education: Applying Theoretical Perspectives to Complex Dilemmas* (3rd edn). Abingdon: Routledge.

Sharp, C., Lord, P., Handscomb, G., Macleod, S., Southcott, C., George, N. and Jeffes, J. (2012) *Highly Effective Leadership in Children's Centres*. Nottingham: National College for School Leadership.

Sharples, J., Webster, R. and Blatchford, P. (2015) *Making Best Use of Teaching Assistants: Guidance Report*. London: Education Endowment Foundation. Available at https://educationendowmentfoundation.org.uk/public/files/Publications/Campaigns/TA_Guidance_Report_MakingBestUseOfTeachingAssisstants-Printable.pdf (accessed 1.7.16).

Silas, D. (2014) *A Guide to the SEN Code of Practice (2014): What You Need to Know*. London: Douglas Silas Solicitors.

Sindelar, P., Shearer, D., Yendol-Hoppey, D. and Liebert, T. (2006) 'The sustainability of inclusive school reform', *Exceptional Children*, 72 (3): 317–31.

Siraj-Blatchford, I. and Manni, L. (2007) *Effective Leadership in the Early Years Sector: The ELEYS Study*. London: Institute of Education.

Siraj-Blatchford, I. and Wah Sum, C. (2013) 'Understanding and advancing systems leadership in the early years'. London: National College for Teaching and Learning. Available at www.yor-ok.org.uk/downloads/Childcare%20Strategy/understanding-and-advancing-systems-leadership-in-the-early-years1.pdf (accessed 26.6.16).

Siraj-Blatchford, I., Sylva, K., Muttock, S., Gilden, R. and Bell, D. (2002) *Researching Effective Pedagogy in the Early Years*. London: HMSO.

Skills Funding Agency (2016) 'Early years teacher'. Available at https://national careersservice.direct.gov.uk/advice/planning/jobprofiles/Pages/earlyyearsteacher.aspx (accessed 1.7.16).

Slee, R. and Allan, J. (2001) 'Excluding the included: a reconsideration of inclusive education', *International Studies in Sociology of Education*, 11 (2): 173–91.

Sousa, D.A. (2015) *The Leadership Brain: Strategies for Leading Today's Schools More Effectively*. Thousand Oaks, CA: Corwin Press.

Standards and Testing Agency (STA) (2015) *2016 Early Years Foundation Stage Assessment and Reporting Arrangements (ARA)*. London: Standards and Testing Agency.

Standards and Testing Agency (STA) (2017) *The Early Years Foundation Stage Profile 2017 Handbook*. London: Standards and Testing Agency.

Standards and Testing Agency (STA) (2016) *Early Years Foundation Stage Handbook*. London: Standards and Testing Agency. Available at www.gov.uk/government/uploads/system/uploads/attachment_data/file/564249/2017_EYFSP_handbook_v1.1.pdf (accessed 8.1.17).

Strike, K. (2007) *Ethical Leadership in Schools*. Thousand Oaks, CA: Corwin Press.

Strike, K., Haller, E. and Soltis, J. (2005) *The Ethics of School Administration*. New York: Teachers College Press.

Stronach, I., Corbin, B., McNamara, O., Stark, S. and Warne, T. (2002) 'Towards an uncertain politics of professionalism: teacher and nurse identities in flux', *Journal of Education Policy*, 17 (1): 109–38.

Sure Start (2002) *Supporting Families Who Have Children with Special Needs and Disabilities*. London: DfES.

Swain, J. and French, S. (2000) 'Towards an affirmation model of disability', *Disability and Society*, 15 (4): 569–82.

Sylva, K., Melhuish, E., Sammons, P., Siraj-Blatchford, I. and Taggart, B. (2004) *The Effective Provision of Pre-School Education (EPPE) Project: Technical Paper 12 – The Final Report: Effective Pre-School Education*. London: DfES/Institute of Education.

Sylva, K., Melhuish, E., Sammons, P., Siraj-Blatchford, I. and Taggart, B. (2010) *Early Childhood Matters: Evidence from the Effective Pre-School and Primary Education Project*. London: Routledge.

Sylva, K., Melhuish, E., Sammons, P., Siraj-Blatchford, I. and Taggart, B. (2012) *The Effective Pre-school, Primary and Secondary Education 3–14 Project (EPPSE, 3–14): Final Report from the Key Stage 3 Phase – Influences on Students' Development from Age 11–14*. London: DfE.

Teacher Development Agency (TDA) (2007) *Professional Standards for Qualified Teacher Status and Requirements for Initial Teacher Training*. London: TDA.

Teaching Agency (2012) *Review of the Early Years Professional Status Standards*. London: Stationery Office.

Thompson, D. (2012) 'Whole school development, inclusion and special educational needs: acknowledging wider debates', in Cornwall, J. and Graham-Matheson, L. (eds), *Leading on Inclusion: Dilemmas, Debates and New Perspectives*. London: Routledge.

Tickell, C. (2011) *Review of the Early Years Foundation Stage*. London: DfE.

Tomlinson, S. (1982) *A Sociology of Special Education*. London: Routledge.

Tomlinson, S. (2012) 'The irresistible rise of the SEN industry', *Oxford Review of Education*, 38 (3): 267–86.

Tutt, R. and Williams, P. (2015) *The SEND Code of Practice 0–25 Years, Policy, Practice and Provision*. London: Sage.

UNESCO (1992) *United Nations Convention on the Rights of the Child*. Paris: UNESCO.

UNESCO (1994) *The Salamanca Statement and Framework for Action on Special Needs Education*. Paris: UNESCO.

UNESCO (1999) *The Salamanca Statement. Five Years On. A Review of the UNESCO Action in the Light of the Salamanca Statement and Framework for Action.* Paris: UNESCO.

UNESCO (2006) *United Nations Convention for the Rights of People with Disabilities.* Paris: UNESCO.

UNICEF (2012) *School Readiness and Transitions.* New York: UNICEF.

UNISON (2016) *Professional Standards for Teaching Assistants: Guidance for Head Teachers, Teachers, Teaching Assistants, Governing Boards and Employers.* London: UNISON.

United Nations (1989) *Convention on the Rights of the Child: UN General Assembly.* New York: United Nations.

Urban, M. (2008) 'Dealing with uncertainty: challenges and possibilities for the early childhood profession', *European Early Childhood Education Research Journal*, 16 (2): 135–52.

Urban, M., Vandenbroeck, M., Van Laere, K., Arianna Lazzari, A. and Peeters, J. (2012) 'Towards competent systems in early childhood education and care: implications for policy and practice', *European Journal of Education*, 47 (4): 508–26.

Wall, K. (2003) *Special Needs and Early Years.* London: Chapman.

Wall, K. (2011) *Special Needs and Early Years: A Practitioner's Guide.* London: Sage.

Ward, U. (2013) *Working with Parents in the Early Years.* London: Sage.

Warnock, H.M. (1978) *Special Educational Needs: Report of the Committee of Enquiry into the Education of Handicapped Children and Young People.* London: HMSO.

Warnock, M. (2005) *Special Educational Needs: A New Look.* London: Philosophy of Education Society of Great Britain.

Weale S. (2016) 'English schools struggling to recruit headteachers, research finds', *Guardian*, 26 January, p.14.

Wearmouth, J. (2016) *Special Educational Needs and Disability: The Basics.* London: Routledge.

Webber, R., Blatchford, P. and Russell. A. (2013) *Teaching Assistants: A Guide to Good Practice.* Oxford: Oxford University Press.

Westwood, P. (2003) *Commonsense Methods for Children with Special Educational Needs: Strategies for the Regular Classroom* (4th edn). London: Routledge/Falmer.

Whalley, M.E. (2011) 'Leading and managing in the early years', in Miller, L. and Cable, C. (eds), *Professionalization, Leadership and Management in the Early Years.* London: Sage. pp. 13–28.

Whalley, M. and the Pen Green Team (2007) *Involving Parents in their Children's Learning.* London: Chapman.

Wigfall, V. and Moss, P. (2001) *More Than the Sum of Its Parts? A Study of a Multi-agency Child Care Network.* London. National Children's Bureau.

Wilde, A. and Avramidis, E. (2011) 'Mixed feelings: towards a continuum of inclusive pedagogies', *Education, 3–13*, 39 (1): 83–101.

Wilson, T. (2016) *Working with Parents, Carers and Families in the Early Years: The Essential Guide.* London: Routledge.

Wolfson, L. and King, J. (2008) *Evaluation of the Extended Pre-school Provision for Vulnerable Two Year Olds Pilot Programme.* Edinburgh: Scottish Government. Available at www.gov.scot/Publications/2008/12/16111725/0 (accessed 25.4.17).

Woods, P.A. (2004) 'Democratic leadership: drawing distinctions with distributed leadership', *International Journal of Leadership in Education*, 7 (1): 3–26.

Worcestershire NHS Trust (2013) 'An evaluation summary of Worcestershire's ECaT programme delivery and outcomes 2009–2013'. Available at www.languageforlearning.co.uk/images/uploads/5270bd57b58df.pdf (accessed 12.12.16).

World Bank (2014) *Analysis of the Function and Structure of the Ministry of Education and Culture of the Republic of Cyprus*. Geneva: World Bank. Available at http://media.phile news.com/PDF/education.pdf (accessed 15.8.17).

World Health Organization (WHO) (2001) *International Classification of Functioning, Disability and Health (ICF)*. Geneva: World Health Organization.

Young, A., Temple, B., Davies, L., Parkinson, G., Bolton, J., Milborrow, W., Hutcheson, G. and Davis, A. (2006) *Early Support: An Evaluation of Phase 3 of Early Support*. London: DfES.

Young Minds (2016) *Strategic Plan 2016–20: Key Objectives*. London: Young Minds. Available at https://youngminds.org.uk (accessed 13.3.17).

# INDEX